City Logistics: Modelling, Planning and Evaluation

I0867705

This volume on city logistics presents recent advances of modelling urban freight transport as well as planning and evaluating city logistics policy measures in the academic research areas and practices. The contributions of eleven chapters have come from eight countries, including Japan, UK, The Netherlands, Italy, France, Singapore, Indonesia, and Brazil. As city logistics aims at creating efficient and environmental-friendly urban freight transport systems, these chapters deal with challenging urban freight transport problems from various point of views of the usage of ITS (Intelligent Transport Systems), multi-agent modelling, public–private partnerships, and the disaster consideration.

This book was published as a special issue of the *International Journal of Urban Sciences*.

Eiichi Taniguchi is Professor of Transport and Logistics in Department of Urban Management, Kyoto University. His research centres on City Logistics and urban freight modelling. He developed vehicle routing and scheduling with time windows models and multi-agent models for evaluating city logistics policy measures.

City Logistics: Modelling, Planning and Evaluation

Edited by
Eiichi Taniguchi

Routledge
Taylor & Francis Group
LONDON AND NEW YORK

First published 2015
by Routledge

2 Park Square, Milton Park, Abingdon, Oxon OX14 4RN
711 Third Avenue, New York, NY 10017, USA

Routledge is an imprint of the Taylor & Francis Group, an informa business

First issued in paperback 2017

British Library Cataloguing in Publication Data
A catalogue record for this book is available from the British Library

ISBN 13: 978-1-138-88545-5 (hbk)
ISBN 13: 978-1-138-06023-4 (pbk)

Typeset in Times New Roman
by RefineCatch Limited, Bungay, Suffolk

Publisher's Note
The publisher accepts responsibility for any inconsistencies that may have arisen during the conversion of this book from journal articles to book chapters, namely the possible inclusion of journal terminology.

Disclaimer
Every effort has been made to contact copyright holders for their permission to reprint material in this book. The publishers would be grateful to hear from any copyright holder who is not here acknowledged and will undertake to rectify any errors or omissions in future editions of this book.

Contents

Citation Information

The chapters in this book were originally published in the *International Journal of Urban Sciences*, volume 18, issue 2 (July 2014). When citing this material, please use the original page numbering for each article, as follows:

Chapter 1

Application of exact route optimization for the evaluation of a city logistics truck ban scheme
Ali Gul Qureshi, Eiichi Taniguchi, Russell G. Thompson and Joel S.E. Teo
International Journal of Urban Sciences, volume 18, issue 2 (July 2014) pp. 117–132

Chapter 2

Ontology-based multi-agent system for urban freight transportation
Nilesh Anand, Ron van Duin and Lori Tavasszy
International Journal of Urban Sciences, volume 18, issue 2 (July 2014) pp. 133–153

Chapter 3

Multi-agent systems modelling approach to evaluate urban motorways for city logistics
J.S.E. Teo, E. Taniguchi and A.G. Qureshi
International Journal of Urban Sciences, volume 18, issue 2 (July 2014) pp. 154–165

Chapter 4

A location-based accessibility analysis to estimate the suitability of urban consolidation facilities
Jesus Gonzalez-Feliu, Josep-Maria Salanova Grau and Adrien Beziat
International Journal of Urban Sciences, volume 18, issue 2 (July 2014) pp. 166–185

Chapter 5

City logistics through the canals? A simulation study on freight waterborne transport in the inner-city of Amsterdam
J.H.R. van Duin, R. Kortmann and S.L. van den Boogaard
International Journal of Urban Sciences, volume 18, issue 2 (July 2014) pp. 186–200

Chapter 6

City logistics long-term planning: simulation of shopping mobility and goods restocking and related support systems
Agostino Nuzzolo, Antonio Comi and Luca Rosati
International Journal of Urban Sciences, volume 18, issue 2 (July 2014) pp. 201–217

Chapter 7
Model of debris collection operation after disasters and its application in urban area
Andie Pramudita and Eiichi Taniguchi
International Journal of Urban Sciences, volume 18, issue 2 (July 2014) pp. 218–243

Chapter 8
London 2012: changing delivery patterns in response to the impact of the Games on traffic flows
Michael Browne, Julian Allen, Ian Wainwright, Andrew Palmer and Ian Williams
International Journal of Urban Sciences, volume 18, issue 2 (July 2014) pp. 244–261

Chapter 9
Developing a local research strategy for city logistics on an academic campus
Thomas Hagen Zunder, Paulus Teguh Aditjandra and Bruce Carnab
International Journal of Urban Sciences, volume 18, issue 2 (July 2014) pp. 262–277

Chapter 10
Collaboration in urban logistics: motivations and barriers
Lindawati, Johan van Schagen, Mark Goh and Robert de Souza
International Journal of Urban Sciences, volume 18, issue 2 (July 2014) pp. 278–290

Chapter 11
An estimation of freight flow using secondary data: a case study in Belo Horizonte (Brazil)
Leise Kelli de Oliveira and Lílian dos Santos Fontes Pereira
International Journal of Urban Sciences, volume 18, issue 2 (July 2014) pp. 291–307

Please direct any queries you may have about the citations to clsuk.permissions@cengage.com

INTRODUCTION

This special issue on city logistics presents recent advances of modelling urban freight transport as well as planning and evaluating city logistics policy measures in the academic research areas and practices. The contributions of 11 papers to this special issue have come from 8 countries, including Japan, UK, The Netherlands, Italy, France, Singapore, Indonesia, and Brazil. As city logistics aims at creating efficient and environmental-friendly urban freight transport systems, these papers deal with challenging urban freight transport problems from various point of views of the usage of ITS (Intelligent Transport Systems), multi-agent modelling, public–private partnerships, and the disaster consideration.

The first paper entitled 'Application of exact route optimization for the evaluation of a city logistics truck ban scheme' by Qureshi, A.G., Taniguchi, E., Thompson, R.G. and Teo, S.E.J. presents the application of the exact solution of vehicle routing and scheduling problem with the time windows (VRPTW) model for evaluating truck ban schemes with ITS. It was found that truck ban on low-speed link of road network resulted in win–win situation of improving the environmental conditions as well as reducing operations costs of freight carriers.

The second paper entitled 'Ontology based multi-agent system for urban freight transportation' by Nilesh, A., van Duin, R. and Tavasszy, L. deals with the behaviour of stakeholders using multi-agent modelling. It focuses on the usefulness of ontology in the development of agent-based models in city logistics domain and demonstrates the effectiveness of agent technology in analysing the urban freight decision-making processes.

The third paper entitled 'Multi-agent systems modelling approach to evaluate urban motorways for city logistics' by Teo, S.E.J., Taniguchi, E. and Qureshi, A.G. presents the multi-agent modelling approaches to evaluate urban freight road alternatives especially providing urban motorways. These models allow us to understand the behaviour of stakeholders, including shippers, freight carriers and administrators in response to the infrastructure provision and management schemes.

The fourth paper entitled 'Estimating the impacts of urban consolidation facilities on delivery times via an accessibility analysis' by Gonzalez-Feliu, J., Salanova Grau, J-M. and Beziat, A. highlights the location-based accessibility analysis to estimate the suitability of urban consolidation facilities. The analysis used three steps, namely generating freight transport demands, estimating the routes, and accessibility calculation. A set of scenarios were examined in the application in Lyon, France.

The fifth paper entitled 'City Logistics through the canals? A simulation study on freight waterborne transport in the inner-city of Amsterdam' by van Duin, R., Kortmann, R. and van den Boogaard, S. discusses the possibility of city logistics through the canals in Amsterdam. The results of simulation showed that a water-borne city logistics concept through the canals of Amsterdam has demonstrated the capability of reducing the congestion in the inner-city and satisfying the requirements of shopkeepers.

The sixth paper entitled 'City logistics long-term planning: simulation of shopping mobility and goods restocking and related support systems' by Comi, A., Nuzzolo, A. and Rosati, L. discusses the city logistics long-term planning using the shopping demand models and urban goods restocking models. The simulation demonstrated that the changes in demographic and socio-economic characteristics could cause the relevant effects, in particular increasing car use in shopping mobility.

The seventh paper entitled 'Model of debris collection operation after disasters and its application in urban area' by Pramudita, A. and Taniguchi, E. presents a new capacitated arc routing model for effective debris collection and transport to disposal sites. Case studies on a test network as well as on realistic instances based on estimates of debris due to likely large-scale natural disaster in Tokyo Metropolitan Area have also been reported under various scenarios such as with or without multiple intermediate depots.

The eighth paper entitled 'London 2012: Changing delivery patterns in response to the impact of the Games on traffic flows' by Allen, J., Browne, M., Wainwright, I., Palmer, A. and Williams, I. addresses road freight transport operations during the London Olympic and Paralympic Games in 2012. The possible actions that could be taken by organizations to reduce the negative impacts were modelled and the results indicated that such actions would help to mitigate the impact of the road restrictions imposed on operators during the Games.

The ninth paper entitled 'Developing a local research strategy for city logistics on an academic campus' by Aditjandra, P., Zunder, T. and Carnaby, B. investigates relative suitability of data and methodology to assess the determinants of urban freight activities based on a case study in a British university campus. The study demonstrated the imperfect data and raised questions that identify new research opportunities with new data collection including: focus group interviews, staff questionnaires, and stated preference surveys.

The tenth paper entitled 'Collaboration in urban logistics: Motivations and barriers' by Lindawati, L., van Schagen, J., Goh, M. and de Souza, R. addresses the collaboration between stakeholders in urban logistics in Singapore. They pointed out that expected benefits and the competitive intelligence risks influence the participation decision in urban logistics.

The eleventh paper entitled 'An estimation of freight flow using the secondary data: a case study in Belo Horizonte (Brazil)'by Oliveira, L. and Pereira, Lilian presents a methodology for estimating freight flow by gathering common available data and applying the method in a study area. The results achieved in Belo Horizonte indicated the effectiveness of the methodology as well as the need for a systematic data collection in order to improve future results.

Eiichi Taniguchi
Department of Urban Management
Kyoto University

Application of exact route optimization for the evaluation of a city logistics truck ban scheme

Ali Gul Qureshi[a], Eiichi Taniguchi[a], Russell G. Thompson[b] and Joel S.E. Teo[a]

[a]Department of Urban Management, Graduate School of Engineering, Kyoto University, C-1 Kyotodaigaku Katsura, Nishikyo, Kyoto; [b]Department of Infrastructure Engineering, The University of Melbourne, Parkville, Australia

This paper presents an application of the exact solution approach for the Vehicle Routing Problem with Soft Time Windows based on the column generation scheme developed earlier by the authors, for evaluating a truck ban scheme from the environmental improvement aspect on a realistic logistics instance based on the Vehicle Information and Communication System data, which is an Intelligent Transportation Systems (ITS) application in Japan. Two different types of truck ban schemes are evaluated, one which denies truck entry on congested links (with average speeds lower than a threshold) and the other with and without the availability of the ITS-based data to freight firms. It was found that the Uniform truck ban on low travel speed links can result in a win-win situation, improving the environmental conditions as well as reducing the operation cost for freight carriers in a scenario where freight carriers do not have access to ITS-based travel time information. While the use of an exact optimization method and with ITS-based historical traffic information still helps in reducing environmental impacts, freight companies are slightly worst-off as far as the operation cost is concerned.

1. Introduction

Transportation demand both in terms of freight and passenger vehicles is increasing due to increased economic and industrial activities in cities. Since most large cities have evolved as a direct consequence of these activities, a high proportion of total goods movement occurs within cities by road transport. For example in Tokyo, Japan, the share of road-based transport is about 99.4% of the total intra-urban freight movement (Bureau of Industrial and Labor Affairs in Tokyo Metropolitan Government, 2009). Door-to-door service industries such as home appliances or utility repair services are also included in the broader definition of the urban logistics. The reliance on road-based transport leads to the typical problems relating to urban freight transport, which include traffic congestion, loading and unloading on-street, vehicle idling and hazardous emissions (Ortuzar & Willumsen, 1995). It is often the case that residents living in areas with a large amount of freight-related truck traffic complain about emissions, such as oxides of Nitrogen (NO_x).

City logistics aims to mitigate the adverse effects of urban freight movement through policy measures, which include promoting the use of advanced information and communication technology and Intelligent Transportation Systems (ITS) technologies, optimizing operations and other regulatory measures (congestion charging, load factor control, street and area truck bans, etc.). The aim of such policies is to improve traffic flow and the environment in city centres. The Vehicle Routing Problem with Time Windows (VRPTW) can be used for evaluating many types of such measures and policies along with route optimization. Route optimization not only serves the logistics firms, but also advances the objectives of other urban freight stakeholders, i.e. city administrators, residents and receivers (Taniguchi, Thompson, Yamada, & Duin, 2001). Route optimization results in the least possible number of vehicles for serving all customers' demands, travelling the minimum possible distance and decreasing the idling time of vehicles. This would result in less demand on road networks and less traffic-related environmental problems. Thus, administrators get less traffic-related problems, residents get cleaner environments and customers get faster deliveries.

The VRPTW involves determining a set of optimum routes covering all demands of a given set of customers without violating the capacity of vehicles and time window constraints that require deliveries to start at each customer i within a pre-specified time window $[a_i, b_i]$. Furthermore, to be more realistic, late deliveries are accepted with some penalty costs in the Vehicle Routing Problem with Soft Time Windows (VRPSTW), where it is assumed that if a vehicle arrives earlier than a_i, it will wait until a_i to start service; however, no penalty is applied for such waiting. Figure 1 shows the penalty function of the VRPSTW.

The VRPTW is defined on a complete graph, as shown in Figure 2(b), where every vertex (customer or depot) is connected with each of the other vertices with a single arc. Most of the VRPTW-related optimization research (especially in the exact optimization domain) base their analysis on benchmark instances developed on complete graphs, such as Solomon's benchmark instances (Solomon, 1987). These instances cover many aspects

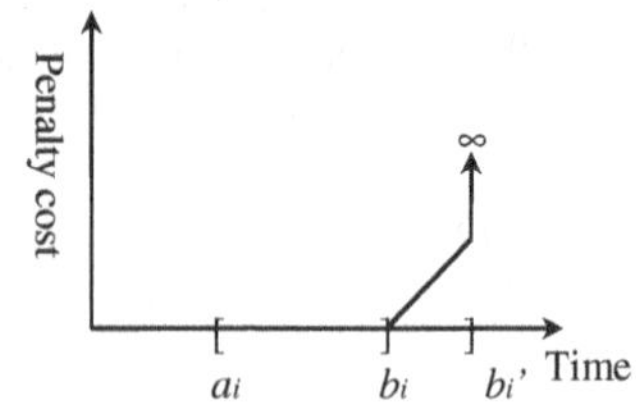

Figure 1. Penalty function of the VRPSTW.

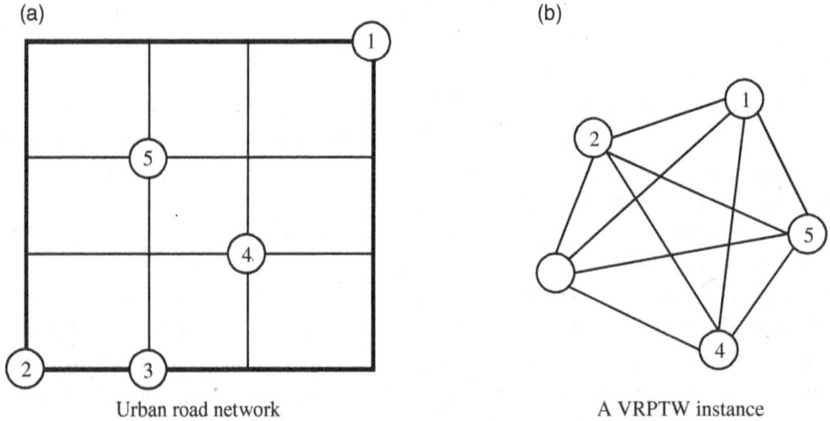

Figure 2. An urban road network and its transformation in a VRPTW instance.

of typical VRPTW; however, these are based on Euclidean distances and thus are devoid of actual traffic characteristics such as travel speeds and travel times. On the other hand, city logistics needs to deal with problems set in real-life road networks (Figure 2(a)) and incorporate prevalent traffic conditions. It is, therefore, advantageous to base the VRPTW analysis on realistic data sets using actual traffic data. It would also enable other solution characteristics to be compared, which are typically based on the actual traffic conditions and not just the solution cost and number of vehicles required.

For example, reducing emissions from urban freight movement is considered very important in city logistics. A single arc between two vertices in the complete graph representation (Figure 2(b)) is equal to a shortest path that may consist of various links in an actual road network (Figure 2(a)) with differing traffic conditions and contributing differently to emissions when vehicles travel on them. Vehicle emissions depend on the travel speed, and therefore, the effect of different city logistics policies on environment can only be evaluated if realistic data sets are used, based on actual traffic data. If instances are based on actual road networks, it would be possible to map-back the optimized VRPTW routes, which can help monitor the trucks' movement. Links with severe problems commonly attributed to freight truck movement can be identified, such as congested links with severe local pollution levels. Advancements in (ITS enable the collection of a large amount of useful road network-related data, thus making it possible to use realistic logistics instances based on these data.

Furthermore, most urban freight-related research has adopted heuristic approaches (for solving the underlying VRPSTW) to evaluate various policy measures (e.g. Taniguchi & van der Heijden, 2000). Heuristics are sometimes faster and easily implemented, yet they do not guarantee to identify the exact solution or even state the gap between the exact solution and a particular feasible solution found using these heuristics (Thompson & Van Duin, 2003). In research, where various policies and schemes are evaluated based on VRPTW solutions, the use of heuristic solutions with an aspect of uncertainty can create doubts in the mind of decision-makers that may hamper the evaluation itself.

Therefore, in light of the above discussion, this paper employs an exact solution approach for the VRPSTW based on the column generation scheme (Qureshi, Taniguchi, & Yamada, 2009), and presents an evaluation of a truck ban scheme for improving the environment on a realistic logistics instance based on the Vehicle Information and Communication System (VICS) data, which is an ITS application in Japan. Here, NO_x emissions have been calculated on roadway links, which are used in the routes of exact VRPSTW solutions, thereby identifying links with severe NO_x levels. Two different scenarios of truck ban schemes are evaluated, one which denies truck entry on congested links (with average speeds lower than a threshold) and the other with and without the availability of the ITS-based data to freight firms.

2. Literature review

As mentioned previously, mostly heuristic techniques have been adopted for solving the VRPSTW. For example, Taillard, Badeau, Guertin, Gendreau, and Potvin (1997) and Gendreau, Guertin, Potvin, and Taillard (1999) presented tabu search-based heuristics for the soft time windows settings mentioning their practical importance. van Duin, Tavasszy, and Taniguchi (2007) used the VRPSTW model and solved it with using tabu search for each freight carrier in a framework of a hybrid freight market, where a fraction of the demand was pre-allotted and another fraction was available in a real-time auction system. Genetic algorithms (GAs) are often employed for solving complex and close to real-life VRPSTW instances in city logistics. For example, Yamada, Taniguchi, and Itoh (2001) combined logistics terminal location, Cooperative Delivery System (CDS) and VRPSTW in a single framework. The combined model was solved using a GA heuristics and the results were compared to a base case that did not use the CDS. Qureshi and Hanaoka (2005) studied a CDS using GA solutions of the associated VRPSTW, where a truck assignment module assigned consolidated routes back to trucks of participating companies. Tamagawa, Taniguchi, and Yamada (2010) used GA-based solutions of the VRPSTW in a multi-agent model to evaluate various city logistics-based schemes such as road pricing and truck ban along with the toll discounts. Using a similar multi-agent model, Teo, Taniguchi, and Qureshi (2012) also investigated the effects of cordon-based and distance-based freight road-pricing schemes and concluded that distance-based pricing may result in less overall emissions in the entire city, whereas the cordon-based scheme has better results in the city centre only.

While the bulk of the research targeting soft time windows is heuristics based, exact solution research incorporating soft time windows has focused on the schedule optimization of a given fixed path considering linear (Sexton & Bodin, 1985) and/or generalized convex penalty functions (Dumas, Somis, & Desrosiers, 1990). Recently, Tagmouti, Gendreau, and Potvin (2007) presented an arc routing problem with soft time windows, where vehicles are not allowed to wait along their routes. In their column generation scheme, they have used a modified labelling algorithm for the Shortest Path Problem with Time Windows and Time Costs sub-problem earlier given by Ioachim, Gelinas, Soumis, and Desrosiers (1998). The vehicle arrival pattern was represented by a continuous variable that resulted in very high computation times and this limited the maximum size of problem solved to 40 customers. Recently, Qureshi et al. (2009) presented a column generation-based exact solution approach for soft time windows that considers late arrival penalties, and efficiently solved instances up to 50 customers under various soft time windows settings.

Almost all of the afore-cited references use Solomon's benchmark instances or test instances based on hypothetical networks which are devoid of the actual traffic conditions. There is little research that has used actual network-based instances in the heuristic analysis of the VRPTW (for example, see Ioannoue, Kritikos, & Prastacos, 2002; Prindezis, Kiranoudis, & Marinos-Kouris, 2003). Fleischmann, Gnutzmann, and Sandvoss (2004) worked with test instances based on the data from Leit-und Information System Berlin, an ITS implemented in Berlin, Germany, that provided travel time data on links every 5 minutes. In Japan, VICS provides such network data, which have been used in various traffic-related studies (Hiramatsu, Nose, Tenmoku, & Morita, 2009), but its application in the logistics field has been limited. Recently, utilizing the VICS data complemented with the data from 66 days operation of probe pickup/delivery trucks, Ando and Taniguchi (2006) applied a probabilistic-VRPTW and its GA solution to an actual delivery system in Osaka, Japan. This paper also adopts test instances based on VICS data and evaluates a truck ban scheme using the exact solution of the underlying VRPSTW using actual traffic conditions.

3. The VRPSTW formulation

The classical VRPSTW is defined on a directed graph $G = (V, A)$ (such as in Figure 2(b)). The vertex set V includes the depot vertex 0 and a fixed set of customers $C = \{1, 2, \ldots, n\}$. The arc set A consists of all feasible arcs (i, j), $i, j \in V$. With every vertex of V, there is an associated demand d_i, with $d_0 = 0$, and a time window $[a_i, b_i]$ representing the earliest and the latest possible service start times. A set of identical vehicles (represented by K), each with a capacity q stationed at the depot, is available to service customers' demands. Both cost c_{ij} as well as a travel time t_{ij} are associated with each arc $(i, j) \in A$. The time t_{ij} includes the travel time on arc (i, j) and the service time at vertex i, and a fixed vehicle utilization cost is added to all outgoing arcs from the depot, i.e. in c_{0j}, $j \in C$. However, as shown in Figure 1, based on a routing decision, the modified arc costs c'_{ijk} depend on the service start time (s_{jk}) at customer j by vehicle k; these costs are calculated as per Equation (1), where c_l is the unit penalty costs for any late arrival and the lateness is also bounded by b'_i.

$$c'_{ijk} = \begin{cases} c_{ij}, & \text{if } a_j \leq s_{jk} \leq b_j \\ c_{ij} + c_l(s_{jk} - b_j), & \text{if } b_j < s_{jk} \leq b'_j. \end{cases} \tag{1}$$

Now the VRPSTW can be mathematically formulated as:

$$\min \sum_{k \in K} \sum_{(i,j) \in A} c'_{ijk} x_{ijk} \tag{2}$$

subject to

$$\sum_{k \in K} \sum_{j \in V} x_{ijk} = 1 \quad \forall i \in C \tag{3}$$

$$\sum_{i \in C} d_i \sum_{j \in V} x_{ijk} \leq q \quad \forall k \in K \tag{4}$$

$$\sum_{j \in V} x_{0jk} = 1 \quad \forall k \in K \tag{5}$$

$$\sum_{i \in V} x_{ihk} - \sum_{j \in V} x_{hjk} = 0 \quad \forall h \in C, \forall k \in K \tag{6}$$

$$\sum_{i \in V} x_{i0k} = 1 \quad \forall k \in K \tag{7}$$

$$s_{ik} + t_{ij} - s_{jk} \leq (1 - x_{ijk})M \quad \forall (i, j) \in A, \ \forall k \in K \tag{8}$$

$$a_i \leq s_{ik} \leq b'_i \quad \forall i \in V, \ \forall k \in K \tag{9}$$

$$x_{ijk} \in \{0, 1\} \quad \forall (i, j) \in A, \ \forall k \in K \tag{10}$$

The model contains two decision variables: s_{jk} determines the service start time at customer j as well as the travel cost of arc (i, j), and x_{ijk} represents whether arc (i, j) is used in the solution $(x_{ijk} = 1)$ or not $(x_{ijk} = 0)$. The objective function (1) minimizes the total cost including the fixed cost for vehicle utilization and the travel cost on the arcs with late arrival penalty costs. Constraint (2) ensures that every customer is only serviced once, while Constraint (3) is the capacity constraint that keeps the cumulative demands along a vehicle's route within its capacity. Constraints (4), (5) and (6) are flow conservation constraints, specifying that every route shall start from and end at the depot; while, on the route, if a vehicle travels to a customer location h, it must also travel from it. Constraint (7) is a time window constraint specifying that if a vehicle travels from i to j, service at j cannot start earlier than that at i. Here, M is a large constant. Constraint (8) represents the relaxed time windows for the VRPSTW and restricts the service start time at all vertices within their relaxed time windows $[a_i, b'_i]$. Finally, Constraint (9) ensures the integrality of the flow variables x_{ijk}.

3.1. *Dantzig–Wolfe decomposition of the VRPSTW*

From the formulation of the VRPSTW given in the previous section, only Constraint (3) couples all the vehicles together, while the rest of the constraints are separable for each vehicle. The Dantzig–Wolfe decomposition (or column generation) scheme decomposes the VRPSTW formulation in a set partitioning problem (Equations (11)–(13)) by taking the coupling constraint (i.e. Equation (3)) in it. The remaining constraints (Equations (4)–(10)) formulate an Elementary Shortest Path Problem with Resource Constraint with Late Arrival Penalties (ESPPRCLAP) as a sub-problem. The rôle of the sub-problem is to provide feasible single vehicle routes (also called paths or columns) to the linear program of the set partitioning master problem. Set P is the set of all such feasible routes. The variable y_p takes value 1 if the route $p \in P$ is selected and 0 otherwise. The cost of route p is denoted by c_p, and a_{ip} represents the number of times route p serves customer i. The objective (Equation (11)) selects a minimum cost set of routes from P such that each customer $i \in C$ is serviced exactly once as per the constraint represented by Equation (12). The integrality constraint is represented by Equation (13); usually a linear programming relaxation of this constraint is solved where y_p can vary anywhere between 0 and 1.

$$\min \sum_{p \in P} c_p y_p \tag{11}$$

subject to

$$\sum_{p \in P} a_{ip} y_p = 1 \quad \forall i \in C \tag{12}$$

$$y_p \in \{0, 1\} \quad \forall p \in P \tag{13}$$

The ESPPRCLAP sub-problem has an objective function that minimizes the reduced cost of a path (Equation (14)) starting and ending at the depot (i.e. a single vehicle route), called a column in the column generation scheme.

$$\min \sum_{(i,j) \in A} \overline{c'_{ij}} x_{ij} \tag{14}$$

subject to Constraints (4)–(10), separated for each vehicle $k \in K$.

The ESPPRCLAP is solved on the same graph as the VRPSTW, taking reduced cost on its arcs. The reduced cost of an arc (i, j) (Equation (15)) is obtained using the corresponding dual variable value π_i (price or shadow cost) for each customer $i \in C$, obtained in the solution of the set partitioning master problem.

$$\overline{c'_{ij}} = c'_{ij} - \pi_i \quad \forall i \in C \tag{15}$$

For more details, please refer to Qureshi et al. (2009).

4. The test logistics instance

To evaluate city logistics measures and policies such as the truck ban scheme proposed in this paper, a range of precise data is required to be collected/obtained. This includes the network data (preferably in digital or geographic information system versions with current restriction/grading of roadway links). Associated travel time data (preferably detailed travel time data from an ITS source covering temporal variations of the travel time on network links), and logistics data (such as depot location, available truck resources and customer's data such as location, demand and time windows) are also needed. As it can be observed that such data would have many local trends, therefore, most of the analysis results may also be valid only for a particular locality. Unfortunately, the logistics data are the most difficult one to get in many circumstances, as it is regarded as classified by the logistics firms.

The VICS aims to provide useful traffic information to users in order to reduce road congestion. VICS was the first such service implemented in the world, commencing operation on 23 April 1996 (Yamada, 1996). Initially it was designed to distribute traffic data collected by prefectural police headquarters and road administrators, using road side infrastructure consisting of radio wave beacons, infrared beacons and frequency modulated multiplex broadcasting. At present, VICS data are augmented with a probe car system, another important ITS application in Japan (ITS Handbook 2007–2008, Japan). Although the use of car navigation systems equipped with VICS has increased in Japan, its use within the freight industry, especially at the route planning (optimization) stage, is not very high, as most of the freight companies operating within urban areas plan their operations manually.

To incorporate actual traffic-related characteristics within the test logistics instances, this study has used a portion of the Osaka road network in Japan. The network consists of 225 nodes and 789 links, all being VICS links. The travel time data for each 5-minute slot were obtained for each of these links for 30 working days. For the static version of the VRPSTW used in this research, we obtained an average value of travel time for each link based on the aforementioned data. Firstly, average travel time for each time slot was obtained over the entire 30 days to make an average day's data, and then the average of all the slots (within working hours) was taken as the value of travel time for a particular link of the network shown in Figure 3.

As mentioned earlier, the VRPSTW is solved on a complete graph, where each arc (i, j) directly connects customer i with customer j; in fact, this arc is the shortest path from customer i to customer j in real network. Therefore, to formulate a VRPSTW instance, the instance based on Osaka road network (Figure 3) was converted into a complete graph (similar to Figure 2(b)) by finding the shortest path between various customers and the depot using Dijkstra's algorithm. Advantageously, it was also possible to map the solution of the VRPSTW onto the real road network, identifying the links of the road network to be used by the delivery vehicles. Hence, a detailed link-based analysis of the environment-related issues was possible, employing useful VICS data. Furthermore, the location of customers is hypothetical for this test instance but it incorporates some local knowledge of the area. Similarly, customers' demand and their time windows were generated randomly, keeping a time windows length of 10 minutes (i.e. $b_i - a_i = 10$ minutes). In calculating costs, the vehicle operating cost (VOC) was taken as 14.02 ¥/minute with a fixed cost of 10417.50 ¥/vehicle. Furthermore, the slope of late arrival penalty curve (i.e. the unit late arrival penalty cost c_l) was set to five times that of the VOC. These parameter settings are based on an interview survey of logistics firms in Japan and have been extensively used in the literature (for example, see Qureshi et al., 2009; Tamagawa et al., 2010; Taniguchi & van der Heijden, 2000; Teo et al., 2012; Yamada et al., 2001).

5. Environment and idling related issues

It is well documented that vehicle emissions such as NO_x, CO_2 and suspended particulate matter are dependent on the speed of the vehicle (Taniguchi et al., 2001), which in turn

Figure 3. The realistic logistics instance.

depends on the geometric conditions of the roads (such as width and gradients), type of roads (such as expressway and local street) and the traffic conditions on the roads. For example, Equation (15) gives the speed–emission (NO_x) relationship for small logistics trucks (up to 2.5 tons) provided by the National Institute for Land and Infrastructure Management, Japan (NILIM, 2003). The corresponding curve is shown in Figure 4; a very steep rise in emission levels can be observed at the low end of the travel speeds. Although the relationship used here is based on a Japanese study, the European Programme on Emissions, Fuels and Engine Technologies (EPEFE, 1995) has also reported a similar trend of NO_x–speed curve for diesel vehicles.

$$\mathrm{NO}_x = l_{ij}\left(1.06116 + 0.000213\, v_{ij}^2 - 0.0246\, v_{ij} + \frac{16.258}{v_{ij}}\right). \tag{16}$$

A path between two customers (i.e. a single arc in the graph $G = (V, A)$, described in earlier sections) may contain links with different speeds, and therefore, it may have different NO_x emissions associated with the various links on it. Furthermore, the effect of waiting time was actively incorporated in calculation of NO_x by considering the vehicle's *engine on* condition while waiting. Yu, Qiao, and Soltani (2006) concluded that an *idling* vehicle emits the same

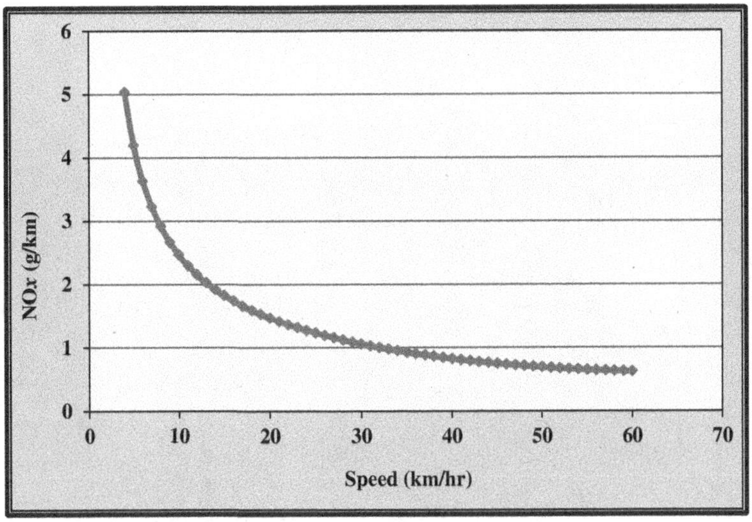

Figure 4. NO_x–speed relationship.

amount of emissions as if it was travelling at a speed of 4.025 km/h (equivalent to 2.5 mph). The *idling* emissions were taken into account in the same manner as that for waiting vehicles in this research.

6. The truck ban scheme

As mentioned earlier, to offset the ill effects of urban goods movement, various city logistics schemes could be used, with truck bans being one such scheme. Truck bans can be implemented in a variety of ways, for example, trucks could be banned from entering a particular area during peak hours only, or restrictions can be levied based on their size. As the VRPSTW formulation given in earlier sections and its exact solution approach consider a single type of truck (2 ton truck), this paper considers a very simple version of the truck ban policy. Usually, the aim of the truck ban policy is to relieve congestion and to reduce local pollution on streets. Streets with low travel speeds (either due to congestion or due to their narrow widths), which generally occur in city centres, are more likely be the places where such policies are expected to be implemented. Therefore, this research considers a uniform truck ban on all streets and road links where the average travel speed is less than 10 kmph. Figure 5 shows the road network links (in red colour) subjected to the truck ban due to their average travel speed being less than 10 kmph. In total, 38 links were subject to the truck ban out of 789 links. It can be observed that most of these links are in central city area, and some of these links also have some customer locations. Therefore, if not banned exclusively, it is possible that freight carriers may use them, specially if they are not aware of the true average travel speed on these links. It is also possible that the policy of truck bans may result in a situation in which one or more customers become inaccessible; however, in that case, it can be assumed that the trucks would stop at a nearby location and the 'last mile' delivery would be done in some environmentally friendly way (even by walking or by tricycles) with additional time and cost requirements, but still resulting in a connected underlying graph required to solve the VRPSTW with exact methods.

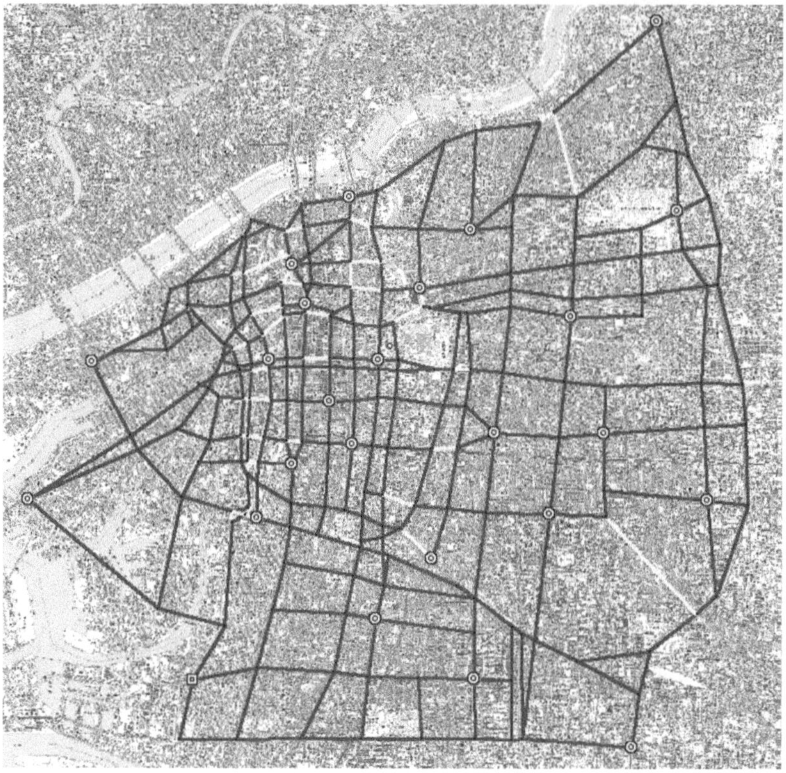

Figure 5. Road network links under truck ban.

Two scenarios were considered as far as the use/availability of the ITS-based travel time data is concerned; Scenario 1 assumes that the freight carriers do not have historical information about travel times on roadway links, and they optimize their operations by minimizing the distance travelled. The corresponding VRPSTW is solved using the exact solution technique on graph *G* where each arc is based on the 'shortest distance' paths assuming a uniform travel speed that equals to the average travel speed of the entire road network (20 kmph in this case). However, when such a solution would actually be executed on the real road network, trucks would experience the actual network travel time and speeds. Therefore, while keeping the link sequences of the 'shortest distance' paths, the VRPSTW solution was evaluated using the actual travel speeds and travel times on these links. In the second scenario, it is assumed that the freight carriers have access to advanced ITS technologies such as VICS, and they have historical information about the travel times on road network links; therefore, they use 'shortest travel time' paths in the exact VRPSTW solutions to optimize their operations.

One immediate consequence of the two scenarios mentioned earlier can be observed from comparing Figures 6 and 7, which show the distribution of links (based on their travel speed) used in the exact VRPSTW solutions of the freight companies in the absence of the truck ban. Clearly, more links with less than 10 kmph travel speed have been used in Scenario 1 compared to Scenario 2. Another evident trend is the relatively higher usage of high travel speed (in range of 26–60 kmph) links in Scenario 2 compared to Scenario 1 both with and without truck ban cases. Therefore, it can be concluded that without access to the ITS-based historical travel time information and to when the freight carriers resort to the

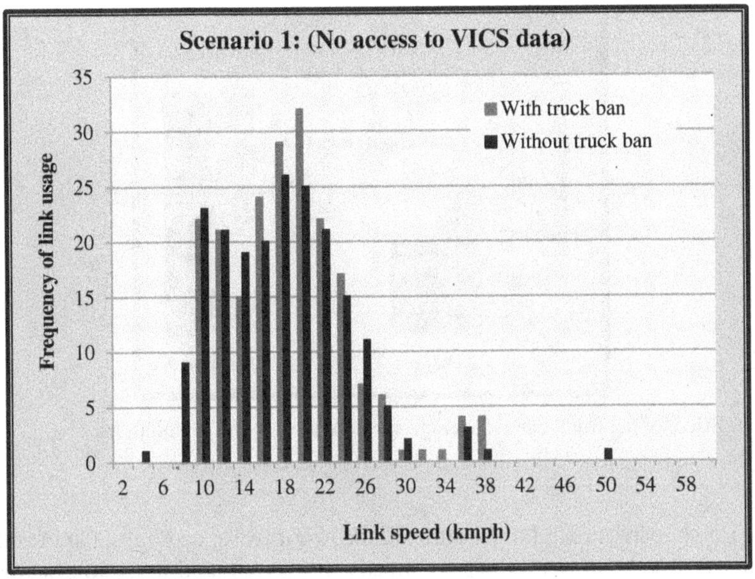

Figure 6. Usage of links of various speeds in exact solutions of Scenario 1.

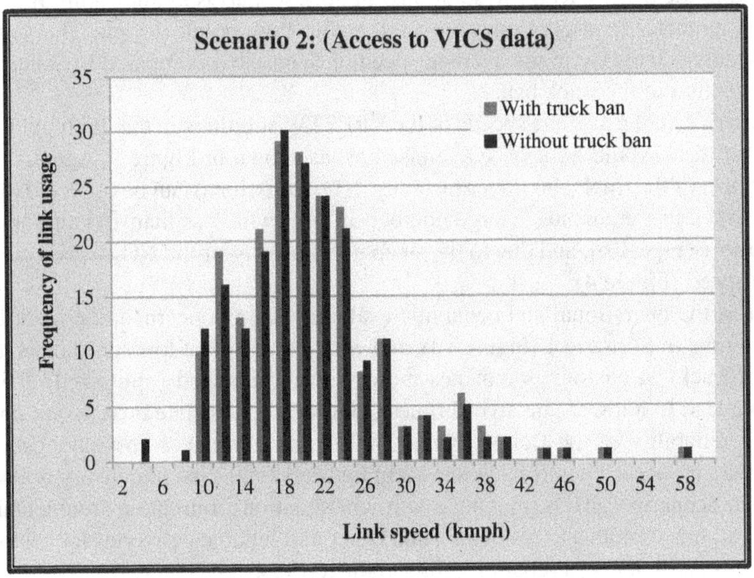

Figure 7. Usage of links of various speeds in exact solutions of Scenario 2.

shortest distance-based optimization, the chance of getting stuck in the slow moving traffic is relatively higher even though they use sophisticated exact optimization techniques.

Furthermore, the truck ban on links with less than 10 kmph speeds (the city logistics policy considered in this paper) had more impact (in the form of change in frequency of used links of a certain speed) in Scenario 1 as compared to Scenario 2, shown by the difference in heights of bars in with and without the truck ban. Therefore, in Scenario 1, more benefits are achieved by the truck ban policy, as even still unaware of the true travel time of the

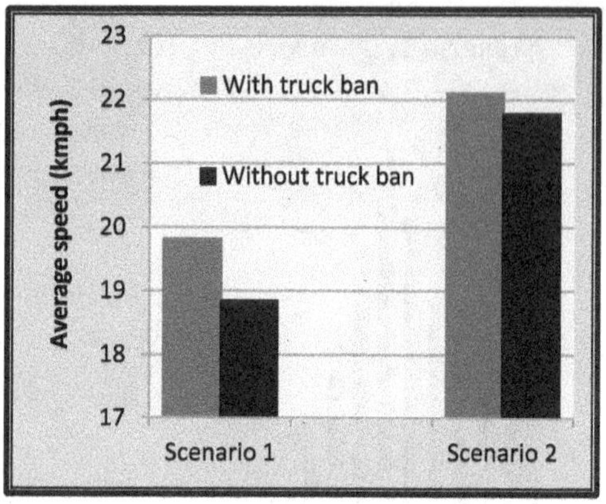

Figure 8. Effect of the truck ban on average speed of the VRPSTW solutions.

links, the freight carriers are forced off from the low travel speed links. On the other hand, in Scenario 2, freight carriers (their optimization process) tend to avoid low travel speed links due to better travel time information, and therefore, a truck ban on low speed links does not affect them a lot. The truck ban leads to an increase in average speeds (over all the links used in the exact VRPSTW solutions) in both scenarios as shown in Figure 8 which is a good indicator in itself from an overall traffic flow point of view. This explains the relatively larger increase in the average speed of Scenario 1 compared to Scenario 2 after the introduction of the truck ban.

The increase in the average speeds of the VRPSTW solutions in the 'with truck ban' case means that there would be less NO_x emissions, as shown in Figure 9. Again, a relatively better impact of the truck ban (in terms of less NO_x emissions) can be observed in Scenario 1, as the truck ban eradicates a large number of links with less than 10 kmph travel speed in Scenario 1 (Figure 6), and due to the steep non-linearity of the NO_x–speed curve in that range of speed (Figure 4).

As far as the operational and economic evaluations are concerned, the truck ban saves operation time in Scenario 1 (Figure 10), and with less usage of low speed links, the actual arrival of trucks at customers matches more with the planned (optimized) arrival times and hence lead to a lower late arrival times (Figure 11). Less late arrivals not only means improved reliability of the freight carrier, but this also achieves cost savings as the late penalties are reduced. Therefore, as shown in Figure 12, the cost of delivery is also slightly reduced in Scenario 1. Thus, making a win-win situation from an environmental point of view (for administrators and residents), and faster and reliable deliveries for customers and cost savings and improved reliability for freight carriers.

For Scenario 2, however, the previous comparison is not that favourable to the truck ban scheme, because all the factors compared, i.e. operation time, late arrival time and consequently the cost, are higher in the 'with truck ban' case, as shown in Figures 10–12, respectively. The main reason for this result is the very high level of optimization resulting from sophisticated exact optimization based on the precise historical travel time information from the ITS. With this historical travel time information available, the shortest paths between the depot and customers, and between customers (i.e. arcs of the complete graph G, which is used in exact optimization of the VRPSTW) are composed of road network links with high average travel times even in without the truck ban. Therefore, the pre-truck ban routing solution in Scenario 2 is already the 'most' efficient in terms of

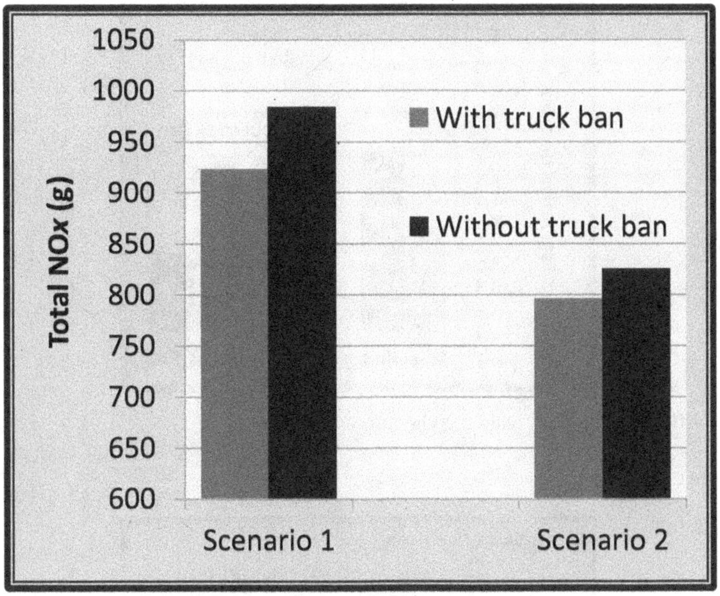

Figure 9. Effect of the truck ban on NO_x emissions.

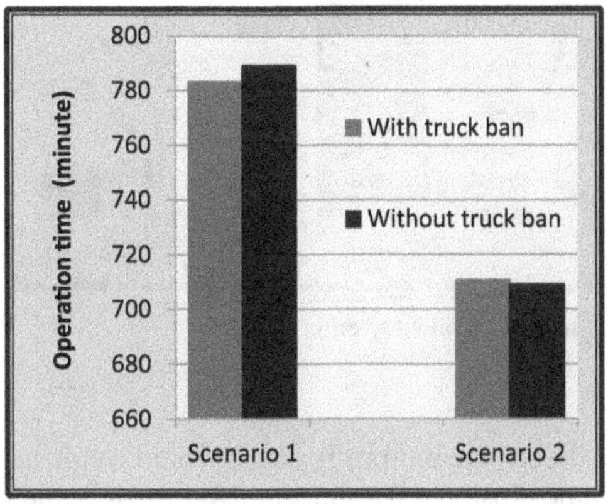

Figure 10. Effect of the truck ban on NO_x emissions.

operation time, late arrival time and the solution cost. Any change in this solution due to truck bans on links used in this solution leads to poorer solutions from all these aspects, which is evident in Figures 10–12. However, it must be noted that the overall increase in costs is insignificant (only 0.2%) as compared to the improvement in the local environment (i.e. a reduction of 3.5% in the NO_x emissions). Finally, the large difference in the operation time and solution cost between the two scenarios shows the benefit (cost saving) of having (or not having) access to the ITS-based historical travel time information. This could be, therefore, used to entice the freight carriers to invest more in their information database as well as in sophisticated optimization methods.

It must also be mentioned here that a truck ban will not always produce the ideal effects as found in this study, where both environmental improvements are obtained and the cost is either improved (Scenario 1) or slightly increased (Scenario 2). This result is due to the fact

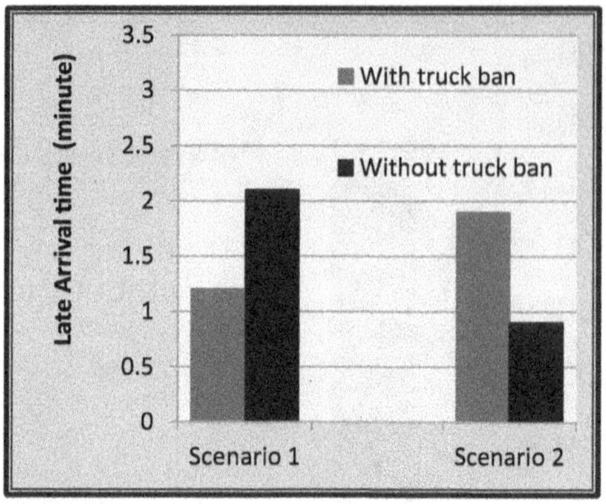

Figure 11. Effect of the truck ban on NO_x emissions.

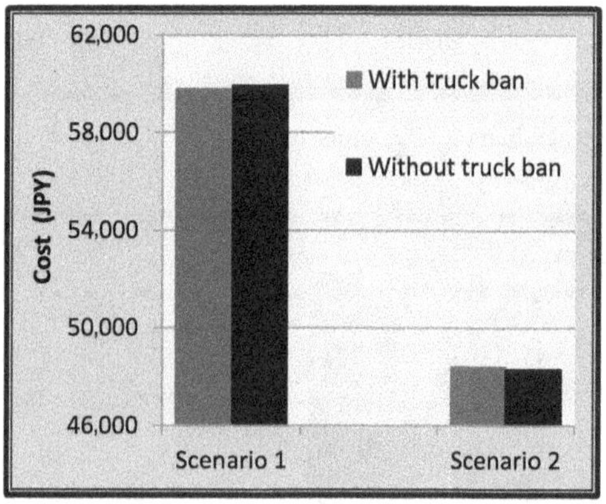

Figure 12. Effect of the truck ban on NO_x emissions.

that the truck ban considered here uniformly bans truck movements only on all 'low speed links' and not on the major roads or the most utilized roads, which is often the case with usual truck ban schemes. Truck ban schemes that ban large trucks on bigger arterial roads and/or in peak traffic periods often lead to a switch from large to many small-sized trucks, resulting in even more traffic on the roads. Such switching of trucks also results in extra costs to the freight carriers, thus making the truck ban scheme less desirable for them. The truck ban considered in this study assumes the use of relatively small-sized (2 ton) trucks both before and after the truck ban scheme. Another feature of the tested truck ban scheme is that it affects only a small number of road network links (only 38 out of 789 in this instance) in a discrete manner (as shown in Figure 5), with alternate routes still being available easily. Therefore, it would not require freight carriers to switch to smaller sized trucks as would have been the case with a general area/road truck ban. Furthermore, if trucks are banned from using arterial roads with relatively higher average travel speeds (in order to improve traffic or as a reaction to higher NO_x levels), it would lead to larger changes in routing plans (if it is highly optimized). This would lead to only the second or even third best routing solutions with a high increase in operational cost as well as in late arrival time (Qureshi, Taniguchi, & Yamada, 2012).

7. Conclusion

This paper presented an evaluation of a truck ban scheme from the environmental improvement perspective as well as from the operational and cost aspects on a realistic logistics instance. An exact solution approach for the VRPSTW based on the column generation scheme was used in the evaluation, which improves the reliability of the evaluation itself. It was found that a uniform truck ban on low travel speed links results in a win-win situation, improving the environmental conditions as well as reducing the operation cost for the freight carrier in a scenario where the freight carrier does not have access to ITS-based historical travel time information. While the use of an exact optimization method and ITS-based historical traffic information gives the ideal exact solution, truck ban on a link used in such an ideal solution would definitely result in the 'the second best' solution. The second best solution, however, would still help in reducing environmental problems, but the freight companies would be slightly worst-off as far as operation costs and the additional late arrival time/penalties are concerned.

Often regulatory policies (such as truck bans) provoke hostility from freight carriers, but as shown, if a proper analysis is done, a better facet of the policy can be presented to them, which shows that the utmost impacts on their operations are insignificant, if they are already optimizing their routes. It is also possible that the truck ban policy on all low speed links (as used in this paper) may result in a scenario in which one or more customers will become inaccessible; however, in that case, it can be assumed that trucks would stop at a nearby location and the 'last mile' delivery would be done in some environmentally friendly way (even by walking or by tricycles) with additional time and cost requirements, but still resulting in a connected underlying graph required to solve the VRPSTW with exact methods.

References

Ando, N., & Taniguchi, E. (2006). Travel time reliability in vehicle routing and scheduling with time windows. *Networks and Spatial Economics, 6*, 293–311.

Bureau of Industrial and Labor Affairs in Tokyo Metropolitan Government. (2009). *Industry and Employment in Tokyo, A Graphic Overview 2009*. Retrieved August 12, 2010, from http://www.sangyo-rodo.metro.tokyo.jp/monthly/sangyo/graphic/2009nen/index.htm

van Duin, J. H. R., Tavasszy, L. A., & Taniguchi, E. (2007). Real time simulation of auctioning and re-scheduling process in hybrid freight markets. *Transportation Research Part B, 41*, 1050–1066.

Dumas, Y., Somis, F., & Desrosiers, J. (1990). Optimizing the schedule for a fixed vehicle path with convex inconvenience costs. *Transportation Science, 24*, 145–152.

EPEFE (1995). *European programme on emissions, fuels and engine technologies* (ACEA, EUROPIA Report). Brussles: ACEA, EUROPIA.

Fleischmann, B., Gnutzmann, S., & Sandvoss, E. (2004). Dynamic vehicle routing based on online traffic information. *Transportation Science, 38*, 420–433.

Gendreau, M., Guertin, F., Potvin, J., & Taillard, E. (1999). Parallel tabu search for real-time vehicle and dispatching. *Transportation Science, 33*, 381–390.

Hiramatsu, A., Nose, K., Tenmoku, K., & Morita, T. (2009). Prediction of travel time in urban district based on state equation. *Electronics and Communications in Japan, 92*, 1–11.

Ioachim, I., Gelinas, S., Soumis, F., & Desrosiers, J. (1998). A dynamic programming algorithm for the shortest path problem with time windows and linear node costs. *Networks, 31*, 193–204.

Ioannoue, G., Kritikos, M. N., & Prastacos, G. P. (2002). A GIS-based decision support system for intra-city vehicle routing with time windows. *The Journal of the Operational Research Society, 53*, 842–854.

ITS Handbook. (2007–2008). Japan, Highway Industry Development Organization (HIDO). Retrieved January 16, 2010, from http://www.hido.or.jp/09kankou/HANDBOOK_all.pdf

National Institute of Land and Infrastructure Management (NILIM), Japan. (2003). *Quantitative appraisal index calculations used for basic unit computation of* CO_2, NO_x, *SPM* (in Japanese). Tsukuba, Japan: Author.

Ortuzar, J. D., & Willumsen, L. G. (1995). *Modeling transport*. England: John Wiley & Sons.

Prindezis, N., Kiranoudis, C. T., & Marinos-Kouris, D. (2003). A business-to-business fleet management service provider for central food market enterprises. *Journal of Food Engineering, 60*, 203–210.

Qureshi, A. G., & Hanaoka, S. (2005). Analysis of the effects of cooperative delivery system in Bangkok. In E. Taniguchi, & R. G. Thompson (Eds.), *Recent advances in city logistics* (pp. 59–73). Oxford: Elsevier.

Qureshi, A. G., Taniguchi, E., & Yamada, T. (2009). An exact solution approach for vehicle routing and scheduling problems with soft time windows. *Transportation Research Part E, 45*, 960–977.

Qureshi, A. G., Taniguchi, E., & Yamada, T. (2012). *Evaluation of a City Logistics Scheme using Exact Optimization for the VRPSTW*. Presented at 4th World Conference of Production and Operations Management (P&OM), Amsterdam.

Sexton, R. T., & Bodin, L. D. (1985). Optimizing single vehicle many to many operations with desired delivery times: II. Routing. *Transportation Science, 19*, 411–435.

Solomon, M. M. (1987). Algorithms for the vehicle routing and scheduling problem with time windows constraints. *Operations Research, 35*, 254–265.

Tagmouti, M., Gendreau, M., & Potvin, J. Y. (2007). Arc routing problem with time-dependent service costs. *European Journal of Operational Research, 181*, 30–39.

Taillard, E., Badeau, P., Guertin, F., Gendreau, M., & Potvin, J. (1997). A tabu search heuristic for the vehicle routing problem with soft time windows. *Transportation Science, 31*, 170–186.

Tamagawa, D., Taniguchi, E., & Yamada, T. (2010). Evaluating city logistics measures using a multi-agent model. *Procedia Social and Behavioral Sciences, 2*, 6002–6012. doi:10.1016/j.sbspro.2010.04.014

Taniguchi, E., & van der Heijden, R. E. C. M. (2000). An evaluation methodology for city logistics. *Transport Reviews, 20*, 65–90.

Taniguchi, E., Thompson, R. G., Yamada, T., & Duin, R. V. (2001). *City logistics; Network modeling and intelligent transport systems*. Oxford: Pergamon.

Teo, J. S. E., Taniguchi, E., & Qureshi, A. G. (2012). Evaluation of distance-based and cordon-based urban freight road pricing on e-commerce environment with multi-agent model. *Transportation Research Record (TRR): Journal of the Transportation Research Board, 2269*, 127–134.

Thompson, R. G., & Van Duin, J. H. R. (2003). Vehicle routing and scheduling. In E. Taniguchi, & R. G. Thompson (Eds.), *Innovations in freight transport* (pp. 47–63). Southampton: WIT Press.

Yamada, S. (1996). The strategy and deployment plan for VICS. *IEEE Communications Magazine, 34*, 94–97.

Yamada, T., Taniguchi, E., & Itoh, Y. (2001). Co-operative vehicle routing model with optimal location of logistics terminals. In E. Taniguchi, & R. G. Thompson (Eds.), *City logistics II* (pp. 139–153). Japan: Institute for City Logistics.

Yu, L., Qiao, F., & Soltani, F. (2006). *Testing and modeling truck emissions while idling* (Research Report 167650-1). Houston, TX: Texas Southern University.

Ontology-based multi-agent system for urban freight transportation

Nilesh Anand[a], Ron van Duin[a] and Lori Tavasszy[a,b]

[a] *Faculty of Technology, Policy & Management, Delft University of Technology, Delft, The Netherlands;* [b] *TNO, Delft, The Netherlands*

Congestion, pollution, and safety are some of the most worrisome side-effects of the urban goods movement activities. These problems are generally attributed to the underlying characteristics of the domain such as heterogeneous stakeholders, their conflicting objectives and resulting distributed decision-making. Such autonomous decision-making stakeholders do not efficiently cooperate and coordinate while performing city logistics activities. The ensuing inefficient use of resources (e.g. goods delivery vehicle, time, etc.) gives rise to the above-mentioned problems. To reduce the negative externalities of urban goods movement, we first must understand the decision-making process of the city logistics stakeholder under different situations. Agent-based simulation modelling technique is such an approach where distributed decision-making of the multiple stakeholders can be included by modelling each entity as an autonomous agent. In this paper, we propose the use of a knowledge data model of urban freight domain – city logistics ontology – to develop an agent-based model. City logistics ontology is a knowledge model which includes city logistics entities (e.g. stakeholders, resources, etc.) and relationships between them in a structured form. The paper focuses on the usefulness of ontology in the development of agent-based model for city logistics domain, and attempts to demonstrate the effectiveness of agent technology in analysing the urban freight decision-making processes.

1. Introduction and motivation

City logistics (henceforth also as urban freight transportation[1]) is often considered a part of the urban transportation domain instead of a domain in itself. Goods movement is treated as passenger movement, though passengers move themselves and goods do not. In fact, the goods movement is the result of demand for goods from the consumers. Owing to the demand from the consumers, the retail firm generates orders for a shipper firm. The shipper needs transportation to deliver goods from the warehouse to the retailers' locations and thus hires a logistics firm for the delivery of goods. The infrastructure needed for goods transportation (e.g. road, rail, etc.) is provided by local, regional, and national governments. Consequently, the presence of multiple heterogeneous stakeholders with different objectives and limited resources gives rise to distributed decision-making system. In such a distributed decision-making system, the stakeholders usually do not share information and each stakeholder is interested in achieving his/her own objective (Thompson & Taniguchi,

2001). No central authority controls the decisions of all stakeholders, leaving all stakeholders to act autonomously. This non-cooperative decision-making leads to inefficient system performance (Friesz & Holguín-Veras, 2005).

Furthermore, city logistics is an open system where interactions between different stakeholders are characterized by communication which is not constant, information sources, and levels change unexpectedly, and even stakeholders appear and disappear frequently. These interactions, which take place between heterogeneous stakeholders at different times under different conditions, create situations which are not known in advance and change over time. The complexity of the city logistics domain is also considerable due to the emergence phenomenon. Emergent behaviour in city logistics appears when a number of stakeholders operate and form a complex behaviour as collective (Puckett Hensher, Rose, & Collin, 2007). The number of interactions between stakeholders increases combinatorially with the increase in the number of stakeholders, potentially allowing for many new and subtle types of behaviour to emerge which can be described as 'aggregate complexity' (Crooks, Castle, & Batty, 2008). Such phenomena make it hard to predict emergent behaviour in the city logistics domain. Thus, a large number of heterogeneous stakeholders participating in distributed decision-making processes add to the complexity and unpredictability of the city logistics domain.

The complexity of the city logistic domain and diverse interests of various stakeholders demand a well-designed approach and active participation of stakeholders in order to formulate effective city logistics-related policy measures (OECD, 2003). It demands an approach which can simulate the details of continuously changing city logistics characteristics in an efficient way and be able to capture the emergent behaviour of the dynamically changing city logistics processes. This approach should help understand ongoing changes in the system. Subsequently, the knowledge about the system and its emergent behavioural processes can be used to invent solutions for city logistics-related problems. Therefore, the method should be able to generate extreme events upon which different policy analysis can be carried out to analyse the possible outcomes of measures. Additionally, the model/method should be able to explain the data-generating process for such events.

Agent-based simulation modelling technique (henceforth also ABM) is an approach where distributed decision-making of multiple stakeholders can be included by modelling each entity as an autonomous agent. Roorda, Cavalcante, McCabe, and Kwan (2009) present a conceptual framework for detailed modelling of actors and their interactions using agent-based modelling system for urban freight transportation. The framework claims that the agent technique can be helpful in representing business decisions ranging from fundamental long-term decisions to short-term operational decisions and is thus sensitive to a variety of technology trends, business trends, and policy scenarios in ways that conventional approaches are not.

In this paper, we propose the use of a knowledge data model – a city logistics ontology – to develop an agent-based model for the city logistics domain. An ontology is essentially a data model representing the domain knowledge in a structured way. The paper focuses on the usefulness of ontology in the development of agent-based model for the city logistics domain, and attempts to demonstrate the effectiveness of agent technology in analysing the urban freight decision-making processes. The remainder of the paper is organized as follows. Section 2 summarizes the literature of urban freight modelling with an emphasis on simulation techniques. In Section 3, we discuss the use of the city logistics ontology as building blocks for developing an agent-based model. Next, we give details about model architecture by describing stakeholder agents, their decision-making, and simulation setup for the model. In Section 5, we implement a scenario to explore the possibility of cooperation between city logistics stakeholders, followed by the outcome and analysis. Finally, in Section 6, we draw conclusions.

2. Literature review

A wide variety of modelling approaches are used in the urban freight domain, including operations research techniques, differential equation modelling, and system dynamics (interested readers are advised to refer Ambrosini & Routhier, 2004; Anand, Quak, van Duin, & Tavasszy, 2012a; Russo & Comi, 2006). However, simulation is one of the most widely used techniques for urban freight modelling. In a survey on simulation for supply chains, Terzi and Cavalieri (2004) conclude that simulation is very helpful as it provides a systematic, quantitative, and objective evaluation of the outcomes resulting from different possible planning scenarios. In essence, the survey agrees that simulation is a very powerful tool for understanding the dynamics of the system. In the article 'a tour-based micro-simulation of urban commercial movements', Hunt and Stefan (2007) state the essential characteristics of modelling techniques for urban commercial movements as (1) its ability to model various aspects of choice behaviour explicitly, (2) to aggregate results ex post as desired, (3) to provide explicit representation of tours, and (4) to include specific constraints acting at the individual level. The authors believe that micro-simulation is very appropriate for such task. Similarly, Liedtke and Schepperle (2004) claim that a micro-simulation freight model could be used as a potential forecast tool and pave the way for more reliable policy assessments than are currently available.

However, when decision-making between independent actors or firms must be modelled, traditional discrete-event simulation is not pragmatic due to limited information exchange between actors in real life. For this purpose, the simulation technique should be able to represent many individuals with autonomous behaviour. The relatively new paradigm of parallel and distributed simulation, an agent-based simulation, allows us to capture interactions between independent actors. It is a special type of discrete event simulation that does not rely on a model with an underlying equation, but can nonetheless be represented formally. Although new to freight modelling, the agent-based technique is successfully implemented in many disciplines (Axelrod, 2006). One of the most important reasons for using this technique is that agent-based models can explicitly model the complexity arising from individual actions and the interactions that arise in the real world, that were either not possible or not readily accommodated using traditional modelling techniques, like discrete event or system dynamic modelling (Borshchev & Filippov, 2004).

Introduction of agent-based models in supply chains is more than a decade old (e.g. Swaminathan, Smith, & Sadeh, 1994). Since then, the field of supply chain management has produced a number of supply chain models with varying types and extents of supply chains using agent technology (for the overview refer Kumar & Srinivasan, 2010). These models aim to capture the decision-making and interactions between entities of the supply chain, and mainly capture the dynamics of the product flows instead of the transport flows. It is self-evident that the focus of modelling a supply chain is different from modelling freight activities, as the former is customer-driven while the latter is the result of macroeconomic activities depending upon the scope of the model (i.e. international, national, regional, or urban). The decision-making incorporated in a supply chain model represents the firm (or at the most partner firms) involved in a supply chain, which does not give insight into goods movement generated due to activities of multiple supply chains – the general focus of freight models. Davidsson, Henesey, Ramstedt, Törnquist, and Wernstedt (2005) give a survey of existing research on agent-based approaches for transportation and traffic management. The survey evaluates the models based on the domain, transport mode, time horizon, usage (i.e. automation system, decision support system), control (i.e. centralized, distributed), agent structure (i.e. static, dynamic), agent behaviour (i.e. benevolent, selfish), maturity level of model and evaluation comparison (i.e. qualitative, quantitative, none). The survey concludes that agent-based modelling approach is very suitable for modeling transport and logistics domains.

In urban freight modelling, only a few agent-based models have been developed previously. The multi-agent model by Taniguchi and Tamagawa (2005) considers five agent types in the model: freight carriers, shippers, residents, administrator, and motorway operators. The model captures the interactions between these stakeholders and establishes a good base of agent technology for urban freight domain. The model by Donnelly (2007) is a hybrid modelling approach based upon aggregate macroeconomic interactions, discrete event micro-simulation, and agent-based modelling for urban freight flows. The model uses data from Portland region and can be seen as the first agent-based model with real-life data. However, due to its vastness the model must make a trade-off between the number of independent agents (i.e. firm, importer, and exporter – which are generalizations of the firm and carrier) and thus models a limited number of interactions. Bergkvist, Davidsson, Persson, and Ramstedt (2005) developed a model for testing the effects of government policies on transport chains. The model includes a variety of information exchanges – i.e. from the case where agents share no information to where it flows freely among the actors. A small test case was employed as a proof of concept. The development of the model is ongoing and it aims at studying cooperation between actors. It takes a logistics chain perspective for modelling agents to represent firms, customers, and a transport coordinator. However, the behaviours of the agents need to be extended to take advantage of the agent structure.

Usefulness of ABM is visibly accepted among city logistics researchers as evidenced by an increasing number of agent-based models found in the city logistics modelling literature. Thus, ABM is certainly a useful methodology, however the effort to develop an ABM is nontrivial when multiple stakeholders must be included (Tamagawa, Taniguchi, & Yamada, 2010). An ABM is developed based on domain-specific knowledge base (Le Ber & Chouvet, 1999), abstracted into agents and their relationships. Often such knowledge bases are conceptual and constructed by the modellers using sources like literature, surveys, and project reports. Such individually constructed knowledge bases are subjective, and often are built with little sharing or reuse – almost everyone starts from a blank slate. In this situation use of ontology for the development of agent-based model can be really rewarding in terms of time and precision. According to Gruber (1995) 'an ontology is a description (like a formal specification of a program) of the concepts and relationships that can exist for an agent or a community of agents'. Accordingly, the city logistics ontology is a structured knowledge base of the city logistics domain which represents potential agents and their relationships with other agents. Such ontology can be used as a knowledge-sharing document and parts of it can be automatically transferred as components of an agent-based model. In this paper, we use this novel approach for developing an agent-based model using the city logistic ontology.

3. Agent-based model architecture using city logistics ontology

To model a city logistics domain using an agent-based simulation technique successfully, it is important to accurately represent the communication between heterogeneous stakeholder-agents of the domain. For accurate communication, the agents of the model should have common knowledge of different terminologies and the types of decisions they are making. From a semantic point of view, these agents should have a common view of the system and should have coordination in their activities. City logistics ontology is such a semantic model and can work as a common platform for communication and information exchange between agents. The ontological classes can represent entities, events, resources, etc. for a specific domain. Anand, Yang, van Duin, and Tavasszy (2012b) developed a generic ontology for city logistics domain (called GenCLOn[2] – Generic city logistics ontology) which represents the domain with eight general classes, namely Stakeholder, Objective, KPI, Resource, Measure, R&D and value-partition. Theses eight classes are further divided into multiple sub-classes to represent the domain in sufficient detail. These classes represent city logistics stakeholders (e.g. shipper, carrier, receivers, etc.), activities (e.g. transiting, goods ordering, etc.), resources (e.g. trucks, roads, etc.) and many other details along with respective associated attributes. Furthermore, the GenCLOn also contains relationships between these classes. For example, it shows a stakeholder receiver is connected with a stakeholder shipper via the activity relation 'goods ordering'. In another example, a stakeholder carrier is connected to resource truck with the relation 'own_by'.

GenCLOn is a multi-stakeholder ontology where multiple stakeholder types existing in the city logistics domain are represented as ontology components. These stakeholder components are associated with their respective objectives, resources, KPIs, and activities. Thus, the GenCLOn represents the system model of individual stakeholder which is important for developing individual stakeholder-agents in the ABM. Furthermore, the individual system model of each stakeholder is connected to the system model of other stakeholders by appropriate links. Thus, the GenCLOn represents multi-stakeholder perspectives in the ontology. Developing an ABM from such a model gives consistency in the relations and communications between the agents.

Figure 1 shows a representative sketch of the system model of a carrier and a shopkeeper. Here the shopkeeper is associated with its shop, goods, and cost via different links. Similarly, the carrier is associated with its respective attributes and components. These individual models represent the functioning of the individual stakeholder and at the same time the link connecting both stakeholders' system models indicates how they are connected in the domain of urban goods movement. Similarly, all the city logistics concepts are connected by appropriate link, and, thus the whole picture comprehensively captures the city logistic domain in an abstract way in the form of GenCLOn.

One way of using this multi-stakeholder city logistics ontology for ABM development is as a knowledge-sharing document. In this case, one can use this structural document to browse through different stakeholders, their objectives, resources, etc. to see how these different concepts are connected and how the interactions can take place during the decision-making for urban goods movement. Such information requires drawing a first sketch of the agents and agent interactions for ABM. Since the GenCLOn is a generic ontology it contains the basic concepts of city logistics domain at a broad level with limited details of each concept. For instance, the ontology may contain the information that a carrier stakeholder owns trucks but does not include the details of the truck such as the engine type, tyre size, or load capacity. Conversely, it may contain many other concepts and relationships which are of no use for a specific model case. Keeping the useful concepts and relationship, one can derive a structural conceptual model that can work as a guiding document for the agent modelling and interaction design.

In another instance, the ontology components (i.e. classes and relationships) can be extracted to be used as building blocks of the ABM. The city logistics ontological classes already contain attributes and relationships that exist between stakeholder-agents of the agent-based simulation system. Using a code generation method one can extract (Java) classes from the city logistics ontology (for technical detail refer to Stevenson & Dobson, 2011 and also refer to note[3]). These classes can be used as agents representing stakeholders (or activates, resources, etc.) in the model. It should be noted that these classes do not represent fully functional agents, but rather act as building blocks of the agent-based model. With additional code representing the specific communication protocols in the class the agent is ready for simulation.

Finally, one can also connect the ontology with simulation, where the relevant information needed for the agent to perform a certain action is obtained directly from the ontology during the simulation run. This is done using the query language (e.g. SPARQL). Thus, the ontology is connected with the model throughout the simulation, unlike in the code generation method, where the ontology is detached after appropriate classes are extracted.

In our case, we developed an agent-based model for city logistics using the previous two techniques. We aim to develop a model depicting fundamental aspects of urban goods movement using city logistic ontology. Therefore, we extracted classes from the GenCLOn to create stakeholder-agents such as carriers, shops, shippers, municipality, and inhabitants. These classes have attributes which are needed for the specific stakeholder. For instance, the shop class of the ontology has ID number, area, stock level, and is connected to the shipper by the 'goods ordering' method.

Until now the structure of the model represents the 'skeleton' of an agent-based model where individual agents and its plans are defined so the agents knows 'what to do'. Next, we add additional communication and interactions between the agents which are not available in the classes extracted from the ontology. These strategies for agent interactions give agents information about 'what to do when'. In the following section, we discuss the main agents of the model and their interactions with other agents.

3.1. *Stakeholder agents and interactions*

The agent-based model developed for urban freight system has multiple agents with 'situated' or 'local' knowledge about the system so it is called SMUrFS – situated multi-agent urban freight system. The key stakeholders involved in the generation and movement of urban freight are represented as agents in SMUrFS. Considering the bottom-up approach for the simulation processes, city inhabitants start the process by demanding goods from

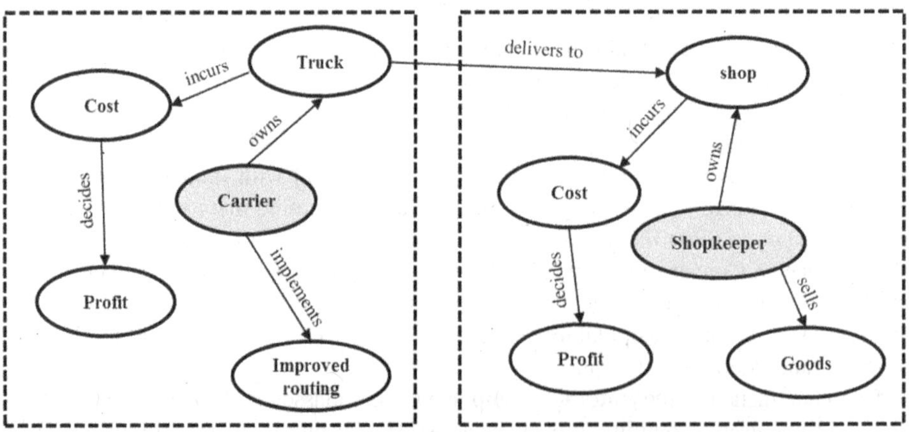

Figure 1. Representative sketch of multi-stakeholder ontology for city logistics domain.

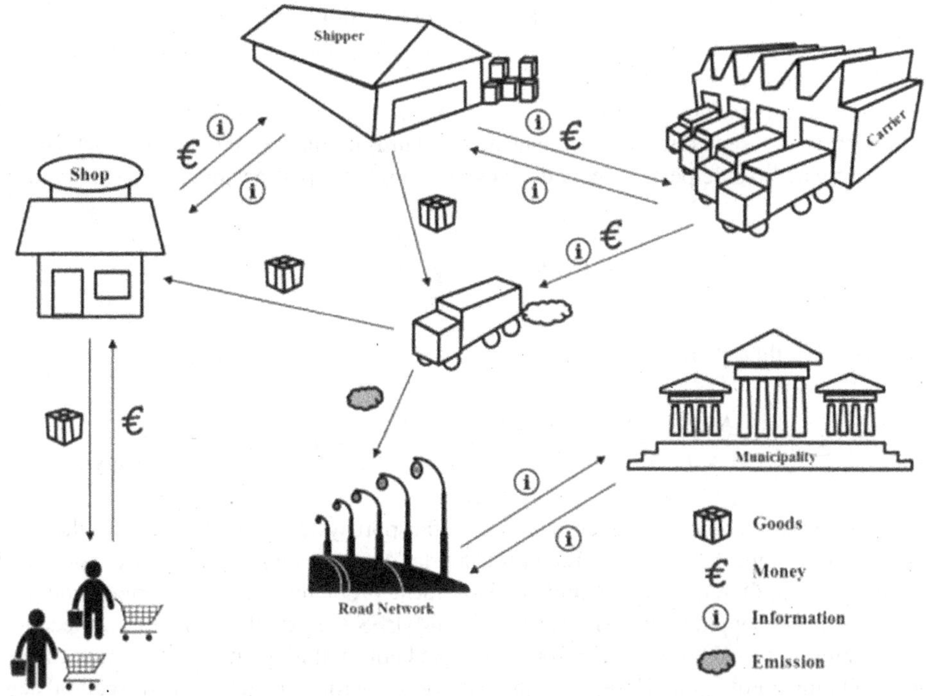

Figure 2. SMUrFS – agents and their interactions.

shops. Shops, in turn, contact shipper-firms that produce and supply goods. The shippers buy transportation service from the carriers who transport goods from the shippers' locations to the shops[4]. The administrator plays a vital role by providing infrastructure for freight vehicle movement and is also responsible for creating an economical and environmentally friendly city area. We have the following types of agents in SMUrFS.

- Person agent
- Shop agent
- Shipper agent
- Carrier agent
- Administrator agent (e.g. municipality)

Figure 2 shows the role of these agents in the model and how these agents interact with each other in terms of goods, money, information, and harmful effects.

Person-agent:
The person-agent represents the inhabitant (e.g. consumer) in the city who buy goods from the shops. The activity of the person-agent starts with a decision about a shopping trip, which is based on the Bernoulli distribution. If it decides to shop, the number of units bought is based on the Poisson distribution. The selection of the shop for buying goods is based on three factors: (1) the size of the shop, (2) the profit-margin of the shop, and (3) the on-shelf availability of the shop (the service level). There are many other factors people consider during shopping in real life, such as the quality of the goods or the ambience of a shop. Because we are modelling people as entities that shop and not investigating shopping

behaviour, only the first three factors are considered. Additionally, the decision about the shop selection is not affected by distance to the shop as all the shops are located in the radius less than a kilometre.

First, the utility of every alternative (i.e. shop) is calculated using these three factors. Next, a probability is assigned to every shop using the multi-nominal logit (MNL) model. Based on this probability, the person-agent decides on a single shop as a shopping destination:

$$P(Shop\, i) = \frac{e^{U_i}}{\sum_{i=1}^{n} e^{U_i}},$$

where U_i = utility of shop i,

$$U_i = f_1 \times \frac{\text{Area}_j}{\text{Max area}} + f_2 \times \frac{\text{Service Level}_j}{\text{Max Service Level}} - f_3 \times \frac{\text{Profit Margin}_j}{\text{Max Profit Margin}}.$$

People are the end-users of the urban freight transport systems and they are also the ones who experience the nuisances of freight transportation in the city, such as noise, pollution, and congestion. Often, people complain about these problems and change their shopping behaviour (e.g. shopping time). However, in the SMUrFS, the person-agents are non-reactive to such nuisances and their concern for the safe and non-polluting city is taken into account by the administrator-agent. Here, the administrator-agent (described later in the section) acts as the people's representative and takes action to solve problems of congestion, pollution, noise by implementing various policy measures.

Shop-agent:
Shopkeepers are one of the most important stakeholders in the city logistics domain. They have a big influence on the urban freight transportation system. In the end, they decide when to order, how much to order, and when they want to have the order delivered. In the SMUrFS model, every shop takes certain decisions during the setup phase and the simulation phase.

Setup phase decisions are:

- Shipper selection
- Maximum stock level
- Monthly demand of shop
- Minimum stock level (i.e. safety stock)

The setup phase decisions are made only once during the simulation (in the beginning), whereas the simulation phase decisions are made repeatedly under certain conditions. The decision about shipper selection is made based on the distance between the shop and the location of the shippers. The area of the shop, maximum stock level and safety stock are the function of their respective distribution functions. At the beginning of the simulation, a monthly demand is estimated as a function of the shop area using the given total demand for the city. During simulation, each shop calculates the monthly demand using a simple moving average formula using demand of last three months.

The simulation phase involves mainly two decisions:

- Re-ordering point (ROP)
- Ordering quantity (OQ)

The reordering point is estimated using the following formula:

$$\textit{Re-order point} = (\textit{average daily demand} * \textit{lead time in days}) + \textit{safety stock}$$

Since the lead time is one day (i.e. goods are delivered next day) the reorder point is equal to the sum of the average daily demand and safety stock. The objective of the shop-agent is to maximize profit. This objective is closely connected to the number of units purchased and inventory cost associated with the stock. Furthermore, customers (i.e. person-agents) are attracted to shops with higher stock availability. In this situation, shops optimize their ordering quantity using the economic order quantity formula:

$$Q = \sqrt{\frac{2OD}{I}},$$

where Q = order quantity, O = ordering costs per order, D = demand per month, I = inventory costs per item per month.

Carrier-agent:
It is not uncommon that a shipper has his/her own private fleet for goods delivery. In that case, a carrier has a close connection with a shipper. In another case, a carrier is an independent logistics provider who collects goods from different shippers and delivers them to retailers. In the case of an independent carrier, her selection is mostly done by the shipper but sometimes a retailer can also influence the selection of a carrier. In the SMUrFS model, we assume that shops are not part of a retail chain and therefore they do not have private fleet. In the model, shipper-agents use independent carriers for delivery of goods to the customers (i.e. receivers). The selection of a carrier is done by the shipper based on the minimum cost for delivery. Carriers play an important role in the city logistics framework as they are not only transporting the goods but also plan the tours. Together with their ability to improve the scheduling of the trucks, they can improve the efficiency of urban freight transport considerably.

The total transportation cost incurred by the carrier is the sum of the fixed costs (e.g. depreciation of trucks, insurance) and variable costs (e.g. driver cost, fuel cost). The variable costs that are associated with the truck usage depend on the average length of a tour, the average number of stops in a tour, the speed of the trucks, and driver's hourly wage. During the auction for the carrier selection, the carrier-agent adds its profit margin to the calculated cost and sends the final price as a bid to the shipper. As every carrier has a limited number of trucks, a carrier stops bidding in the auction once the total demand won from shippers exceeds the total capacity of the trucks. During the simulation phase, a carrier receives the order from shipper, and transport goods from the shipper to the shops.

Shipper-agent:
The shipper is responsible for supplying goods to the retailers. There are different types of supply chains with different echelons and thus there can be more than one type of shipper. For this model, we assume only one type of shipper, who has goods available in the warehouse located outside the city area. We also assume that the goods are always available when a shop is ordering. In the SMUrFS model, a shipper-agent first decides its monthly demand by estimating the demand from its customer shops. Next, it starts the auction to hire the carrier-agent for goods delivery. In this auction the shipper-agent sends the estimated demand to the carriers. The carriers calculate the costs of transportation for the auctioned demand. The shipper chooses the carrier with the cheapest bid and uses this price to calculate the ordering

costs for the shops. During the simulation phase, the shipper-agent collects all orders from its shops and sends the orders to the hired carrier.

Administrator- agent:
The municipal government is the administrator in the city and can influence the urban freight activities by implementing various policies, measures, and regulations. The administrator is also responsible for the economic and environmental sustainability of the city and thus must consider the effects of policies on businesses as well as inhabitants. For example, improving conditions for businesses may lead to more freight-related transport activities. The subsequent increase in air and noise pollution and safety-related issues affects the livelihood of city habitants. Conversely, implementing strict restrictions on freight vehicle movements reduces business activities in cities and therefore also jobs and supply of goods to city habitants. Thus, the objective of the administrator is to find policies that strike a balance between economic and environmental goals. In the SMUrFS model, the administrator-agent represents the municipality. The administrator-agent gathers information about the number of trucks entering into the city, the pollution level based on total truck-kilometre travelled as KPIs for an environmentally sustainable city.

In contrast to the detailed categorization of various stakeholders in the ontology, in the SMUrFS model, we combine different sub-types of stakeholders under one main stakeholder type. For example, instead of modelling different types of receivers (e.g. hotels, supermarkets, offices, individuals) we consider a single type of receiving agent as a shop-agent. Furthermore, the different stakeholder types exhibit simple and mostly homogeneous behaviour. For example, each shop agent orders goods using the ROP and EOQ formulas.

Admittedly, these are strong assumptions which will limit the range of possible outcomes of the model. Nonetheless, the main objective of this research is to demonstrate the use of an integrative ontology in the development of an agent-based model. Subsequently, we want to prove that such an integration provides structural consistency in the relationships between the agents of the model. Such a methodology provides an innovative way to develop a valuable decision support tool which, by allowing autonomous decision-making by stakeholders, explicitly incorporates distributed decision-making in the urban freight domain.

In the light of this objective, assuming simplistic behaviour is justified at this stage of model development. Once the model is extended to evaluate real-life situations and scenarios, the inclusion of more complex behaviour of stakeholders becomes important. It should be noted that an increase in the behavioural space also increases the complexity of the model, and consequently the complexity of the analysis of emergence in the model outcomes.

3.2. *Model simulation setup*

The detailed sequence diagram for the SMUrFS is shown in Figure 3. Here, Figure 3(a) illustrates the set-up phase and Figure 3(b) illustrates the simulation phase. The model starts with a setup phase, where each shop-agent selects a shipper-agent. Next, shop-agents estimate their maximum stock level, safety stock level, and monthly demand for the shop. Shipper-agents estimate monthly demand and conduct an auction to select the carrier-agent. Shipper-agents announce the demand and each carrier-agent calculates the price for delivery. The shipper-agent hires the carrier-agent who bids the lowest price in the auction. Based on that price, the shipper-agent determines an ordering cost and sends it to its shop-agents.

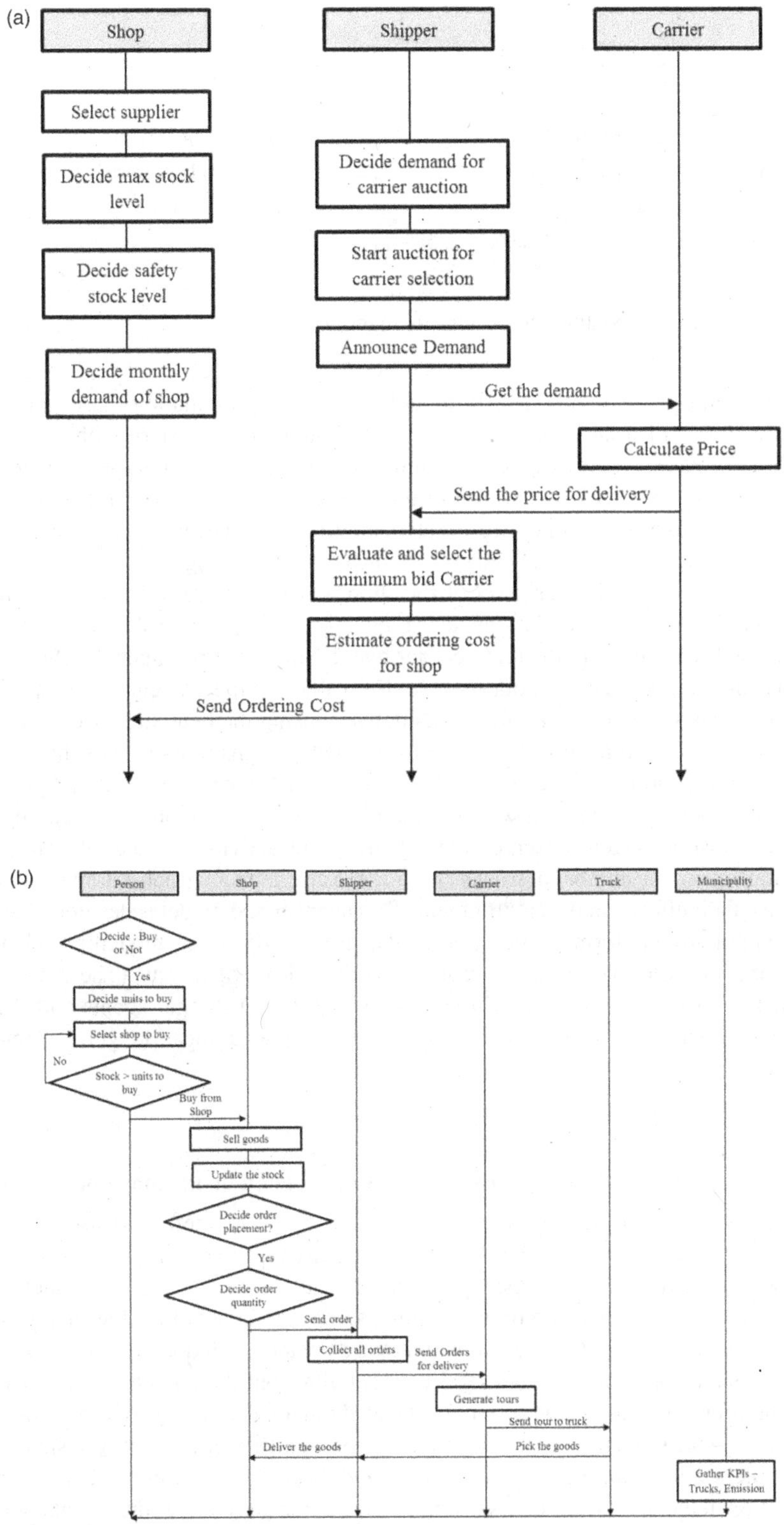

Figure 3. SMUrFS model sequence diagram: (a) setup phase and (b) simulation phase.

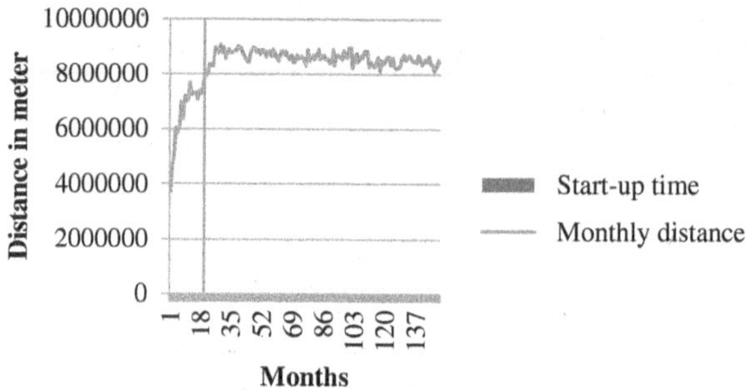

Figure 4. Plot for the monthly truck-kilometre in the city.

After the setup phase is complete, the model enters into the simulation phase and simulates the daily activities of urban goods movement. The simulation phase starts with person-agents buying goods. Based on the assigned probability function, each person-agent selects a shop-agent and buys goods if the stock level of the shop is enough to satisfy the demand of the person-agent. This process is iterated for all person-agents. At every shopping iteration, the stock level of each shop-agent is updated. At the end of shopping activity each shop-agent checks the stock level. If stock level of the shop is below the re-ordering point, then the shop-agent places an order to the selected shipper-agent. Next, each shipper-agent collects all orders and sends them to the hired carrier-agent. Since a carrier-agent might be serving more than one shipper-agent, it collects order from all her shipper-agents. Subsequently, the carrier-agent starts making tours for goods delivery using the heuristic-based Tabu search vehicle routing algorithm. Finally, each carrier-agent assigns tours to its vehicles-agents, who then deliver goods to the shops. Once shop-agents receive the ordered goods they update their stock level. On the next day simulation starts with person-agents buying goods.

The administrator-agent observes the urban freight activities in the city and collects information about the number of trucks entering the city and total truck-kilometres travelled to estimate their effects on the environment. This agent-based model is developed using the Repast Simphony platform[5] which allows the use of GIS-based modelling. To test the GIS feature in ABM, we used the road network of Rotterdam city (The Netherlands). Nevertheless, it is a 'toy model' with 100 shop-agents, 10 shipper-agents and 7 carrier-agents. Other data used for parameters such as the shop area, location, goods demand are synthetic data.

4. Exploring cooperation in decision-making for urban goods movement

One of the reasons for city logistics-related problems is the inefficient use of resources (e.g. trucks, parking area, etc.). Poorly coordinated city logistics activities cause inefficient utilization. For instance, shopkeepers place orders without any knowledge about the ordering patterns of other shops who order from the same shipper. On the other hand, shippers work under strict delivery-time pressure and thus dispatch small quantities of goods. These stakeholders are connected by goods delivery activities but there is no way to share other important information about the activities of stakeholders. Knowledge of other information can promote more efficient use of resources in goods delivery operations. For stakeholders, most business-related information is sensitive and they may not want to share such information. Nonetheless, sharing less sensitive information may allow these stakeholders to coordinate their activities more efficiently.

Most city logistics measures, implemented in practice, aim at curbing the use of urban freight delivery vehicles. Instead, the measures should facilitate an enhancement of urban goods movement practices that also reduces harmful effects. For instance, according to Crainic, Ricciardi, and Storchi (2009), streamlining freight distribution activities can lead to fewer goods delivery vehicles in the city and can, in turn, reduce congestion, pollution in the urban areas. In the words of the authors:

> The consolidation of loads of different shippers and carriers within the same vehicles, associated to some form of coordination of operations within the city are among the most important means to achieve these goals. The use of so-called green vehicles and the integration of public transport infrastructure (e.g. light rail and barges on rivers and water canals) may enhance these systems and further reduce truck movements and related emissions in the city. But consolidation and coordination are the fundamental concepts of city logistics.

The presumably effective, but less explored area of city logistics domain is cooperation and consolidation. Consolidation can only be achieved if different stakeholders want cooperation. Cooperation between different actors should result in the win–win situation. In essence, the objectives and business models of the stakeholders should allow them to synchronize their activities. In this section, we describe and implement a scenario promoting cooperation between stakeholders. This scenario offers the stakeholders an opportunity to modify their urban freight-related activities so they can achieve their own objectives while reducing the negative impacts of their city logistics activities.

Last-minute order scenario

In the base scenario, the shops place an order if the stock level reaches the re-order point. The shipper collects the orders from all shops and gives the carrier. The carrier does the scheduling, routing, and sends trucks to deliver the goods. One of the reasons for the high number of delivery vehicles in the city area is the poor loading-rate of the trucks. Increasing the loading-rate can result in fewer goods delivery vehicles delivering the same amount of goods. The loading-rate can be increased by better consolidation, adjusting/improving delivery schedules and routing. However, not much can be achieved using the above techniques when shops place orders on different days. For example, if 3 bookshops on the same street order goods on different days, then (assuming short lead time – a day) the goods delivery vehicle has to come to that street three times in a week. However, if two shops instead place orders on the same day, then the loading-rate of the truck will be higher (assuming other conditions are not changed) and one less truck enters the street. The last-minute scenario is about opening up communication between the shops and carrier which might increase the loading-rate of the truck, and in turn improve the efficiency of the entire system without leaving any stakeholder worse off. The following texts describe the last-minute order scenario and discuss the necessary conditions for shops and carriers to participate.

The last-minute order scenario explores the possibility of other shops (which did not order goods) on the route of the established truck tour placing an order to increase the loading-rate of the truck. However, if a shop places an order several days before its actual ordering time (which is at ROP), then the shop incurs extra inventory cost for those days. Hence, the shop is willing to place an early order provided the extra inventory cost is compensated. Suppose the extra inventory cost of a shop placing an early order is I_{extra}.

Now, whenever a shop places an order, the carrier gets some revenue from the shipper: the normal cost of delivery contracted between the shipper and carrier. Since the truck is making an extra stop, the carrier incurs an extra stop cost. However, since the carrier takes last-minute orders from shops along the truck route, the truck is not driving any extra distance and incurs no extra distance cost. Thus, if a shop places a pre-order the carrier gets extra revenue. Suppose, as per the contract between shipper and carrier, the carrier gets revenue C_d per order delivery. Here C_d consist of the actual cost to the carrier and some percentage of profit. Thus, C_d takes following form:

$$C_d = p_s * (C_f + C_r),$$

where C_f is the fixed cost, C_r the running cost, and p_s the profit margin of the shipper.

Total revenue for delivering n number of goods orders without last-minute orders

$$T_d = (p_s * (C_f + C_r)) * n.$$

Therefore, total revenue for delivering n_l (where $n_l > n$) number of orders with last-minute orders

$$T_{dl} = (p_s * (C_f + C_r)) * n_l,$$

However, the running cost is less as there is no extra distance driven by the truck. Thus, if the reduced running cost is C_r^* , then the actual revenue should be

$$T_{dl}^* = (p_s * (C_f + C_r^*)) * n_l.$$

Thus, if the net extra profit is called P_{extra} then,

$$P_{\text{extra}} = T_{dl} - T_{dl}^* = (p_s * (C_r - C_r^*)) * n_l > 0 \quad since\ C_r > C_r^*.$$

Here the shop placing a pre-order is incurring an extra inventory cost, whereas the carrier is making extra profit. If the carrier is willing to compensate the extra inventory cost of the shop, it will be a win–win situation. Assuming the carrier is willing to share its profit with the shop, then it will accept only the last-minute order from the shop if

$$P_{\text{extra}} \geq I_{\text{extra}}.$$

Thus, the necessary economic condition for the successful implementation of the last-minute order scenario is that the extra profit made by the carrier must be greater than or equal to the extra inventory cost of the shop.

Along with the economic constraints, some physical constraints must be evaluated before placing the order and accepting the order. The shop can place an order only if the summation of its order quantity and current stock level is less than the maximum capacity of the shop. Likewise, the carrier can accept the order only if the addition of the new order does not exceed the truck capacity.

In the simulation, the carrier sends a message to every shop along the route asking if it wants to place a last-minute order. The shops who receive the message check the shop capacity constraint and send the extra inventory cost as well as ordering quantity to the carrier. The carrier-agent first checks the economic constraint (i.e. $P_{\text{extra}} \geq I_{\text{extra}}$) for each shop and declines all shops which do not satisfy it. Next, it accepts orders from the shops that maximize the loading-rate of the truck.

Owing to the simple setting of this scenario, the administrator agent does not play any active role. However, the administrator agent is capable of playing an active role and can influence outcomes. For example, the administrator agent can provide some fiscal incentives to shops en route (who are not already placing an order due to the higher inventory cost) to place an order to increase the loading-rate and observe the outcome in terms of KPIs. The administrator can review its incentive structure to reach its goal – say 20% reduction in the truck-kilometres travelled – and modify its incentive strategy at certain interval. Such extension of the 'last-minute ordering scenario' is the subject of ongoing work.

Table 1. Setup values for the experiment.

Parameter	Value
Average total demand per month	500,000
Vehicles per carrier	30
Vehicle capacity (units/truck)	1500
Number of shops	100
Number of carriers	7
Number of shippers	10
Price per goods-unit (euro)	50
Start-up time (months)	20
Simulation time (months)	150

Table 2. Paired samples statistics.

		Mean	*N*	Std. deviation	Std. error mean
Pair 1	MonthlyDistance	8607644.18	130	221533.351	19429.760
	LM_MonthlyDistance	8480792.89	130	257653.670	22597.722
Pair 2	MonthlyOrders	2600.37	130	68.344	5.994
	LM_MonthlyOrders	2611.60	130	76.486	6.708
Pair 3	UnitsShopped	496212.40	130	4216.469	369.809
	LM_UnitsShopped	492727.32	130	5027.269	440.921
Pair 4	MonthlyTrucks	421.28	130	8.343	0.732
	LM_MonthlyTrucks	411.45	130	10.009	0.878

LM implies data for the last-minute order scenario.

5. Analysis and discussion

Table 1 lists the model parameters for the simulation setup. The scenario ran for 150 months, each consisting of 30 days. The first 20 months are considered start-up time until the system reaches steady-state. With a start-up time of 20 months, there are 130 data points available for each parameter, which is a reasonable number of data points to compare the base situation with the last-minute order scenario. With 130 data entries per parameter, there are 129 degrees of freedom in the test. This means that 129 observations plus the total number of observations are needed to specify the sample, the 130th being determined by subtraction (BMJ Group, 2012).

For the base case reference scenario and the last-minute scenario, following variables are logged:

- Total distance travelled by trucks per month (in meters)
- Total number of orders per month
- Total number of trucks entering the city per month
- Total number of units shopped per month

In Table 2, the mean and standard deviation are given for every variable in both situations, also the number of data points for every variable in both models is given ($N = 130$). The test results are presented in Table 3.

In Table 3, the first column shows the paired variables, which are compared with each other. The second column shows the difference in the value of the means of the two compared variables. Column 3 shows the standard deviation of the difference of the mean. Column 4 shows the standard error of the difference of the mean. The fifth and sixth columns show

Table 3. Paired samples test.

		Paired differences							
					95% confidence interval of the difference				
	Mean	Std. deviation	Std. error mean		Lower	Upper	t	df	Sig. (2-tailed)
Pair 1	MonthlyDistance - LM_MonthlyDistance	126851.285	339345.522	29762.571	67965.309	185737.261	4.262	129	0.000
Pair 2	MonthlyOrders - LM_MonthlyOrders	−11.231	106.845	9.371	−29.771	7.31	−1.2	129	0.233
Pair 3	UnitsShopped - LM_UnitsShopped	3485.077	6537.039	573.336	2350.717	4619.437	6.079	129	0.000
Pair 4	MonthlyTrucks - LM_MonthlyTrucks	9.838	13.206	1.158	7.547	12.13	8.494	129	0.000

LM implies data for the last-minute order scenario.

the 95% confidence interval of the difference. The t-value of the test with 129 degrees of freedom (column 8) is shown in the 7th column. The last column shows the significance level or p-value of the test.

In the paired t-test, the null hypothesis is that the paired variables have the same distribution. If the p-value of the test is lower than 0.05, the null hypothesis is rejected, which suggests that the paired variables have different distributions. If the p-value of the test is equal to or higher than 0.05, the null hypothesis is accepted, which suggests that the paired variables have the same distribution.

When the information from Tables 2 and 3 is combined, the individual conclusions are as follows:

- The distance travelled by trucks in the city per month is lower in last-minute orders scenario
- The number of orders per month is statistically the same in both models.
- The number of units shopped per month is lower, when last-minute orders are allowed.
- The number of trucks entering the city per month is significantly lower in last-minute orders scenario

Interpretation

Interpreting the results per pair does not allow us to explain high-level model behaviour. Since the different variables influence each other, combining individual conclusions offers a better explanation of the behaviour of the model and the real system.

The distance travelled by trucks in the city is lower in the last-minute order model, but so is the number of trucks. To see if this explains the lower distance per month, we examine the average distance per truck. In the reference scenario, the average distance per truck is $8607644.18/421.28 = 20432.12\,\text{m/truck}$. In the last-minute orders scenario, the average distance per truck is $8480792.89/411.45 = 20611.96\,\text{m/truck}$. So with the last-minute orders, a truck drives 179.84 m more per tour, on average. This calculation implies that fewer trucks, each travelling a greater distance, reduce the total distance travelled by all trucks in the city. Additionally, these data suggest that tour planning can be done more efficiently as more shops are listed per tour.

The number of trucks entering the city is lower with the last-minute orders, but the number of units bought is also lower with the last-minute orders. To see if this explains the lower number of trucks per month, the differences of the averages are compared. The average difference of the units shopped per month is 3485.077. With a vehicle capacity of 1500 units per truck and a loading-rate of 0.6 approximately, four trucks worth of units are shopped less. The average difference of the number of trucks per month is 9.838 trucks. This suggests that fewer trucks are required to transport same number of units in last-minute ordering scenario. At the beginning of the scenario description, we assumed that poor coordination in ordering lead to increased truck-kilometre travelled and more trucks in the city. Another explanation for this situation could be poor routing or high number of carriers. Nonetheless, the analysis of our results shows that allowing shops to place last-minute order reduces the number of goods delivery trucks (six trucks per month), which implies an increase in the loading-rate. This means that the trucks in the last-minute scenario have a higher average loading-rate than when there are no last-minute orders.

An explanation for the higher loading-rates comes from the number of orders. The number of orders is statistically the same in both models, but the number of trucks used is lower. This means that there are more orders per truck. The average order size for the model without last-minute orders is $496212.40/2600.37 = 190.82$ units per order. The average order size for the model with last-minute orders is 492727.32/2611.60 = 188.67 units per order. It is likely that smaller orders can fill a truck better than larger orders, which results in a higher loading-rate for the truck.

In summary, by opening the communication link between a shop and a carrier agent, the last-minute scenario offers the shops the option of placing an order after the tour is generated. Consequently, the shops decide whether to place a last-minute order by calculating different associated costs. This option results in a negligible increase in total orders placed by shop agents, which implies that shops are ordering more number of times than they do in the reference scenario. When the carrier gets last-minute orders from multiple shops along the tour route, it only selects shops which maximize carrier's revenue and loading-rate of the truck.

In this setting, a system emerges where shops place an order for the slightly smaller quantity than the normal ordering quantity (since the shop is pre-ordering). Consequently, more than 30% (approximately 800) orders placed during the month are the last-minute orders, which allows for better consolidation of goods due to a change in ordering patterns by shop agents. In conclusion, the last-minute order scenario decreases the distances travelled by trucks in the city per month. It also decreases the number of trucks in the city per month and which can be explained primarily by higher loading-rates for the trucks.

6. Conclusions

Congestion, pollution, and safety are some of the most pressing problems of urban areas. Along with the large number of passenger transport vehicles, the urban goods delivery vehicles significantly contribute to these problems. The problems related to urban goods transportation activities are primarily attributed to underlying characteristics such as heterogeneous stakeholders, their conflicting objectives and the resulting system of distributed decision-making. Such autonomous decision-making stakeholders do not efficiently cooperate and coordinate their activities. The ensuing inefficient use of resources (e.g. goods delivery vehicle, time, etc.) gives rise to the above-mentioned problem.

To reduce the negative externalities of urban goods movement, we must first understand the decision-making process of the city logistics stakeholder under different situations. The discipline of city logistics modelling is dedicated to understanding the effects of various changes in the urban distribution system without actually changing the system. Various types of modelling systems exist for the analysis of the city logistics domain and its respective policies. Nonetheless, the agent-based modelling technique is very advantageous for such analysis because it can model city logistics-related entities (e.g. stakeholders, resources) and activities in a natural way. It allows one to depict the stakeholders as independent agents with different behaviours. Thus, the novelty of using agent technology is its capability to capture emergence and distributed decision-making in varying situations. Policies analysed using this technique are more robust as they are evaluated under dynamically changing conditions of city logistics.

City logistics modellers already take an interest in the agent technology, as evident by the growing number of agent-based models developed for urban freight analysis. Notably, many fields (e.g. energy, land planning) which are now fairly mature in agent-based modelling started with developing 'toy models' for analysing their respective domain. In the same vein, agent-based models in city logistics domain are mostly 'toy models' where different stakeholders of the city logistics domain interact in an artificial city.

In this paper, we present the approach of using city logistics ontology for the development of an agent-based model for urban freight domain. City logistics ontology is a knowledge model which includes city logistics entities (e.g. stakeholders, resources, etc.) and the relationships between them in a structured form. This approach takes ontology as a starting point for developing agent-based model by using ontological components as building blocks for agent-based model. Extraction of these entities and relations readily supplies the basic structure of the agent-based simulation model in the form of the classes and relationship. Such flexibility can reduce the modelling time when the modeller is familiar with the ontology and extraction process. Furthermore, even just using the city logistics ontology as a structural conceptual model offers advantages over the verbal conceptual model. Because the GenCLOn is a validated ontology (Anand, Duin, & Tavasszy, 2014), the model developed from it also has structural integrity.

The current version of the model uses real GIS data from the city of Rotterdam. GIS compatibility of the model facilitates easy transformation to real life cases. For instance, with the appropriate data (e.g. shops locations, delivery frequency), the model can be used for a real city. Furthermore, the integration of the validated city logistics ontology promises structural validity of agents and their interactions. The model is built up from very simple ground rules (i.e. change your shipment size as to maximize profits) and so far, the behaviour of the model has been evaluated allowing students to play simulation game. Students were asked to make choices based on the ground rules. The approach and outcomes of this game is reported in Anand, Meijer, van Duin, & Tavasszy (2013).

Nonetheless, there are certain limitations to using ontology for the ABM development. First, the structure of the ontology is mirrored in ABM, and so if the modeller wants to explore/model information exchange or relationships other than those depicted in the ontology, he/she has to modify the code or modify the ontology. Secondly, extracting the code is not very complicated, but modifying it for the simulation can be tricky. Sometimes the time saved by extracting code is offset by the time spent modifying it. This is especially true for researchers with limited programming knowledge. In our opinion, a better way of using an ontology for the ABM development is to extract part of the ontology needed for the model, and modify it to address your requirements and finally extract the model or run the model directly from the ontology. This method offers high consistency in the model and more flexibility for model extension.

Acknowledgements

We thank three anonymous referees from this journal for providing a range of very useful suggestions for improving the earlier version of this paper. We also wish to acknowledge help of Caroline Jaffe for improving language of this article.

Funding

Support from Netherlands Organization for Scientific Research (NWO) for funding this research (Project: Sustainable Accessibility of the Randstad) is greatly acknowledged.

Notes

1. City logistics can refer to a wide variety of activities including supply chain management, but also to transportation activities, including goods movements, service oriented trips of vans, construction related vehicle movements and waste collection. Nonetheless, the current research community has a focus on vehicle movements related to goods delivery and hence it is often referred as urban freight transportation. This research concentrates on vehicle movements related to goods delivery and hence we also use phrase 'urban freight transportation..
2. GenCLOn is developed using open source software Protégé – http://protege.stanford.edu/

3. http://www.incunabulum.de/projects/it/owl2java
4. It should be noted that there is wide variety within this categorization. For an in-depth categorization refer to Anand et al. (2012b).
5. For more detail visit – http://repast.sourceforge.net/

References

Ambrosini, C., & Routhier, J. (2004). Objectives, methods and results of surveys carried out in the field of urban freight transport: An international comparison. *Transport Reviews, 24*(1), 57–77.

Anand, N., Duin, J. H. R., & Tavasszy, L. (2014). *Quality of semantic data for the city logistics domain: A comparison with the stakeholders' perspectives.* Paper presented at the Transportation Research Board 93th Annual Meeting, Washington DC.

Anand, N., Quak, H., van Duin, R., & Tavasszy, L. (2012a). City logistics modeling efforts: Trends and gaps-a review. *Procedia-Social and Behavioral Sciences, 39*, 101–115.

Anand, N., Yang, M., van Duin, J. H. R., & Tavasszy, L. (2012b). GenCLOn: An ontology for city logistics. *Expert Systems with Applications, 39*(15), 11944–11960. http://dx.doi.org/10.1016/j.eswa.2012.03.068.

Anand, N., Meijer, D., van Duin, J. H. R., & Tavasszy, L. (2013). *Validation of an agent based model using participatory gaming approach: A case of city logistics.* Proceedings of Conference on Agent-Based Modeling in Transportation Planning and Operations, Virginia Tech, Blacksburg, Virginia.

Axelrod, R. (2006). Agent-based modeling as a bridge between disciplines. *Handbook of Computational Economics, 2*, 1565–1584.

Bergkvist, M., Davidsson, P., Persson, J., & Ramstedt, L. (2005). A hybrid micro-simulator for determining the effects of governmental control policies on transport chains. *Multi-Agent and Multi-Agent-Based Simulation*, 3415, 236–247.

BMJ Group. (2012). The t tests. Retrieved November 6, 2012, from http://www.bmj.com/about-bmj/resources-readers/publications/statistics-square-one/7-t-tests.

Borshchev, A., & Filippov, A. (2004). *From system dynamics and discrete event to practical agent based modeling: reasons, techniques, tools.* Paper presented at the Proceedings of the 22nd international conference of the system dynamics society. Retrieved from http://www.econ.iastate.edu/tesfatsi/systemdyndiscreteeventabmcompared.borshchevfilippov04.pdf

Crooks, A. T., Castle, C. J., & Batty, M. (2008). Key challenges in agent-based modelling for geo-spatial simulation. *Computers, Environment and Urban Systems, 32*(6), 417–430.

Crainic, T., Ricciardi, N., & Storchi, G. (2009). Models for evaluating and planning City Logistics systems. *Transportation science, 43*(4), 432–454.

Davidsson, P., Henesey, L., Ramstedt, L., Törnquist, J., & Wernstedt, F. (2005). An analysis of agent-based approaches to transport logistics. *Transportation Research Part C, 13*(4), 255–271.

Donnelly, R. (2007). *A hybrid microsimulation model of freight flows.* Paper presented at the 5th international Conference on City Logistics, Kyoto, pp. 235–246.

Friesz, T. L., & Holguín-Veras, J. (2005). Dynamic game-theoretic models of urban freight: Formulation and solution approach. In A. Reggiani & L. A. Schintler (Eds.), Methods and Models in Transport and Telecommunications (pp. 143–161). Berlin: Springer.

Gruber, T. R. (1995). Toward principles for the design of ontologies used for knowledge sharing. *Int. J. Hum.-Comput. Stud., 43*(5–6), 907–928. doi:10.1006/ijhc.1995.1081.

Hunt, J. D., & Stefan, K. J. (2007). Tour-based microsimulation of urban commercial movements. *Transportation Research Part B: Methodological, 41*(9), 981–1013.

Kumar, V., & Srinivasan, S. (2010). A review of supply chain management using multi-agent system. *International Journal of Computer Science*, 7(5), 198–205.

Le Ber, F., & Chouvet, M. P. (1999). An agent-based model for domain knowledge representation. *Data & Knowledge Engineering, 29*(2), 147–161.

Liedtke, G., & Schepperle, H. (2004). Segmentation of the transportation market with regard to activity-based freight transport modelling. *International Journal of Logistics Research and Applications, 7*(3), 199–218.

OECD. (2003). Delivering the goods: 21st century challenges to urban goods transport. Paris: Author. Retrieved from http://www.internationaltransportforum.org/pub/pdf/03DeliveringGoods.pdf

Puckett, S. M., Hensher, D. A., Rose, J. M., & Collins, A. (2007). Design and development of a stated choice experiment for interdependent agents: Accounting for interactions between buyers and sellers of urban freight services. *Transportation, 34*(4), 429–451.

Roorda, M., Cavalcante, R., McCabe, S., & Kwan, H. (2009). A conceptual framework for agent-based modelling of logistics services. *Transportation Research Part E: Logistics and Transportation Review*, *46*(1), 18–31.

Russo, F., & Comi, A. (2006). Demand models for city logistics: a state of the art and a proposed integrated system. In E. Taniguchi & R. Thompson (Eds.), *Recent advances in city logistics* (pp. 91–105). Amsterdam: Elsevier.

Stevenson, G., & Dobson, S. (2011). *Sapphire: Generating Java runtime artefacts from OWL ontologies.* Paper presented at the Advanced Information Systems Engineering Workshops. Retrieved from http://link.springer.com/chapter/10.1007/978-3-642-22056-2_46

Swaminathan, J. M., Smith, S. F., & Sadeh, N. M. (1994). *Modeling the dynamics of supply chains.* Paper presented at the Proceedings of AAAI-94 SIGMAN Workshop on Intelligent Manufacturing Systems. Retrieved from http://www-preview.ri.cmu.edu/pub_files/pub2/swaminathan_j_m_1994_1/swaminathan_j_m_1994_1.pdf

Tamagawa, D., Taniguchi, E., & Yamada, T. (2010). Evaluating city logistics measures using a multi-agent model. *Procedia – Social and Behavioral Sciences, 2*(3), 6002–6012. doi:10.1016/j.sbspro.2010.04.014.

Taniguchi, E., & Tamagawa, D. (2005). Evaluating city logistics measures considering the behavior of several stakeholders. *Journal of the Eastern Asia Society for Transportation Studies, 6*, 3062–3076.

Terzi, S., & Cavalieri, S. (2004). Simulation in the supply chain context: a survey. *Computers in Industry, 53*(1), 3–16.

Thompson, R. G., & Taniguchi, E. (2001). City logistics and freight transport. In A. Brewer, K. J. Button, & D. A. Hensher (Eds.), Handbook of logistics and supply chain management (pp. 393–405). Amsterdam: Elsevier Science Ltd.

Multi-agent systems modelling approach to evaluate urban motorways for city logistics

J.S.E. Teo, E. Taniguchi and A.G. Qureshi

Department of Urban Management, Graduate School of Engineering, Kyoto University, C-1 Kyotodaigaku Katsura, Nishikyo, Kyoto, Japan

Government road authorities are constantly faced with the challenges of urbanization and traffic congestion requiring them to make good decisions for infrastructure developments. Several developed and developing countries have focused their concerns on building motorways for private and public transports for intercity connectivity and economic growth in the past. However, very few evaluation models were concerned about urban motorways for the benefit of urban freight transport. There may not even be an evaluation model for urban motorways development, which has considered the routing behaviour of truck movements in urban areas, especially if the main purpose for the urban motorway is for improving city logistics. Faced with the problems and concerns of the road authorities in Japan regarding capacity increase measures or other freight management schemes, this paper is an initial step to explore and provide the methodology to support the road authorities in their decision for urban motorway alternatives.

1. Introduction

Transportation infrastructure is vital to the economy and connecting people, which led to several countries including the USA (US Department of Transportation, 2013) and China (Transport Business International, 2013) to announce their plans to fund the infrastructure projects. Large amount of budget has been allocated to road and bridge improvements and construction, for example, the USA has assigned about $305 billion over the next six years (US Department of Transportation, 2013). Due to the large financial investments typically involved in roads and bridge construction, transportation authorities and planners perform extensive evaluation and impact studies to justify and support their decisions on the location and construction of the new motorways. Besides the purpose of increasing the road capacity for private cars and public transport, motorways may help to reduce the inner city pollution level. In the context of urban freight movement or city logistics (Taniguchi, Thompson, Yamada, & van Duin, 2001), delivery trucks may use urban motorways as alternative paths to improve on their delivery time.

Urban freight transport has gained more attention in many cities of the world due to the concentration of more population into urban areas as well as social and environmental problems relating to urban freight transport. The typical problems we face in urban areas are concern about: (1) how we can create efficient urban freight transport systems with higher services and lower costs and (2) how we can ensure the better environment, safer community and well-being of people who are living there. The idea of city logistics has been proposed (Crainic, Ricciardi, & Storchi, 2009; Taniguchi et al., 2001) for establishing efficient and environmentally friendly urban freight transport systems towards sustainable and liveable cities by balancing the above-mentioned two issues. The essential aspect of city logistics is that although the logistics activity is mainly carried out by private companies, the intervention of public authorities are required to achieve the goals of city logistics by implementing government-driven policy measures (PIARC Technical committee B.4 freight transport and inter-modality, 2012). In the procedure of public private partnerships for identifying current problems, discussing appropriate approaches and measures as well as evaluating them are important. Sharing data and information among stakeholders and assessing the policy measures before implementing them would also be essential. In this context, modelling city logistics policy measures, including truck ban, access control, road pricing, setting urban distribution centres, off-peak hour delivery, load factor controls and new motorways construction plays a crucial role for the evaluation.

Few studies in the past have studied the impact of urban motorways on urban freight movement and the effect on the stakeholders in the city. Although it may seem that motorways are the natural choice to improve road capacity and travel speed, but the selection of the new motorways, given several options, is usually difficult to determine. A cheaper motorway construction may not lead to a useful infrastructure if it does not attract road users, especially if the motorway is intended to relieve urban freight traffic and eliminate 'rat-running' in the city centre. This paper seeks to provide a unique modelling framework to support government transport authorities in decision-making especially on the location of constructing new motorways to improve freight activities and reduce negative environmental impact. The model in our research has incorporated an autonomous road administrator while considering the objectives of the stakeholders involved within the urban freight environment.

2. Literature review

A recent publication by Cambridge Systematics, Inc. (2013) provides a summary of the current practice of integrating freight in the highway planning process in the USA, which focused on three major points. The first is about freight self-assessment, which includes existing logistics patterns, logistics bottlenecks and needs identification. The second element is concerned about the stakeholder outreach where public and private freight stakeholder groups are formed. The third major point is about data analysis like forecasting freight volumes and evaluating existing performance measures. These are the major elements that are common for the macro-level evaluation of freight policies. Studies in the past reflected three groups of people, who have concerns related to new motorway developments. One group typically supported the plans for the development, while the second group felt the necessity of such projects but were not convinced on the economic growth and development that such motorways will bring. The last group of people were the critics, who were against the investment and totally disagreed with the theoretical and empirical studies (Rephann & Isserman, 1994). These are the groups of people that the evaluation models for motorway investments can consider. There are many existing models developed that has provided support for government road authorities with a motorway investment plan for bridge preservation, road safety improvements, pavement maintenance, intelligent transport systems and new constructions (Li, Madanu, Zhou, Wang, & Abbas, 2010). Transportation investments look at two analytical steps of project evaluation and selection and projection selection usually involves choosing the best economically projects with maximum benefits

(Li et al., 2012). Cook and Seiford (1984) introduced an ordinal ranking model to select the best option for motorway corridor based on some corresponding qualitative dimension. A benefit–cost analysis to evaluate new capacity motorway projects was proposed by An and Casper (2011) where they considered the logistics benefit, which included the time and shipping cost savings. However, there are limited papers that studied the micro-level of evaluating impact of new urban motorways while considering the objectives of carriers, shippers, administrator and residents and the effects they have on urban freight activities. This research aims to contribute to the literatures to cover the initial step of covering the topic on micro-level analysis of freight carriers' optimized and current practise of last-mile operations and the impact of new motorways on other major stakeholders.

3. Methodology

Based on the literature reviews, none of the models have considered the routing behaviour for carriers when considering urban motorway options relating to freight operations. Our research hopes to consider such activities of the carriers and the interactions of the stakeholders within the context of city logistics especially when the purpose of constructing a motorway is to improve urban freight traffic.

In a recent research, the evaluation of cordon-based and distance-based urban freight road pricing was done using a multi-agent systems (MAS) modelling approach incorporating vehicle routing problem with time window (VRPTW) model solved with insertion heuristics, Q-learning algorithm and second price auctioning model (Teo, Taniguchi, & Qureshi, 2012a). It is observed that researchers, who tend to use the MAS approach, inevitably attempt to include several cross-disciplinary models, which was helpful to model the rationality of urban freight agents' behaviour.

The flexibility of MAS modelling makes it an attractive modelling alternative for complicated problems. Davidsson, Holmgren, Persson, and Ramstedt (2008) and Holmgren, Davidsson, Persson, and Ramstedt (2012) developed the Transportation and Production Agent-based Simulator (TAPAS) that consists of a physical simulator and a decision-maker simulator to evaluate the impact on shippers, carriers and customers due to the implementation of schemes such as fuel taxes, road tolls and vehicle taxes. They recommended that more sophisticated optimization algorithm can be used for the agents' decision-making and agents' learning from experience can be included, along with other recommendations in their study.

A vehicle routing problem with time window – dynamic (VRPTW-D) and Monte Carlo learning model were found to increase the profit of carriers and decrease the shippers' costs with the MAS modelling approach (Taniguchi, Yamada, & Okamoto, 2007). Further evaluation of city logistics schemes such as road pricing and cooperative freight transport systems could also be done using the same methodology. In another research, a VRPTW-forecasted (VRPTW-F) model with the combination of Q-learning algorithm, which is a form of reinforcement learning, was used to evaluate truck ban and motorway toll policy schemes on the impact on administrators, carriers, shippers, residents and motorway operators (Tamagawa, Taniguchi, & Yamada, 2010). In a complex logistics environment having several stakeholders acting on their own interest, it is unavoidable that most modellers face problems anticipating future situations and instilling fixed solutions to all problems may not be the best option. This is the reason why reinforcement learning is one of the important topics in MAS modelling especially in modelling the evaluation of new motorways in the context of urban freight activities or city logistics as shown in Figure 1.

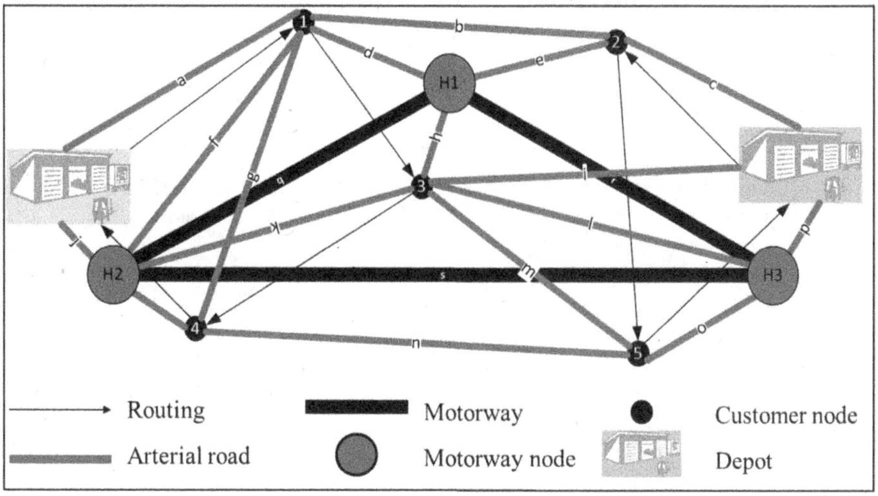

Figure 1. An example of an urban motorway road network in city logistics.

Reinforcement learning has two most critical distinct features that differentiate itself with other learning which are the trial-and-error search and delayed reward (Sutton & Barto, 1998). The simple idea of learning through experimenting and experiencing the consequences makes reinforcement learning close to reality of how human beings learn in any given environment. In this sense, it is expected that the learning model includes the ability to sense the environment, take actions that will change the state and must include the goals that direct the actions. These three aspects provide a suitable condition for research in the area of city logistics due to the involvement of multiple stakeholders that require goal-directed action policies. Another area of consideration is the issue of exploitation and exploration actions. When an agent learns from experience, the next dilemma is to consider whether to take the action that provides the best results every time or to try a new action that has the possibility of achieving a better result. Exploring a new action gives the agent a more complete experience and in some scenarios where competition is involved, it is more rational to switch between actions to make the environment more unpredictable, especially when the agents are in a competitive market.

4. Modelling framework

One of the unique features in this research is the use of object-oriented programming structure with the concept of MAS modelling as compared to previous modelling approach (Teo et al., 2012a; Teo, Taniguchi, & Qureshi, 2012b). Similar attempt by Nilesh, Yang, van Duin, and Tavasszy (2012) was done to facilitate developers to understand the modelling framework for city logistics in MAS models. The framework shown in Figure 2 is the modelling structure used in this research. The arrows connecting each of the class refers to the transfer of information and interaction. Within each class are the associated objects where each of them has their own actions.

The administrator's reinforcement Q-learning algorithm is shown in Equation (1). The algorithm will provide updated learning values for the administrator's action. The administrator's action consists of new urban motorway alternatives. Each alternative includes bi-directional links in the road network. There are three scenarios tested in this research.

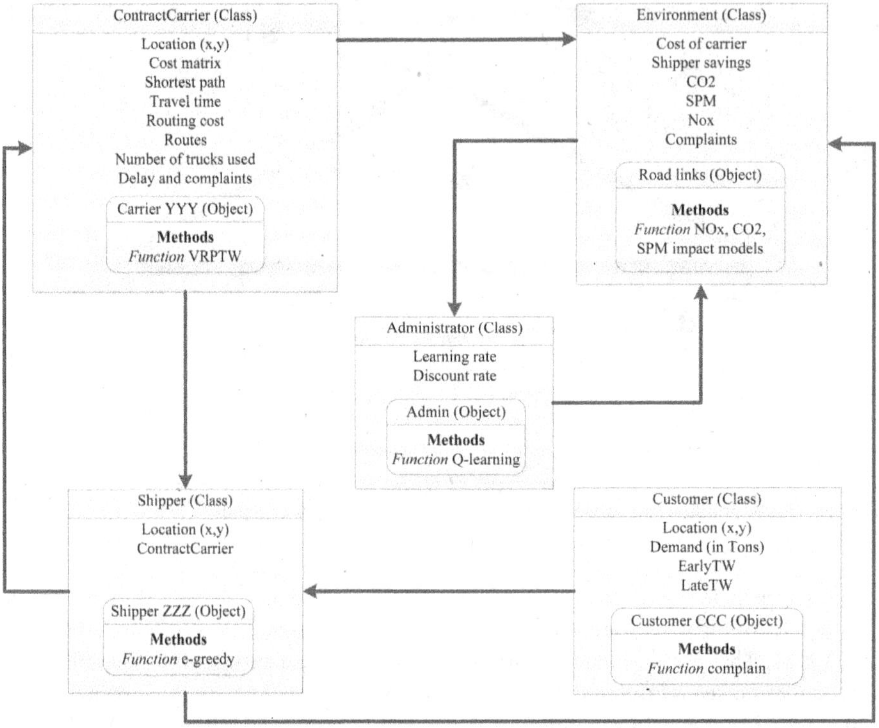

Figure 2. Object-oriented programming MAS framework.

The first scenario is the base case where the administrator was an inactive agent and did not learn from the emissions. In the second and third scenarios, the administrator received emission information from the environment and learnt using the Q-learning algorithm for different motorway connection pattern for each scenario, respectively. The emission level of carbon dioxide, nitrogen oxide and suspended particulate matter are calculated using the equations as found in Equations (2)–(4) (NILIM, 2003).

$$Q_n(s_{n,t}, a_{n,t}) \leftarrow (1-\alpha_n)\, Q_n(s_{n,t}, a_{n,t}) + \alpha_n \left[r_{n,t} + \gamma_n \min_{a_{n,t+1} \in A_n} Q_n(s_{n,t+1}, a_{n,t+1}) \right], \tag{1}$$

where $Q_n(s_{n,t}, a_{n,t})$ is the expected emission level received by administrator n in state t due to action in state t; $Q_n(s_{n,t+1}, a_{n,t+1})$ the expected emission level received by administrator n in state $t+1$ due to the action in state $t+1$; γ_n the discount rate for administrator $n(0 < \gamma_n < 1)$; α_n the learning rate of administrator $n(0 < \alpha_n < 1)$ and $r_{n,t}$ the immediate emission level received by administrator n in state t.

$$\mathrm{CO_2} = l_{ij}\left(278.448 + 0.048059v_{ij}^2 - 5.1227v_{ij} + \frac{2347.1}{v_{ij}}\right), \tag{2}$$

$$\mathrm{NO}_x = l_{ij}\left(1.06116 + 0.000213v_{ij}^2 - 0.0246v_{ij} + \frac{16.258}{v_{ij}}\right), \tag{3}$$

$$\mathrm{SPM} = l_{ij}\left(0.03442 - 0.000039391v_{ij}^2 + 0.0036777v_{ij} + \frac{1.2754}{v_{ij}}\right), \tag{4}$$

where CO_2 is the expected carbon dioxide emission in grams; NO_x the expected nitrogen oxide emission in grams; SPM the expected suspended particulate matter in grams; l_{ij} the length of road link between nodes i and j in kilometres and v_{ij} the speed of vehicle traveling on road link between nodes i and j.

5. Experiment set-up

This research sets up the basic structure with a simplistic road network as shown in Figure 3. This road network is not meant to be a generic representation of realistic cases but is meant to explain how the modelling framework and methodology can be applied. The hypothetical network consists of two shippers with two contract carriers and 21 customers. In the experiment, each of the customers generated dynamic demands, early and late time window for each day. The shippers are assumed to receive all information regarding their customers and passed on this information to the carriers for delivery service. For this experiment set-up, carrier at Node 1 is contracted to shipper at Node 5, while carrier at Node 12 is contracted to shipper at Node 25. This type of contracts reflects the typical industry practice where shippers and carriers are engaged in long-term contracts for regular deliveries. The flow of delivery involves each carrier to pick-up all demands with full truck load as much as possible from their contracted shipper and return to the depot for repacking. The delivery service to the customers is based on the optimized routing using insertion heuristics and the other parameters that were used are shown in Table 1. The learning and discount rates of the administrator are set at the mean of 0.5 in this initial experiment. The demand of customers are assumed to be less than the capacity of the truck for simplicity of one visit to service each customer at the given time window. As for the speed of the motorways, they are set at a higher travelling speed than the normal road links, which are commonly found in real scenarios. The simulation of the MAS model was done for 1080 days, which was about 3 years.

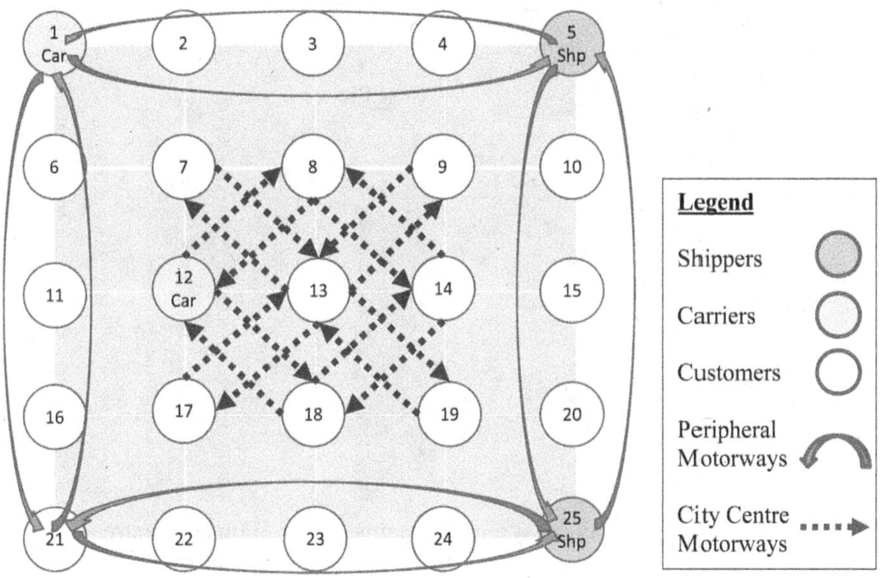

Figure 3. Hypothetical road network with motorway options.

Table 1. Parameters for experiment.

Learning rate of administrator, α_n	0.5
Discount rate of administrator, γ_n	0.5
Maximum capacity of trucks (units)	200
Maximum demand for each customer (units)	100
Length of each road link (km)	5
Length of peripheral motorway (km)	20
Length of city centre motorway (km)	7
Speed of typical truck (km/hr)	30
Speed of peripheral motorway (km/hr)	80
Speed of city centre motorway (km/hr)	60

6. Results and discussion

The current analysis shows the plots of the SPM, CO_2 and NO_x emissions for the entire network. It is assumed that the peripheral highway links provided a travel velocity of 80 km/hr that could entice the carriers to change their path choice. It is shown in Figures 4–6 that the CO_2, SPM and NO_x has increased by 10% after the implementation of peripheral motorways and by 20% after the implementation of city centre motorways. One likely cause of an increase for peripheral motorways is due to the trucks choosing a combination of normal roads and motorways resulting in faster travel time but leading to the consequence of longer distance travelled on the motorways. However, the introduction of the highway schemes have led to fewer complaints by the customers, with the least complaints encountered due to lesser late deliveries with the city centre motorways as shown in Figure 7. In a survey done on two Italian regions, Friuli Venezia Giulia and Marche, it was found that the shippers viewed quality attributes of freight transport services such as reliability and safety more than the cost (Danielis, Marcucci, & Rotaris, 2005). Such findings were also similar to the survey done in Switzerland and other reports reviewed by Fries, de Jong, Patterson, and Wiedmann (2010) where shippers view on-time reliability more important than cost.

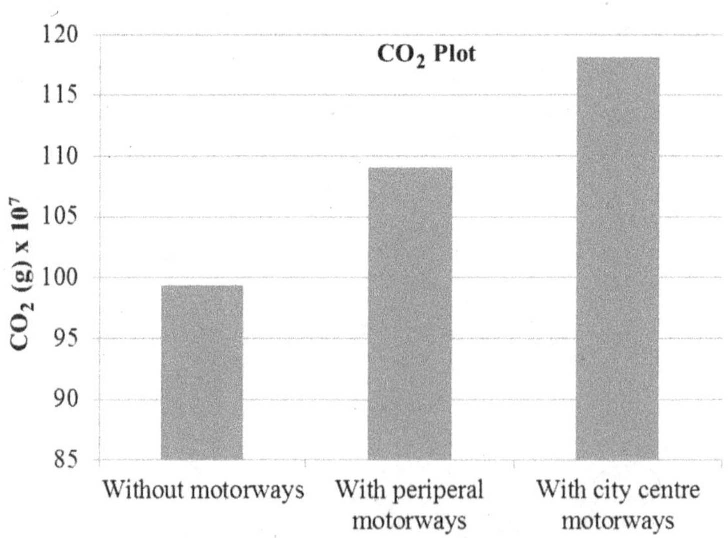

Figure 4. Average CO_2 emission comparison for different motorway schemes.

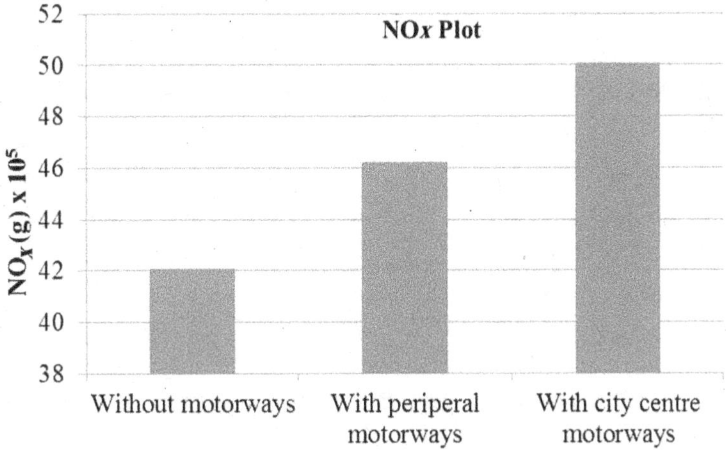

Figure 5. Average NO_x emission comparison for different motorway schemes.

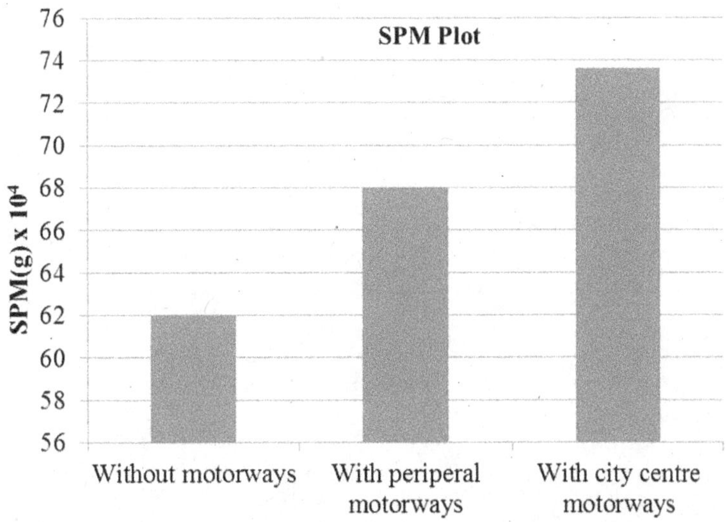

Figure 6. Average SPM emission comparison for different motorway schemes.

Carriers are also considered the last players in the supply chain that could affect the reputation of the shippers from the perspectives of the customers (Patier & Alligier, 2003). To study the impact of how policy schemes can be introduced to cope with the problems, it is necessary to understand the behaviours of the consumers. It was found that consumers in France have several expectations including short delivery times within specified time slots and on-time delivery (Patier & Alligier, 2003). Therefore, the complaints should be validated further especially when it shows the advantage that the introduction of highway created fewer complaints.

Figure 8 shows the savings for shippers as compared to the case if they have chosen the alternative carrier to deliver their goods. The savings experienced by the shipper is the difference between the calculated cost of the alternative carrier and the real cost paid to their own contracted carrier. Figure 8 shows that the contracted carriers provided savings without the highway schemes, which meant that it is a cost-effective way for delivering

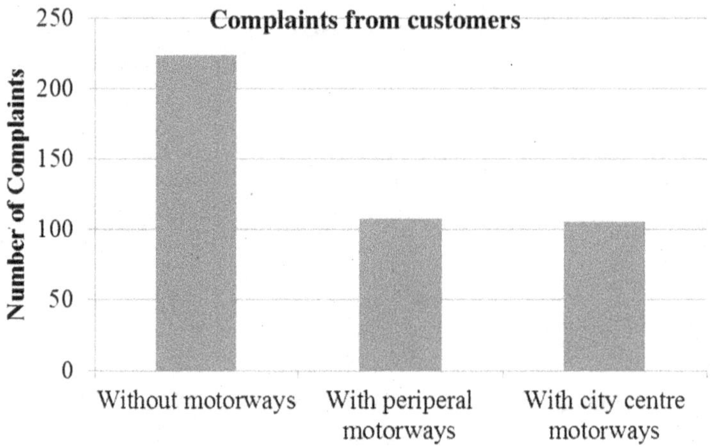

Figure 7. Average complaints comparison for different motorway schemes.

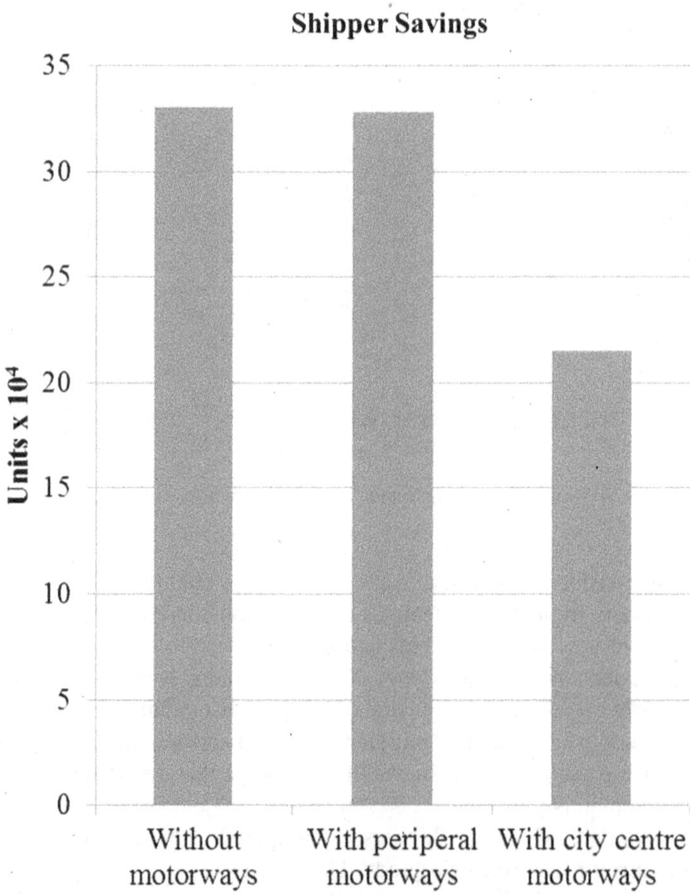

Figure 8. Average savings comparison for different motorway schemes.

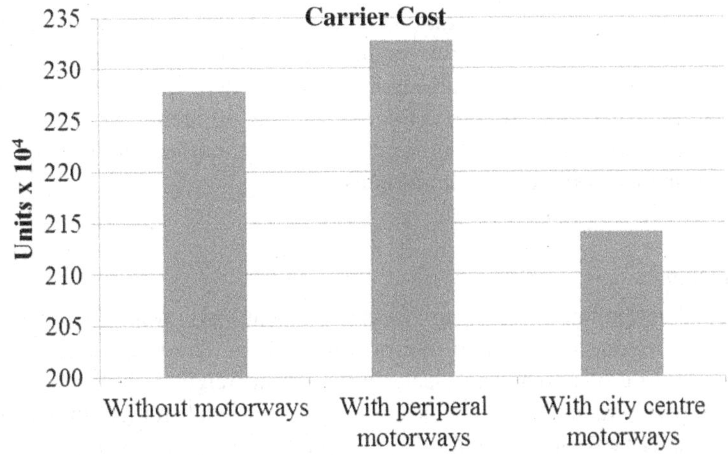

Figure 9. Average carrier cost comparison for different motorway schemes.

their goods if they continue to be contracted to their current carrier. The introduction of motorways has caused the savings to increase further as shown in the figure, especially for the city centre motorway scheme. The city centre motorways may have provided a faster delivery service to the customers. An alternative analysis can be done to consider the effect of having auctioning within the MAS model and how it can translate to more cost savings for the shippers. Such auctioning and e-marketplace are gaining more interest, like a recent project initiative in Singapore for a synchronized last-mile delivery (De Souza, Goh, Lau, Ng, & Tan, 2013). The results shown in Figure 9 shows the lower carrier cost when the city

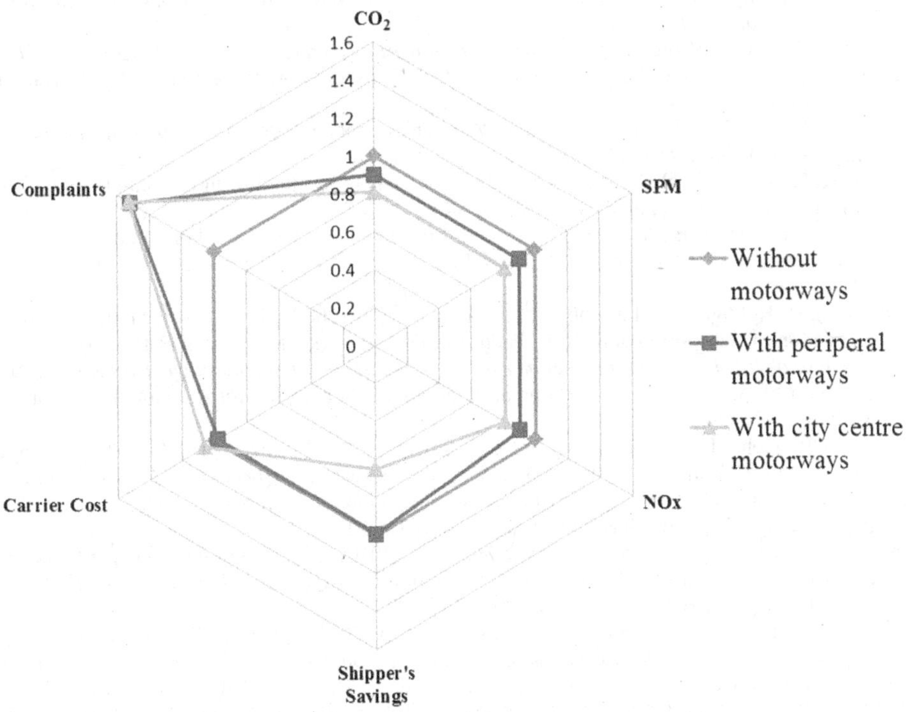

Figure 10. Radar plot for all performance measures.

centre motorways are constructed. This could be the effect of carriers opting to use the city centre motorways that resulted in lesser routing cost and late penalty cost. This experiment have shown how the MAS model can be used to evaluate the highway corridor options and as shown in Figure 10, there will be a trade-off for the different schemes and it seemed that city centre motorways benefit carriers the most but may not be desired by the road authorities since there will be a rise in the emission.

7. Conclusion

Developed and developing countries are facing an urgent need for improving or expanding their infrastructure due to the rapid rate of urbanization. The increase in the migration of population into urban areas has escalated the urban freight activities in recent years. This research was initiated due to the lack of evaluation models for handling new highway corridors for the purpose of improving urban freight transport and city logistics. The results in this paper are meant to provide an understanding of how the methodology is applied in this research and to verify the logics underlying the model. The advantage of this model is the incorporation of an autonomous administrator to represent the road authorities and the logical behaviour of the stakeholders involved in urban freight and city logistics. Future contributions in this area of research may include the modelling approach on realistic road networks such as the Osaka city network and some integration of micro and macro simulation software for generating the dynamic travel time for the MAS model.

References

An, M., & Casper, C. (2011). Integrating travel demand model and benefit-cost analysis for evaluation of new capacity highway projects. *Transportation Research Record: Journal of the Transportation Research Board, 2244*, 34–40.

Cambridge Systematics, Inc. (2013). *SHRP 2 C15 Integrating Freight Considerations into the Highway Capacity Planning Process*. Washington, DC: Transportation Research Board of the National Academies.

Cook, W. D., & Seiford, L. M. (1984). An ordinal ranking model corridor. *Computers, Environment and Urban Systems, 9* (4), 271–276.

Crainic, T. G., Ricciardi, N., & Storchi, G. (2009). Models for evaluating and planning city logistics systems. *Transportation Science, 43*, 432–454.

Danielis, R., Marcucci, E., & Rotaris, L. (2005). Logistics managers' stated preferences for freight service attributes. *Transportation Research Part E Logistics and Transportation Review, 41*, 201–215.

Davidsson, P., Holmgren, J., Persson, J. A., & Ramstedt, L. (2008, May 12–16). Multi agent based simulation of transport chains. In L. Padgham, D. Parkes, J. Müller, & S. Parsons (Eds.), *Proceedings of 7th international conference on autonomous agents and multiagent systems (AAMAS 2008)* (pp. 1153–1160). Estoril, Portugal: International Foundation for Autonomous Agents and Multiagent Systems.

De Souza, R., Goh, M., Lau, H.-C., Ng, W.-S., & Tan, P.-S. (2013, June 17–19). Collaborative urban logistics – synchronizing the last mile a Singapore research perspective. In E. Taniguchi & R. G. Thompson (Eds.), *Proceedings of the 8th international conference on city logistics*, Bali, Indonesia (pp. 536–546). Kyoto: Institute for City Logistics.

Fries, N., de Jong, G. C., Patterson, Z., & Wiedmann, U. (2010). Shipper willingness to pay to increase environmental performance in freight transportation. *Transportation Research Record: Journal of the Transportation Research Board, 2168*, 33–42.

Holmgren, J., Davidsson, P., Persson, J. A., & Ramstedt, L. (2012). TAPAS: A multi-agent-based model for simulation of transport chains. *Simulation Modelling Practice and Theory, 23*, 1–18.

Li, Z., Kaul, H., Kapoor, S., Veliou, E., Zhou, B., & Lee, S. H. (2012). New methodology for transportation investment decisions with consideration of project interdependencies. *Transportation Research Record: Journal of the Transportation Research Board, 2285*, 36–46.

Li, Z., Madanu, S., Zhou, B., Wang, Y., & Abbas, M. (2010). A heuristic approach for selecting highway investment alternatives. *Computer-Aided Civil and Infrastructure Engineering, 25*(6), 427–439.

Nilesh, A. N., Yang, M., van Duin, J. H. R., & Tavasszy, L. (2012). GenCLOn: An ontology for city logistics. *Expert Systems with Applications, 39*(15), 11944–11960.

NILIM, National Institute of Land and Infrastructure Management (2003). *Quantitative Appraisal Index Calculations Used for Basic Unit Computation of CO_2, NO_x, SPM (in Japanese)*. Tsukuba City, Japan.

Patier, D., & Alligier, L. (2003, June 25–27). On-line retailing in France: Current and future effects on city logistics. In E. Taniguchi & R. G. Thompson (Eds.), *Logistics systems for sustainable cities. Proceedings of the 3rd international conference on city logistics*, Madeira, Portugal (pp. 381–395). The Netherlands: Elsevier.

PIARC Technical committee B.4 freight transport and inter-modality (2012). *Public sector governance over urban freight transport*. La Défense cedex, France: World Road Association.

Rephann, T., & Isserman, A. (1994). New highways as economic development tools?: An evaluation using quasi-experimental matching methods. *Regional Science and Urban Economics, 24*, 723–751.

Sutton, R. S., & Barto, A. G. (1998). *Reinforcement learning: An introduction*. Cambridge: MIT Press.

Tamagawa, D., Taniguchi, E., & Yamada, T. (2010). Evaluating city logistics measures using a multi-agent model. *Procedia Social and Behavioral Sciences, 2*, 6002–6012.

Taniguchi, E., Thompson, R. G., Yamada, T., & van Duin, R. (2001). *City logistics: Network modelling and intelligent transport systems*. Rotterdam, The Netherlands: Pergamon.

Taniguchi, E., Yamada, T., & Okamoto, M. (2007). Multi-agent modeling for evaluating dynamic vehicle routing and scheduling systems. *Journal of the Eastern Asia Society for Transportation Studies, 7*, 933–948.

Teo, J. S. E., Taniguchi, E., & Qureshi, A. G. (2012a). Evaluation of distance-based and cordon-based urban freight road pricing in e-commerce environment with multiagent model. *Transportation Research Record: Journal of the Transportation Research Board, 2269*, 127–134.

Teo, J. S. E., Taniguchi, E., & Qureshi, A. G. (2012b). Evaluating city logistics measure in e-commerce with multiagent systems. *Procedia – Social and Behavioral Sciences, 39*, 349–359.

Transport Business International (2013). China planning 120 billion transport investment. *Transport Business International*. Retrieved from http://www.transportbusiness.net/content/view/1259/33/

US Department of Transportation (2013). *Budget Highlights Fiscal Year 2013*.

A location-based accessibility analysis to estimate the suitability of urban consolidation facilities

Jesus Gonzalez-Feliu[a], Josep-Maria Salanova Grau[b] and Adrien Beziat[c]

[a]Centre National de la Recherche Scientifique, UMR 5593, Institut des Sciences de l'Homme, Lyon, France; [b]Center for Research and Technology Hellas, Hellenic Institute of Transport, Tessaloniki, Greece; [c]IFSTTAR, SPLOTT, Marne-la-Vallée, France

This paper proposes a location-based accessibility analysis framework to assess the suitability of urban consolidation platform location scenarios. First, an overview of urban consolidation is presented to identify the main types of platforms and the related scientific work. Then, the proposed framework is presented on the form of a three-step procedure. The first step is to generate goods transport demand using a delivery-to-commodity model. The second consists in estimating routes both for serving the consolidation platforms supplied by shippers and for delivering customers afterwards, using a VRP algorithm. The third step consists in performing an accessibility calculation. Starting from the distances travelled obtained by the vehicle routing algorithm, travel times (including vehicle running and stopping times) are estimated, after which a location-based accessibility indicator based on transport cost is obtained. To illustrate the framework proposed, an example of application for the city of Lyon (France) is presented. Therefore, three sets of scenarios are assessed and discussed. Finally, practical issues of the proposed method are presented.

1. Introduction

Urban consolidation is a popular subject in city logistics as shown by recent works (Allen, Browne, Woodburn, & Leonardi, 2012; Arvidsson & Browne, 2013; Janjevic, Kaminsky, & Ballé Ndiaye, 2013; Macharis & Melo, 2011; Morana, Gonzalez-Feliu, & Semet, 2014; Verlinde, Macharis, & Witlox, 2012). Indeed, many scientific works and experiments have been proposed and communicated in recent years (for an overview on this subject, see Allen et al., 2012; Boudouin, Morel, & Gardat, 2014; Janjevic et al., 2013; Verlinde et al., 2012). However, many scholars and practitioners have concluded on the difficulties of finding standard and economically viable consolidation solutions (Gonzalez-Feliu & Morana, 2010; Ville, Gonzalez-Feliu, & Dablanc, 2013; Zunder & Marinov, 2011), mainly in the form of City Distribution Centers (CDC), and on the need for good decision support tools to help decision-makers in making their choices in terms of logistics solutions for delivery in cities (Faure et al., 2013). Such conclusions are reinforced by the complex current situation in terms of city-centre accessibility (Crozet, Mercier, & Ovtracht, 2012) and the wide variety of consolidation alternatives (Janjevic et al., 2013; Verlinde et al., 2012). Moreover, public authorities' requirements for integrating goods transport in urban planning require support in order to analyse the interaction between their land-use choices and transformations in trip behaviour for both personal and commercial trips. In this context, one of the main questions that arise is that of improving the choice of consolidation points for deliveries in urban zones, mainly in the case of collaborative schemes.

Regarding passenger transport, city planners rely on two main methods for support. The first is that of Transport and Land Use Interaction (LUTI) models (Wegener, 2004). A LUTI model represents the links and interactions between the use humans make of land (in general in urban areas) and transport networks (for basic notions on this subject, see for example De La Barra, 1989). More specifically, a transport model (e.g. a four-step model in the sense of Ortuzar and Willumsen (1990) requires land-use inputs that are considered as exogenous (thus obtained from other methods not integrated in the model), whereas LUTI combines a land-use model with a transport model, which are integrated and need only policy-based data as inputs. The second method is to use accessibility-based tools (Crozet et al., 2012), which do not forecast land-use consequences in an integrated way but translate policies into scenarios, after which accessibility indicators are estimated to assess such scenarios. To the best of our knowledge, neither approach is widely deployed in urban logistics. However, the second category of methods seems us to offer an advantage in comparison to LUTI at the strategic level, namely the quantity of data needed and the efforts made to develop accessibility-based methods are much lower than those of LUTI tools. Therefore, they are suitable for situations where aggregated data and general trends are needed to support planners when taking strategic decisions.[1]

The aim of this paper is to propose a locational accessibility analysis framework to carry out a combined city planning and transport analysis of CDC locations, and apply it to a realistic urban consolidation situation for the city of Lyon (France). The main objective of the proposed framework is not to find optimal locations of CDCs but identify a set of potential locations to then carry out more detailed assessments with suitable tools. First, an overview of urban consolidation is presented, providing the main consolidation solutions and focusing on urban consolidation centres. Afterwards, we present a location-based accessibility analysis methodology to assess the suitability of the location of an urban consolidation centre. This methodology has the following structure. First, transport demand is generated using a three-step delivery-to-commodity model to estimate for each establishment to be delivered the daily number of deliveries and their corresponding quantities of commodity. Second, a heuristic vehicle routing method for estimating realistic routes on the basis of the CDCs considered is proposed, followed by the estimation of the total distance travelled on all routes. Third, a location-based accessibility indicator is built from the resulting distances travelled. The total travel times of each route, including both trips and stops, are calculated, after which an accessibility indicator is estimated. To illustrate the method, an example of application for the city of Lyon is proposed. Three sets of tests are presented and discussed to state on the usefulness and potential of accessibility analysis for urban goods transport.

2. Urban consolidation: an overview

Until the 1980s, each carrier made its own deliveries from their own terminals, which were located at varying distances from the final destinations of deliveries (Ville et al., 2013). In response to societal and consumer demands, new consolidation schemes have emerged in the last three decades to deliver the congested and dense urban sections. Such schemes mainly aim to decrease the number of vehicles, greenhouse gas, pollution and noise, as well as increase productiveness. According to the latest works on the subject (Allen, Thorne, & Browne, 2007; Allen et al., 2012; Boudouin, 2006; Boudouin et al., 2014; Janjevic et al., 2013; Tario, Ancar, Panero, Shin, & Lopez, 2011; Verlinde et al., 2012; Ville et al., 2013), such schemes are based on different infrastructures. We attempt here to make a unified classification by aggregating and summarizing such works. The typology proposed is composed of three categories: single carrier-based organization platforms, multi-carrier platforms for individual purposes and multi-carrier platforms for goods flow pooling.

Carrier-based flow organization platforms are facilities belonging to a single carrier (or used by only one carrier) for its organizational purposes. They obey a rationale of economic performance and are in general planned by carriers following supply chain management strategies. Such platforms are seen in different locations and have different scopes. Three main sub-categories can be identified. The first is that of inter-town/regional platforms serving close locations in urban areas. In general, they are regional-based platforms, mainly warehouses for distribution companies or consolidation facilities for transport carriers which do not serve only urban areas but can play an important role in urban logistics when located in the peripheries of medium and large cities. Most logistics and transport operators have such types of platforms, and in large metropolitan areas they are spread following different strategies (Tario et al., 2011) and their distribution needs to be taken into account in urban planning (Dablanc, 2014). The second one is that of urban distribution centres for single-company purposes which are platforms entirely destined to deliver the urban zones of a conurbation. Although they are less developed than the first subcategory, they are quite operational in big cities, for example in Paris, with the Samada-Monoprix rail consolidation platform (Delaître & De Barbeyrac, 2012) and the Presstalis consolidation platforms for press distribution (Morana et al., 2014). The third subcategory is that of micro-distribution centres for single-company purposes which are small platforms located near the final delivery to which goods are transported by large vehicles before being split into loads for smaller trucks or vans that deliver to the dense urban zones near the centre. Some examples are the Chronospost Paris urban distribution centre and the urban logistics space of Lyon Cordeliers for Deret Transport and Logistics.

Multi-carrier individual-based flow organization platforms are logistics zones planned in general with the support of public authorities for delivery in urban areas. They are shared by two or more carriers but without merging their supply chains. Two subcategories can be defined. Peri-urban logistics zones are industrial areas dedicated exclusively to logistics, located in the periphery of conurbations, which host several shippers and/or logistics operators together (Boudouin, 2006). Such integrated zones allow the various logistics stakeholders to be located near their final customers, thereby limiting their logistics costs. However, each carrier is organized in its allocated space, and, a priori, no merging of flows and practices is observed. Their delivery practices remain unchanged (Boudouin et al., 2014). Urban micro-logistics zones follow the same principle, but they are smaller and are in general located near the delivery zones. The two main examples are the logistics hotels (Boudouin et al., 2014) and the proximity logistics spaces (Boudouin, 2006).

The third category is that of multi-carrier consolidation platforms. These platforms allow flow and supply chain merging to pool goods for last mile deliveries in urban zones in order to reduce the number of vehicles and environmental nuisances. Four types of infrastructures can be defined. The first is that of public CDCs, and the second that of private CDCs. They work quite similarly (Gonzalez-Feliu & Morana, 2010; Ville et al., 2013), but the main difference is that of their status. In the first case, CDCs operate for collective utility, with strong support from the public authorities and by companies that ensure a public (or assimilated) service. In the second case, the contribution of public authorities is limited or absent, and they operate according to the imperatives of economic viability. Examples of known public CDCs are those of La Rochelle (Trentini & Malhéné, 2010), Monaco and Genoa (Gonzalez-Feliu, 2008), and Vicenza (Ville et al., 2013). Private CDCs are mainly observed in Germany (Gonzalez-Feliu, 2008), but also in some Italian cities (Moran et al., 2014) and in Japan (Dablanc, 2011). The third type is that of collaborative urban consolidation centres, which instead of a single outbound operator propose that they collaboratively manage the terminal transport in collaboration with each other. Although some experiments have been reported (Montpellier, Evora, and Bologna), they have now been stopped due to the difficulties of managing collaboration between competitors. The fourth category is that of micro-consolidation centres, which work as CDCs but for smaller areas, mainly city centres or dense urban zones (Janjevic et al., 2013).

Last but not least is the category of neighbourhood and building infrastructures. They are not classical consolidation platforms but allow a level of consolidation near the final place of consumption, avoiding non-deliveries because of the receiver's absence and aggregating part of the demand, thus reducing the number of stops, the length of routes and even the number of vehicles (Boudouin et al., 2014; Ducret, 2013). Such infrastructures are of three types that will not be developed here since they are related to terminal and/or end-consumer transport and in general do not involve motorized outbound transport: shopping centres and in-bound office building logistics facilities, pickup points and freight lockers.

Regarding urban consolidation, three main groups of works can be observed in the literature. The first focuses on computer modelling and simulation. Such works use operations research methods mainly derived from vehicle routing frameworks (Toth & Vigo, 2002). Two main approaches are shown: single-tier systems (van Duin, Quak, & Munuzuri, 2008) in which freight is directly shipped from CDCs, and two-tier systems (Crainic, Ricciardi, & Storchi, 2004, 2009) in which new intra-modal transfers are organized between the CDC and the final destination of goods. Most works remain theoretical or conceptual (Crainic et al., 2004, 2009; Crainic, Perboli, Mancini, & Tadei, 2010; Crainic, Errico, Rei, & Ricciardi, 2012; van Duin, Quak, & Muñuzuri, 2010; Thompson & Hassall, 2012), although several real applications have been observed (Faure et al., 2013; Gonzalez-Feliu & Salanova, 2012). The second includes quantitative evaluation and assessment methods. Such works use quantitative economics and econometrics techniques to assess scenarios and evaluate the suitability of urban consolidation platforms, once the location has been chosen and the main strategic decisions (size, service patters, etc.) approved by public authorities (Ambrosini, Gonzalez-Feliu, & Toilier, 2013; van Duin et al., 2008). In both cases, the estimation of routes is performed only from the CDC, and the inbound part is seldom taken into account explicitly. The third contains qualitative and discussion works to assess the suitability and the limits of urban consolidation, and can be based on case studies (Dablanc, 2014; Gonzalez-Feliu & Morana, 2010; Hesse, 2004; Tario et al., 2011; Trentini & Malhéné, 2010; Ville et al., 2013) or literature-based approaches (Allen et al., 2012; Arvidsson & Browne, 2013; Dablanc, 2011; Janjevic et al., 2013; Zunder & Marinov, 2011). As shown by several authors, consolidation centres are often inefficient and ensuring their deployment and economic viability comes up against difficulties (Allen et al., 2012; Gonzalez-Feliu & Morana, 2010; Gonzalez-Feliu, Salanova Grau, Morana, & Mitsakis, 2013; Zunder & Marinov, 2011). When examining the development of such platforms in-depth, their locations were decided a priori without analysis of the best area for location, and although some authors have indicated accessibility analysis as a good tool for supporting such decisions (Crainic et al., 2010; Gonzalez-Feliu, 2008, 2012), they used indicators that do not take into account the nature of routes (i.e. less-than-truckload). To fill this gap in knowledge, we propose an accessibility analysis with an algorithm easy-to-use and implement by city planners.

The scope of the research covers the two connected transport systems related to a CDC: the inbound one, which is in general planned by each transport carrier, brings goods from their origin (usually a warehouse or a carrier's platform) to the CDC; the outbound trip, planned by the CDC-based service provider, delivers freight from the CDC to its final destination. As seen above, the outbound transport system can consist of direct shipping or a complex hierarchic scheme. We make the assumption here that outbound transport follows direct shipping strategies, since this paper focuses specifically on how both inbound and outbound transport are related. Of course, inbound transport is in general planned by companies, but it can be interesting to take a systemic vision since public policy actions can orient private carriers' choices.

3. The methodology proposed

To plan public or private urban consolidation facilities, city planners must make *ex ante* assessments in order to define the most suitable locations and estimate the consequences of such consolidation, either quantitatively or qualitatively (Gonzalez-Feliu, 2012). However, few methods are available nowadays to perform such analyses from the standpoint of public planning and adapted to urban planners' needs. For these reasons, we propose an *ex ante* assessment methodology based on accessibility.

3.1. *An overview of accessibility analysis*

The notion of accessibility is widely used in both transport planning and urban development analysis. It can be defined as 'the extent to which land-use and transport systems enable individuals to reach destinations by means of a transport mode' (Geurs & van Wee, 2004). According to this definition, three categories of accessibility indicators can be defined.

The first category is that of infrastructure-based indicators that deal with service level related to a transport infrastructure (Ewing, 1993; Linneker & Spence, 1992). The main examples of infrastructure-based accessibility indicators are congestion levels and average travel speeds on a road network (Geurs & van Wee, 2004). The second is that of location-based measures that describe the level of accessibility to spatially distributed activities. Two main groups of indicators can be distinguished in this category: distance-based indicators (Ingram, 1971; Pirie, 1979) and gravity accessibility measures (Hansen, 1959; Ingram, 1971; Vickerman, 1974). The third category is that of person-based measures which define accessibility at the individual level (Burns, 1979). Such indicators can be derived from space–time geography theory (Hägerstrand, 1970; Miller, 1999; Recker, Chen, & McNally, 2001) or be based on the concept of utility (Ben-Akiva & Lerman, 1979; Martínez, 1995).

Regarding urban goods distribution, up to now few works have dealt with accessibility and most of them remained quite theoretical. However, to the best of our knowledge, they have all dealt with location-based indicators. Gravity-based accessibility is the preferred approach and is mainly related to vehicle route optimization (Crainic et al., 2010; Gonzalez-Feliu, 2008, 2012). Such indicators are related to the difficulty of reducing transport costs, not to access to a territorial configuration. Moreover, these works appear to be carrier-oriented.

In this work, we aim to define an indicator capable of allowing city planners to pursue an accessibility analysis related to the location and development of urban consolidation platforms. Taking into account the three categories of indicators and their main applications, it seems that location-based indicators are the most suitable. However, gravity indicators are based on O–D distances, which are adapted to people transport or FTL[2] strategies, but seems less suitable for urban goods transport since most trips are included in LTL schemes (routes) which associate several destinations (located at different zones of the conurbation) with the same origin.

For this reason, a location-based indicator seems to us the most suitable option to include in analysing the LTL[3] nature of urban goods transport. To do this, we propose to define this indicator by first defining the demand to be delivered using consolidation centres, then build the corresponding routes, and finally estimate the distances travelled, the travel times and the stop times to identify the total duration of each route. Finally, the selected location accessibility indicator is estimated. We present the detailed methodology in the following subsections.

3.2. *Motivation and position of the research proposed*

The proposed framework aims to support accessibility analysis based on location-based indicators. This choice has been made because these indicators are usually estimated for people transport, calculated using O-D commodity matrices which can be assimilated with direct trips, whereas urban freight transport is organized by routes containing several trips. However, urban goods transport presents a variety of paths and routes, which is not always easy to identify directly using O-D matrices. To illustrate this, in Table 1 we propose a synthesis of the characteristics observed for urban routes. These results were extracted from the French National Survey on Urban Goods Movement (Ambrosini, Patier, & Routhier,

Table 1. Main characteristics of urban goods paths.

Route size category (in number of deliveries)	Classical third party transport (%)	Small parcel LTL transport (%)	Shipper's own account (%)	Receiver's own account (%)	Total
Percentage of routes					
FTL routes (1 delivery)	4.01	–	4.66	1.29	9.96
2–10 deliveries	9.18	1.55	18.50	0.65	29.88
11–20 deliveries	5.43	4.79	11.13	0.50	21.85
21–30 deliveries	3.75	4.79	4.79	–	13.33
31 deliveries and more	2.98	21.22	0.78	–	24.98
Total	25.35	32.35	39.86	2.44	100.00
Percentage of deliveries					
FTL routes (1 delivery)	0.52	–	0.55	0.16	1.23
2–10 deliveries	3.09	0.68	6.39	0.14	10.30
11–20 deliveries	4.40	3.95	9.29	0.54	18.18
21–30 deliveries	4.84	6.29	6.29	–	17.42
31 deliveries and more	5.62	45.82	1.43	–	52.87
Total	18.47	56.74	23.95	0.84	100.00
Percentage of weights					
FTL routes (1 delivery)	9.81	–	10.92	3.03	23.76
2–10 deliveries	27.22	0.13	14.74	0.89	42.98
11–20 deliveries	15.01	0.51	7.12	0.10	22.74
21–30 deliveries	2.52	0.59	1.60	–	4.71
31 deliveries and more	2.48	3.28	0.05	–	5.81
Total	57.04	4.51	34.43	4.02	100.00

Table 2. Main characteristics of routes in Bilbao City (Pluvinet, Gonzalez-Feliu, & Ambrosini, 2012).

	Mean	Median
Number of delivery stops	21	15
Duration of a delivery stop (min)	17	14
Length of a route (km)	57	54
Duration of a route (h)	4.27	3.70

2010) and projected for a standard medium-sized city using the calibration and extension coefficients proposed for forecasting the results of different situations.

Table 1 shows that more than 90% of transport paths are organized in routes, so FTL transport forms the minority. It represents about 10% of the routes and about 2% of the deliveries, but almost 25% of the total weights (since truckload transport involves heavier weights than parcel delivery transport). Most routes are composed by two or more destinations, which makes it difficult to associate them with an indicator calculated on the basis of direct trips (i.e. of truckload schemes).

For these reasons, we feel it is appropriate to propose an accessibility indicator calculated on a route basis and not on an O–D trip. Moreover, it is also important to include stop times in the indicator estimation as it is an important element of goods transport (about 30% and 60% of the total route travel time according to the French National Surveys on Urban Goods Movement).

The main contribution of this paper is to define a location accessibility indicator from routes. According to the literature (Geurs & van Wee, 2004), three main types of indicators can be estimated: distance indicators, time indicators and cost indicators. According to Pluvinet et al. (2012), neither travelled distances nor times follow the same patterns related to the type of roads vehicles travel (Table 2).

We observe that, for the selected data set, the average distance of the routes travelled is 57 km, resulting in an average duration of about 4 h 15′. The number of delivery stops is about 21 and the average duration of these stops is 17 min.

If we focus on the type of urban space, more precisely the type of road within the urban area, we observe different patterns. Most of the transportation time is spent on residential roads, mainly in city centres (almost 50% of the total time, excluding pickup/delivery stops), but they correspond to less than 30% of the distances travelled. The same applies for urban motorways, where long distances are travelled (about 50% of the total distance of routes), taking up only 20% of the total travel time of the routes. Main roads represent a similar percentage for both travelled distances and times (about 25%).

From these results, we can state that vehicles travel short distances in city centres but take longer times due to congestion. On the other hand, vehicles travel long distances on urban motorways, taking shorter times because of the high travel speeds on these infrastructures. In vehicle routing optimization, and more precisely from the standpoint of strategic planning, transport routes are usually estimated on the basis of travelled distances (Gonzalez-Feliu, 2012). However, in order to take into account the contribution of potential congestion to the accessibility of city centres, a combination of distances and times can be used when defining a location accessibility indicator. To do this, we can define a travel cost (in euros) for goods transport defined as a function of both travelled distances and route duration. This type of indicator, used for people transport (Geurs & van Wee, 2004), is also based on O-D matrices and does not take into account stop times. However, some evaluation works associate such costs with goods transport routes (including stops). Such works can become a basis for defining a more adapted indicator for urban goods transport that would take into account the route characteristics of such transport schemes, and also the load breakups associated with the CDC.

3.3. *The framework proposed*

The methodology is expected to be used to assess the suitability of locating one or more urban consolidation platforms. More precisely, it has to allow the assessment of a wide set of scenarios to take into account several location alternatives and compare them. The method is presented as a sequential framework and is organized as follows:

(1) *Demand estimation.* Using a demand estimation model, the demand entering the system is based on the urban consolidation platform to be located. Once the demand is known, it is associated with both its origin (an urban logistics zone or regional logistics facility) and its destination, as well as with a transport carrier.
(2) *Route construction.* Once the demand is defined, routes are constructed using a vehicle routing approach. From those routes, the travelled distances of each route's set of paths are estimated.
(3) *Route distance and time estimation.* Travel and stop times can be defined using an empirical procedure, by knowing the demand to be delivered at each destination and the travelled distances. From those unitary times, the total duration of each route (including the running and stopping times of the route) is estimated.
(4) *Accessibility indicator calculation.* Knowing the total travel time of the route, a location-based accessibility indicator is defined by aggregating route durations.
(5) *Iterations.* Steps 2–4 are repeated for each scenario in order to obtain a set of results and start the accessibility analysis. A comparative analysis is then carried out to assess the suitability of the locations proposed.

The demand generation model (step 1) is an emission model (contrary to most of the models in the literature which are attraction-based, see Comi, Delle Site, Filippi, & Nuzzolo, 2012; Gonzalez-Feliu & Routhier, 2012 for an overview). It follows a sequential procedure in two steps. First, the number of deliveries to be shipped by a premise is generated using the procedure proposed in Gonzalez-Feliu, Ambrosini, and Bonnafous (2014). Second, to assign a quantity to each delivery, a procedure based on frequency distribution to randomly generate suitable demands (in weight) has been developed. Such a procedure is presented in the appendix for reasons of readability.

The route construction procedure is a VRP algorithm which uses classical methods. We do not intend to propose in this step a methodical innovation but adapt existing tools to the application problem. The method is presented in Gonzalez-Feliu and Salanova (2014) and has been applied here without major scientific contributions, as a possible method, which shows that other methods can also be used to estimate routes. The choice of this type of algorithm, which is not optimal but remains a quick way to estimate the total travelled distance, is motivated by three facts. The first is that we need a fast algorithm in order to simulate tens and even hundreds of instances in a few seconds. Moreover, we need to compare situations using the same basis, so this algorithm is fast and has a similar behaviour if instances are similar (which is the case here). The second is that the algorithm reproduces in a suitable way the driver's behaviour and if we compare such routes to a set of real ones, we observe that the travelled distances and the composition of routes are similar to reality.

A realistic assessment of routes before optimization is suitable for defining a potential set of locations for a wide range of suitable areas. The third is that the problem of urban consolidation taking into account both inbound and outbound flows in a systemic way has been given little attention in the literature (an issue dealt with only by Gonzalez-Feliu & Salanova, 2012; Gonzalez-Feliu & Salanova Grau, 2014), but this type of approach can be a satisfying tool for an exploratory study. Whatever the case we are aware that the vehicle route algorithm can be improved, but current methods must be adapted to the problem by taking into account the combinatorics of the problem.

In this paper we aim to focus on the definition of the time accessibility indicator (steps 3 and 4). Those steps are presented in the following subsections.

3.4. *Estimation of travelled distances and durations of each route*

After constructing routes, the total travelled distances of each one can be estimated directly from the route construction procedure, since we know each distance between two stops of a route. Given $R_k = \{o_k, d_{k1}, d_{k2}, \ldots, d_{kn}, o_k\}$, the ordered set of points served by the route (o_k being the origin, and c_{kj} each destination of the route, in the order determined by the route construction algorithm). The distance between two points i and j is defined as $\text{dist}(i, j)$ and is given (we recall that these distances are used to construct the routes, see the appendix). The total travelled distance of a route can then be estimated as follows:

$$\text{dist}_k = \sum_{i<n} \text{dist}(d_{ki}, d_{ki+1}) + \text{dist}(o_k, d_{k1}) + \text{dist}(d_{kn}, o_k),$$

In other words, the total travelled distance of a route is composed of an initial and a final trip, plus $n-2$ trips linking each destination to its successor. Once the routes have been estimated and each route trip distance calculated, we can estimate the total travel times of a route. Note that we can define two types of times for a route:

- Travel time t^r_{ij} taken by the vehicle while running, defined as the time that a vehicle takes between two locations i and j of a route.
- Stop time t^s_i taken by vehicles parked for loading or unloading, defined as the time taken by a truck driver to pick up or deliver goods at a location i.

For each route taken by large and small vehicles k, the total travel time t_k is calculated as follows:

$$t_k = \sum_{i,j} t^{rk}_{ij} + \sum_{i} t^{sk}_{i}.$$

The overall travel time of all routes t is then estimated as the sum of the duration t_k of each route k.

3.5. *Accessibility definition*

Once both the travelled distances and duration of each route have been estimated, we can start estimating the accessibility indicator. Since we chose to define a cost-based indicator, the first step is to estimate the total cost of a route. To do this, we define a generalized cost of each route in euros. This cost is related to both the travelled distance (mainly fuel and tyre usage, among others) and the duration of the route (labour costs, insurance, etc.), and can be estimated using standard ratios (Gonzalez-Feliu, Basck, & Morganti, 2013). The generalized cost C_k for a route k can then be formulated as follows:

$$C_k = 0.35\ \mathrm{dist}_k + 34.52 t_k,$$

where d_k is the total travel distance and t_k the total duration of route k, estimated as presented above. The two proposed parameters have been adapted to the urban context from the latest ratios published by the French Road Institution (Comité National Routier, 2012) by completing them using a global positioning systems database (Pluvinet et al., 2012). The estimation method is described in Gonzalez-Feliu et al. (2013) and Gonzalez-Feliu, Basck et al., 2013).

In a scenario including consolidation, i.e. when one or more load breakups occur, we need to add to this cost a cost related to the load breakup. In this research, investment costs related to the deployment of urban consolidation centres are not considered, since we propose an accessibility indicator based only on transport organization. The aim of the framework is not to study the economic viability of CDCs (other frameworks are available for this aspect, see van Duin et al., 2008; Vaghi & Percoco, 2011; Morana et al., 2014) but to compare between them different location possibilities to identify their potential locations for CDCs. In this context, we can neglect investment costs to ensure a homogeneous comparison between alternatives, and assume that financial elements are generally included in a previous phase (i.e. before accessibility analysis). In other words, if a comparison between potential sites for developing a CDC is needed, etc.

Route costs have been defined above in order to take into account both loading and unloading costs. We assume that the cross-docking cost at a CDC can be broken down into two: the unloading cost of vehicles delivering goods to the CDC and the loading cost of the CDC final delivery vehicles that will bring goods from the CDC to the city. Following those assumptions, both costs are included in the route costs estimated above. We can finally estimate the total cost for a scenario.

Given a scenario e, the total cost C^e associated with it is given by the following relation:

$$C^e = \sum_k C_k.$$

Finally, we can estimate a location-based accessibility indicator for scenario e, defined as follows:

$$A_e = \frac{W}{C_e},$$

where T_e is the total travel time of all routes for scenario e and W a constant that allows giving a value between 1 and 100. In this study, we chose to use a relative accessibility, i.e. to take all scenarios of the analysis and estimate all accessibilities with respect to the minimum cost (which will give the maximum accessibility). In other words, we set $W = 100.A_{\max}$ where $A_{\max}$ is the maximum accessibility of all simulated scenarios. This choice is motivated by the fact that the proposed analysis framework is aimed to support location decisions from a large set of potential locations, so to have a scale easy to read we propose to give the value of 100 to the most accessible location then we decline the other accessibilities with respect to that maximum value.

4. An example of application: non-food retail in Lyon

To illustrate the proposed method, we present an example of application for a real urban area. To do this, we simulate a set of scenarios to assess using the proposed method. The chosen urban area is that of Lyon, from where we dispose a set of standard databases. The first is that of a file containing all the considered establishments in the assessment. They can belong to three categories. The first is that of establishments to deliver, in other words the retailers receiving goods. The second is that of CDC's. The third is that of carriers using the CDC. Concerning retailers, they were geo-located so longitude and latitude values have been assigned to each of them. Concerning the set of possible CDCs, their locations are in general in the near periphery of the city, mainly in industrial and logistics areas but also in wholesaling or service zones where a space can be dedicated to urban consolidation. In total, we have identified 148 possible locations, all characterized by their longitude and latitude (in the same units than retailers). Concerning location of the depots corresponding to the expected carriers bringing goods to the CDC, instead on considering a large set of locations, we suppose they are located in five main zones, each characterized also by a longitude and a latitude. We consider that all carriers in each location will collaborate to share vehicles visiting the CDCs. In this way, a number of vehicles are assigned to each zone. They are of two types: big vehicles that can be used to deliver CDCs, and small vehicles that are used to deliver retailers from CDCs. The assignment of small vehicles to CDCs has to be decided, whereas big vehicles are systematically assigned to a specific zone. We need also to define travel distance between each pair of locations (for all depots, CDCs' locations and retailers). To do this, a travel distance is assigned to each O-D pair and reported on a separate file. This distance is not estimated with the method used at Lyon's planning authority, Grand Lyon (see Gonzalez-Feliu and Mercier (2013) for more details).

With this information, we associate a demand (in kg) to each retailer using the proposed demand generation model. From this demand, an overall number of 439 deliveries every day are selected. Note that from this set of demands, each zone has a different set of retailers to deliver. Moreover, some retailers receive goods from two or more different zones. The characteristics of in the city logistics system described above are presented in Tables 3 and 4.

Afterwards, the scenarios to be simulated can be built and assessed. Three groups of tests are performed. The first is intended to locate one consolidation centre among the different locations; the second, two facilities; and the third, three platforms. For each group of tests the different possibilities are simulated, except (for the second and third sets) those having two satellites within very close distances and thus unsuitable for a solution with fewer CDCs.

Table 5 gives the number of scenarios simulated for each group, as well as minimum, maximum, mean and medium values of accessibility. We observe that the most accessible scenarios are those of group 1. Indeed, it seems that, in the specific configuration and given the total daily demand to deliver to the chosen retailers of the inner city of Lyon

Table 3. Characteristics of the simulated operators.

Zone of origin	Number of big vehicles	Capacity (tons)	Number of retailers
1	2	7.5	95
2	3	4.0	115
3	2	7.5	86
4	2	4.0	78
5	4	2.5	65
Number of small vehicles to associate to CDCs		Capacity (tons)	
	12	0.8	
	20	0.9	
	14	1.2	

Table 4. Statistics per type of road (adapted from Pluvinet et al., 2012).

	Distance	Duration	Mean speed
Residential	16.5	2.5	7 km/h
Main road	14.2	0.9	15 km/h
Motorway	26.2	0.9	31 km/h
Total	57.0	4.3	15 km/h

Table 5. Synthesis of the three groups of tests.

Group of tests	Number of tests	Min accessibility	Max accessibility	Mean accessibility	Median accessibility
1 (one CDC)	148	9.9	100.0	35.4	34,3
2 (two CDCs)	3248	10.3	42.8	20.2	16.7
3 (three CDCs)	40403	8.8	44.6	18,4	15.6

(136 customers with a total commodity quantity of 27 508 kg), the mean (and median) values of configurations with only one consolidation centre seem to be more accessible. More precisely, a configuration with one CDC has a mean accessibility of 35.4 and a median accessibility of 34.3, which are close. Configurations with two CDCs have a mean accessibility of 20.2 (about 43% lower) and a median accessibility of 16.7 (about 51% lower). Configurations with three CDCs have a mean accessibility of 18.4 (about 48% lower) and a median accessibility of 15.6 (about 55% lower).

Moreover, the accessibilities are somewhat higher than those of the other two groups. Indeed, the maximum accessibility found (and then set to 100) is on a configuration with one CDC. Maximum accessibilities with two and three CDCs are less than half with respect to the overall maximum accessibility. Minimum accessibilities are close for all three groups of scenarios, although the configuration with two CDCs has a higher minimum accessibility (Table 5).

Those results can then be used by practitioners as follows. First, when comparing all three groups of scenarios, we observe that configurations with one CDC seem more robust than those of the two other groups. Indeed, the first group has average, median and maximum accessibilities that are higher than the other two groups, so for the given configuration, one CDC will be more suitable than more than one. This will have an impact on costs, since constructing and planning a network of CDCs have higher costs than doing it for only one, and from the accessibility analysis, overall operational costs will be lower with a single-CDC configuration (we remember that the estimated accessibility indicator is inversely proportional to transport costs).

Second, having selected the group of scenarios, planners can examine the different configurations (in this case 148) to choose a smaller set of possible locations. We report in Figure 1 the statistical distribution of accessibilities for each set of scenarios. We observe that the second and three groups, whose number of instances is higher than for the first group, tend to a Rayleigh distribution. This is not the same for the first. Focusing on the first group, we can determine from the frequency distribution diagram a set of five or six suitable locations.

To do this, it is important to follow experience and practice rules. In other words, the proposed method can rank the main possibilities of location, then planners can define which are the most suitable locations using their experience as well as their knowledge of their

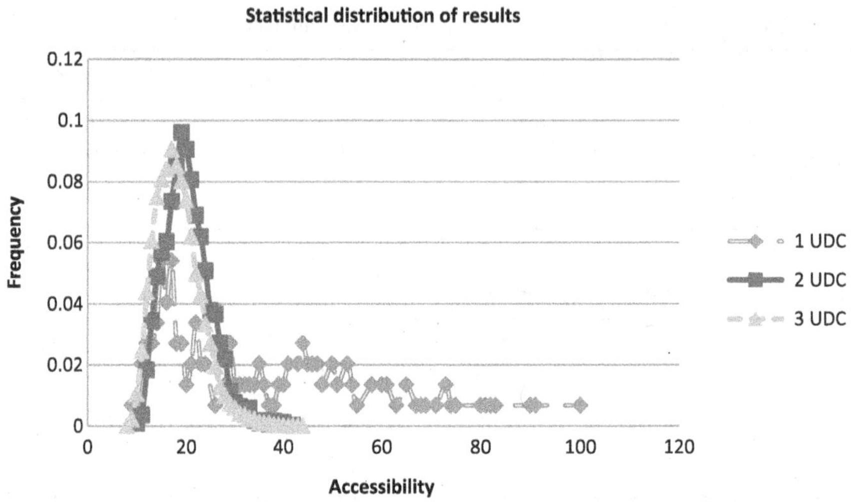

Figure 1. Frequency distribution diagram of accesssibilities for all thre groups of tests.

territories and related demographic and socio-economic issues. For example, once knowing which is the best 25% of possible locations, planners can analyse in-depth the most suitable places to locate a CDC, taking into account the infrastructure's availability, the land cost, the reticence of stakeholders and the visibility of the location, among others.

However, these exploratory results, which merit further investigation and analysis, show that for the given customers and delivery quantities, the best configurations are those with a single consolidation centre. This can be explained by two factors. The first is the quantity to be delivered, which must be linked to the means given to companies to deliver it (in the proposed assessment, no approach to estimate cost is performed, and only a distance-based analysis is carried out). Indeed, the quantities delivered are small but given the fleets of each operator, the concentration at a single consolidation centre is a suitable solution. Nonetheless, this must be matched against the geographical characteristics of the urban territory. In this case, we have five carriers, each of them located in a different area of the conurbation. Since there no concentration of carriers at two points and with all the carriers serving the whole city, in some cases delivering to the same customers, the scenarios with one consolidation centre allow each carrier to concentrate all their deliveries in large trucks making direct shipping shuttle trips. If more than one consolidation centre is defined, each carrier must deliver to two or more points, and the distribution demand will make it more or less difficult to optimize the entire distance (if the demand to be delivered to one platform is higher than a truck capacity, the carrier must use a second truck, and possibly set out routes, increasing the distances travelled). Such increases in distance are not always offset by the reductions obtained by terminal transport (from consolidation centres to customers) since the distances travelled are greater in the periphery than in the main city. Single-platform scenarios are thus on average more suitable than multiple-platform ones, and three-platform scenarios appear more compact (the differences between them are less than in the other two groups, with the means and medians being closer).

5. Conclusion

In this paper, we presented a method to support strategic decisions in terms of urban consolidation centre location. To do this, we proposed an infrastructure-based accessibility indicator estimated using a semi-greedy algorithm to highlight the nature of route-based freight transport in urban areas. The method allows simulating the transport demand using a delivery to the commodity generation model, then assigning it to routes using a semi-greedy algorithm. Finally, an infrastructure-based accessibility indicator was calculated. A practical example of this is provided and numerous scenarios were simulated and assessed by the method in order to produce comparative results and study the possibilities of locating urban consolidation platforms. The proposed results show that the method can show in a comparable way the suitability of a big quantity of configurations in terms of CDC locations. This can be done to select from a large set of alternative the group of potential CDCs (for example five) following suitability and accessibility criteria, so in a quantitatively justifiable way. After selecting a small group of possible locations for CDCs from a large set of possibilities, planners can study in-depth the consequences of locating the CDCs in the selected places, both from a quantitative and a qualitative way, at a strategic planning level. The quantitative simulations can be made using simulation models (Comi & Rosati, 2013) or operations research methods (van Duin et al., 2008, Hemmelmayr et al., 2012) and can give the quantifiable effects of locating a CDC in the selected place (mainly economic and environmental). However, to remain in a sustainable development perspective, it is important to also take into account the social dimension. To do this, qualitative studies to define the determinants, facilitators and limits of locating a CDC in the selected place can be done (Gonzalez-Feliu, 2012).

Finally, it is important to recall that this method aims to support decision-making, not to substitute the decision-maker in taking the choices. An accessibility analysis can be used to decide on the suitability or not of locating platforms and the result of example proposed lacked clarity. Indeed, in urban areas of the size of Lyon several platforms can be considered for urban distribution; however, in the example given single-platform configurations seem more suitable than multiple-platform configurations. Whatever the case, the strategies followed by public authorities may lead them to define more than one platform. In this case, accessibility analysis can be useful for choosing a good and balanced configuration. In conclusion, we emphasize that a decision support method is intended to help decision-makers make their choices, not to substitute them. Thus, decision-makers must always have the freedom and possibility to choose the solution that best satisfies their objectives, and this method should help them to understand the impacts of such choices.

Last but not least, the possibilities of replication of the analysis remain to be addressed. The sets of scenarios proposed here is an example of application, and the method can be applied to other urban contexts. This is possible for the following reasons. The first is that the used tools (the demand generation model, the VRP algorithm and the accessibility indicator estimation) need standard data that do not strongly depend on the context. Moreover, they are connected in a way that the only required data are the inputs of the demand generation model as well as the hypotheses of CDC location configurations. Those inputs data are latitude and longitude coordinates, a typology of establishments (based on the European Nomenclature of Economic Activities (NACE) codes for activity characteristics) and a number of employees. The results of the used tools (Gonzalez-Feliu & Routhier, 2012; Gonzalez-Feliu & Salanova Grau, 2014) show that they can be applied to other realties, at least in Europe (as for example Switzerland, Sweden or Italy), since the generation patterns in terms of the number of deliveries per week remain similar in West Europe. For this reason, the proposed methodology can be used also when only little basic information is available, if geographical coordinates are known. Moreover, at a strategic level, the given level of accuracy and aggregation is enough for the expected aim of the proposed methodology (select a small set of configurations for CDCs' location from an extended group of possibilities on a quantifiable way). However, it will be interesting to adapt and apply it to other realties outside Europe. To do this, further data are needed, but the methodology uses standard approaches (the demand generation model uses the same patterns than Holguín-Veras et al., (2011), which is applied to a USA context, and the VRP algorithm has been proven to be flexible and adaptable to most contexts, as shown in Toth and Vigo, (2002), so the adaptation is possible with a limited effort. Further work envisages comparing European and USA contexts using the proposed methodology, as well as studying the suitability of accessibility analysis in other contexts.

Notes

1. We do not assert that LUTI models are not useful. They can be extremely powerful tools for examining specific situations at a mesoscopic level, and are mainly used in tactical planning. What we do assert is that in strategic planning performed by city planners, accessibility tools provide sufficiently detailed information for planning purposes and seem easier to understand by decision-makers and their technical support teams.
2. Full Truckload.
3. Less than Truckload.
4. http://www.insee.fr

References

Allen, J., Browne, M., Woodburn, A., & Leonardi, J. (2012). The role of urban consolidation centres in sustainable freight transport. *Transport Reviews, 32*(4), 473–490.

Allen, J., Thorne, G., & Browne, M. (2007). *Good practice guide on urban freight.* Bestufs: Rijswijks.

Ambrosini, C., Gonzalez-Feliu, J., & Toilier, F. (2013). A design methodology for scenario-analysis in urban freight modeling. *European Transport/Trasporti Europei, 54*(7), 1–21.

Ambrosini, C., Patier, D., & Routhier, J. L. (2010). Urban freight establishment and tour based surveys for policy oriented modelling. *Procedia-Social and Behavioral Sciences, 2* (3), 6013–6026.

Anand, N., Quak, H., van Duin, R., & Tavasszy, L. (2012). City logistics modeling efforts: Trends and gaps-a review. *Procedia-Social and Behavioral Sciences, 39*, 101–115.

Arvidsson, N., & Browne, M. (2013). A review of the success and failure of tram systems to carry urban freight: The implications for a low emission intermodal solution using electric vehicles on trams. *European Tranpsort/Trasporti Europei, 54*(5), 1–18.

Ben-Akiva, M., & Lerman, S. R. (1979). Disaggregate travel and mobility choice models and measures of accessibility. In D. A. Hensher & P. R. Sopher (Eds.), *Behavioural travel modeling* (pp. 654–679). Andover: Croom Helm.

Boudouin, D. (2006). *Urban logistics spaces: Methodological guide.* Paris: La Documentation Française.

Boudouin, D., Morel, C., & Gardat, M. (2014). Supply chains and urban logistics platforms. In J. Gonzalez-Feliu, F. Semet, & J. L. Routhier, (Eds.), *Sustainable urban logistics: Concepts, methods and information systems* (pp. 1–20). Heidelberg: Springer.

Burns, L. D. (1979). *Transportation, temporal and spatial components of accessibility.* Lexington-Toronto: Lexington Books.

Comi, A., Delle Site, P., Filippi, F., & Nuzzolo, A. (2012). Urban freight transport demand modelling: A state of the art. *European Transport/Trasporti Europei, 51*(7), 1–17.

Comi, A., & Rosati, L. (2013). CLASS: A city logistics analysis and simulation support system. *Procedia – Social and Behavioral Sciences, 87*, 321–337.

Comité National Routier. (2012). *Evolution du prix du gazole et incidence sur le prix de revient. Situation au 30 juillet 2012.* Paris, France. Retrieved from http://www.cnr.fr/content/download/357/3457/version/15/file/Note%20gazole%2001%20ao%C3%BBt%202012.pdf

Crainic, T. G., Errico, F., Rei, W., & Ricciardi, N. (2012). Integrating C2E and C2C traffic into city logistics planning. *Procedia-social and behavioral sciences, 39*, 47–60.

Crainic, T.G., Perboli, G., Mancini, S., & Tadei, R. (2010). Two-echelon vehicle routing problem: A satellite location analysis. *Procedia-Social and Behavioral Sciences, 2*(3), 5944–5955.

Crainic, T. G., Ricciardi, N., & Storchi, G. (2004). Advanced freight transportation systems for congested urban areas. *Transportation Research Part C: Emerging Technologies, 12*(2), 119–137.

Crainic, T. G., Ricciardi, N., & Storchi, G. (2009). Models for evaluating and planning city logistics systems. *Transportation science, 43* (4), 432–454.

Crozet, Y., Mercier, A., & Ovtracht, N. (2012). Accessibility: A key indicator to assess the past and future of urban mobility. In K. T. Geurs, K. J. Krizek, & A. Reggiani (Eds.), *Accessibility analysis and transport planning: Challenges for Europe and North America* (pp. 263–279). Northampton, MA: Edward Eldgar Publishing.

Dablanc, L. (2011). Freight transport, a key for urban economics. Guidelines for practitioners. In C. Macharis & S. Melo, (Eds.), *City distribution and urban freight transport. Multiple perspectives* (pp. 13–36). Cheltenham: Emerald.

Dablanc, L. (2014). Logistics sprawl and urban freight planning issues in a major gateway city. In J. Gonzalez-Feliu, F. Semet, & J. L. Routhier, (Eds.), *Sustainable urban logistics: Concepts, methods and information systems* (pp. 49–69). Heidelberg: Springer.

De La Barra, T. (1989). *Integrated land use and transport modeling.* Cambridge, UK: Cambridge University Press.

Delaître, L., & De Barbeyrac, L. (2012). Improving an urban distribution centre, the French case of samada monoprix. *Procedia-Social and Behavioral Sciences, 39*, 753–769.

Ducret, R. (2013, October 6–8). Parcel deliveries in urban areas: Changes and challenges in the parcel delivery sector in Europe – the French case. V METRANS international conference on urban freight, Long Beach, California.

van Duin, R., Quak, H., & Munuzuri, J. (2008). Revival of the cost benefit analysis for evaluating the city distribution center concept? In E. Taniguchi, & R. G. Thompson (Eds.), *Innovations in city logistics* (pp. 97–114). New York: Nova Science.

van Duin, J. H. R., Quak, H., & Muñuzuri, J. (2010). New challenges for urban consolidation centres: A case study in The Hague. *Procedia-Social and Behavioral Sciences, 2* (3), 6177–6188.

Ewing, R. (1993). Transportation service standards – As if people matter. *Transportation Research Record, 1400*, 10–17.

Faure, L., Battaia, G., Marques, G., Guillaume, R., Vega-Mejia, C. A., Montova-Torres, J. R., … Quintero-Araujo, C. L. (2013) How to anticipate the level of activity of a sustainable collaborative network: The case of urban freight delivery through logistics platforms. In *Proceedings of the 7th IEEE international conference on digital ecosystems and technologies, DEST 2013*, Menlo Park, CA (pp. 126–131).

Geurs, K. T., & van Wee, B. (2004). Accessibility evaluation of land-use and transport strategies: Review and research directions. *Journal of Transport Geography, 12*(2), 127–140.

Gonzalez-Feliu, J. (2008). *Models and methods for the city logistics – The two-echelon capacitated vehicle routing problem* (PhD. Thesis). Politecnico di Torino, Turin, Italy.

Gonzalez-Feliu, J. (2012). Freight distribution systems with cross-docking: A multidisciplinary analysis. *Journal of the Transportation Research Forum, 51*(1), 93–109.

Gonzalez-Feliu, J. (2013, October 4–6). Determinants and variants in urban goods demand strategic modelling: Commodity versus trip as data collection and modelling unit. *INFORMS Annual meeting 2013*, Minneapolis, MN.

Gonzalez-Feliu, J., Ambrosini, C., & Bonnafous, A. (2014). *An alternative to O-D matrix estimation for urban goods transport demand generation.* 63th transportation research board annual symposium compendium of proceedings, TRB, Washington. Retrieved from http://trid.trb.org/view.aspx?id=1289212

Gonzalez-Feliu, J., Ambrosini, C., & Routhier, J. L. (2012). New trends on urban goods movement: Modelling and simulation of e-commerce distribution. *European Transport/Trasporti Europei, 50*(6), 1–23.

Gonzalez-Feliu, J., Basck, P., & Morganti, E. (2013), Urban logistics solutions and financing mechanisms: A scenario assessment analysis. *European Transport/Trasporti Europei, 54*(11), 1–16.

Gonzalez-Feliu, J., & Morana, J. (2010). Are city logistics solutions sustainable? The cityporto case. *TeMA. Journal of Land Use, Mobility and Environment, 3*(2), 55–64.

Gonzalez-Feliu, J., & Routhier, J. L. (2012), Modelling urban goods movement: How to be oriented with so many approaches? *Procedia Social and Behavioral Science, 39*, 89–100.

Gonzalez-Feliu, J., & Salanova, J. (2012). Defining and evaluating collaborative urban freight distribution systems. *Procedia-Social and Behavioral Science, 39*, 172–183.

Gonzalez-Feliu, J., & Mercier, A. (2013, October 6–8). *A double people-freight accessibility approach for urban retailing and leissure planning at strategic level*, V METRANS International Conference on Urban Freight, Long Beach, California.

Gonzalez-Feliu, J., & Salanova Grau, J. (2014, March 25). VRP algorithms for decision support systems to evaluate collaborative urban freight transport systems. *I-ESA 2014 Workshop on Collaborative Solutions for City Logistics*, Albi, France.

Gonzalez-Feliu, J., Salanova Grau, J. M., Morana, J., & Mitsakis, E. (2013). Urban logistics pooling viability analysis via a multicriteria multiactor method. In M. V. Petit-Lavall, F. Martinez-Sanz, A. Recalde-Castells, & A. Puetz (Eds.), *La nueva ordenación del Mercado del transporte* (pp. 867–882). Madrid: Marcial Pons.

Hägerstrand, T. (1970), What about people in regional science? *Papers of the Regional Science Association, 24*, 7–21.

Hemmelmayr, V. C., Cordeau, J. F., & Crainic, T. G. (2012). An adaptive large neighborhood search heuristic for two-echelon vehicle routing problems arising in city logistics. *Computers & operations research, 39*(12), 3215–3228.

Hansen, W. G. (1959). How accessibility shapes land use. *Journal of the American Institute Planners, 25*, 73–76.

Holguín-Veras, J., Jaller, I., Sanchez-Diaz, M., Wojtowicz, J. M., Campbell, S., Lawson, C. T., & Levinson, H. S. (2012). *NCFRP 25 freight generation and freight generation models database*. Retrieved March 25, from http://transp.rpi.edu/~NCFRP25/FTG-Database.rar

Holguín-Veras, J., Jaller, M., Destro, L., Ban, X. J., Lawson, C., & Levinson, H. S. (2011). Freight generation, freight trip generation, and perils of using constant trip rates. *Transportation Research Record: Journal of the Transportation Research Board, 2224*, 68–81.

Ingram, D. R. (1971). The concept of accessibility: A search for an operational form. *Regional Studies, 5*, 101–107.

Janjevic, M., Kaminsky, P., & Ballé Ndiaye, A. (2013). Downscaling the consolidation of goods–state of the art and transferability of micro-consolidation initiatives. *European Transport/Trasporti Europei, 54*(4), 1–23.

Linneker, B. J., & Spence, N. A. (1992). Accessibility measures compared in an analysis of the impact of the M25 London orbital motorway on Britain. *Environment and Planning A, 24*, 1137–1154.

Macharis, C., & Melo, S. (2011) *City distribution and urban freight transport. Multiple perspectives*. Cheltenham: Emerald.

Martínez, F. J. (1995). Access: The transport-land use economic link. *Transportation Research Part B, 29*(6), 457–470.

Miller, H. J. (1999). Measuring space–time accessibility benefits within transportation networks: Basic theory and computational procedures. *Geographical Analysis, 31*(2), 187–212.

Morana, J., Gonzalez-Feliu, J., & Semet, F. (2014). Urban consolidation and logistics pooling. In J. Gonzalez-Feliu, F. Semet, & J. L. Routhier (Eds.), *Sustainable urban logistics: Concepts, methods and information systems* (pp. 187–210). Heidelberg: Springer.

Ortuzar, J. de D., & Willumsen, L. G. (1990). *Modeling transport*. Chichester: John Wiley & sons.

Pirie, G. H. (1979). Measuring accessibility: A review and proposal. *Environment and Planning A, 11*, 299–312.

Pluvinet, P., Gonzalez-Feliu, J., & Ambrosini, C. (2012). GPS data analysis for understanding urban goods movement. *Procedia-Social and Behavioral Sciences, 39*, 450–462.

Recker, W.W., Chen, C., & McNally, M. G. (2001). Measuring the impact of efficient household travel decisions on potential travel time savings and accessibility gains. *Transportation Research A, 35*(4), 339–369.

Tario, J. D., Ancar, R., Panero, M., Shin, H. S., & Lopez, D. P. (2011). *Urban distribution centers a means to reducing freight vehicle miles traveled* (Final Report). New York: NYU.

Thompson, R. G., & Hassall, K. P. (2012). A collaborative urban distribution network. *Procedia-Social and Behavioral Sciences*, *39*, 230–240.

Toth, P., & Vigo, D., (2002), *The vehicle routing problem*. Philadelphia: SIAM.

Trentini, A., & Malhéné, N. (2010). Toward a shared urban transport system ensuring passengers & goods cohabitation. Tema. *Journal of Land Use, Mobility and Environment, 3*(2), 37–44.

Vaghi, C., & Percoco, M. (2011). City logistics in Italy: Success factors and environmental performance. In C. Macharis & S. Melo (Eds.), *City distribution and urban freight transport: Multiple perspectives* (pp. 151–175). Northampton: Emerald.

Verlinde, S., Macharis, C., & Witlox, F. (2012). How to consolidate urban flows of goods without setting up an urban consolidation centre? *Procedia-Social and Behavioral Sciences, 39*, 687–701.

Vickerman, R. W. (1974). Accessibility, attraction, and potential: A review of some concepts and their use in determining mobility. *Environment and Planning A, 6*, 675–691.

Ville, S., Gonzalez-Feliu, J., & Dablanc, L. (2013). The limits of public policy intervention in urban logistics: Lessons from Vicenza (Italy). *European Planning Studies, 21*(10), 1528–1541.

Wegener, M. (2004). Overview of land-use transport models. In D. A. Hensher, K. J. Button, K. E. Haynes, & P. R. Stopher (Eds.), *Handbook of transport geography and spatial systems* (pp. 127–146). Amsterdam: Elsevier.

Wonnacott, T. H., & Wonnacott, R. J. (2001). *Introductory statistics.* New York: John Wiley & Sons.

Zunder, T., & Marinov, M. (2011). Urban freight concepts and practice: Would a traditional UCC scheme work? *Transport Problems, 6*(1), 87–95.

Appendix. The demand generation model

There is a wide variety of models in the literature (for recent surveys, see Anand, Quak, van Duin, & Tavasszy, 2012; Comi et al., 2012; Gonzalez-Feliu & Routhier, 2012; Holguín-Veras et al., 2012). Such models use three main units: the commodity, i.e. the quantity of goods to be transported, the vehicle trip or the delivery itself. The last seems the most complete since it includes a large set of characteristics such as nature of goods, mode of management, quantity to be delivered, type of packaging, etc. (Gonzalez-Feliu et al., 2014). To the best of our knowledge, although some authors speak about 'delivery models' (Comi et al., 2012) only one model uses the general definition (Gonzalez-Feliu et al., 2014). However, in that approach, the delivery is not fully characterized, since three elements are lacking: nature, type of packaging and quantity of goods. Since this paper's scope is parcel deliveries, which are belonging to one specific category of natures (non-perishable and non-fragile manufactured products) and to one specific type of packaging (parcel), we aim to propose a new procedure to assessing a weight to each delivery in order to build vehicle routing instances.

First, let us recall the general methodology of the model (Ambrosini et al., 2013; Gonzaelz-Feliu et al., 2014). First, having a classification of economic activities in 36 classes (following the French classification that aggregates European NACE codes[4]), a category class model (Holguín-Veras et al., 2011) is applied. Each class takes into account the category of the establishment, the mode of management (own account or third party transport and their variants), among others. After that, origins and destinations are matched in order to obtain realistic commodity O-D pairs (i.e. reporting the origin of the shipment to its destination and not the vehicle trip). However, those O-D trips are quantified in number of deliveries and not in a quantity to deliver. The complete method is described in Gonzalez-Feliu et al. (2014).

To complete this information, we propose a probability distribution randomly generation procedure obtained after a statistical analysis of a route database extracted from the French Surveys on Urban Goods Movement.

First, we extract from the database all deliveries corresponding to third-party transport mobilizing parcels, for non-perishable and non-fragile manufacturing goods. We calculate for each category of establishment (36 categories) the average weight of a delivery as well as the corresponding standard error. As standard errors are usually higher than average values, we propose a probability distribution that results of the addition of two half-distributions (see Figure A1).

The upper part follows a normal distribution $N^{+}(E, \sigma)$ and the lower part another normal distribution $N^{-}(E, \sigma')$ where E is the mean quantity of freight per delivery (for each category), σ the corresponding standard error and σ' is calculated as follows:

$$\sigma' = \frac{E}{3},$$

where σ' has been estimated in this way to propose a probability distribution whose minimum value is 0, and avoid in this way negative values (Wonnacott & Wonnacott, 2001). This distribution can be justified by the fact that the variability of the quantity of goods to deliver for each category of establishment is important (as seen from Table A1). In this context, a random generation following a frequency distribution like presented above seems more suitable than using only average weights on

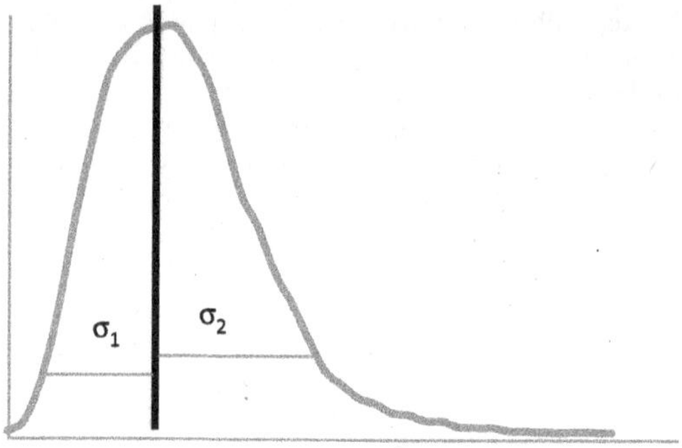

Figure A1. Example of the frequency distribution retained for the proposed model.

each delivery since the proposed procedure allows to represent the variability of the demand when distributing it in the space.

We observe that only six of the 36 classes do not have a number of individuals that ensures us a statistically significant frequency distribution (Wonnacott & Wonnacott, 2001). For the other categories, the proposed frequency distribution allow to randomly assign a demand (in kg) to each delivery obtained with the procedure obtained in Gonzalez-Feliu et al. (2014). In this way we can then propose a realistic set of demands for urban goods transport.

Table A1. Statistical characteristics of the delivery simple in terms of weight per delivery.

			Weight per delivery		
0 Code	Category	Sample	E	σ	σ'
1	Agriculture	4	85.8	58.9	28.6
2	Craftsmen	47	91.8	129.5	30.6
3	Construction industry	47	4432.1	9660.5	1477.4
4	Industry – chemical	31	886.2	3685.5	295.4
5	Industry – production/intermediary goods	212	167.2	1033.8	55.7
6	Industry – consumption products	102	583.5	2989.6	194.5
7	Tertiary – transport	55	986.9	3781.8	329.0
8	Wholesalers – production/intermediary goods	189	266.9	2177.9	89.0
9	Wholesalers – non-food products	161	96.9	262.6	32.3
10	Wholesalers – foods and groceries	81	1503.0	3523.6	501.0
11	Hypermarkets/big department stores	103	880.4	4025.3	293.5
12	Supermarkets	71	1107.6	3998.1	369.2
13	Specialized department stores	58	354.0	1005.2	118.0
14	Minimarkets	11	95.5	185.7	31.8
15	Retailers – clothes, shoes, accessories	227	71.7	213.8	23.9
16	Retailers – butchers	56	83.6	112.4	27.9
17	Retailers – groceries	9	195.0	164.0	65.0
18	Retailers – bakeries	33	441.5	527.9	147.2
19	Hotels, coffees, catering (Ho.Re.Ca.)	67	68.5	133.3	22.8
20	Retailers – pharmacies	122	44.5	52.4	14.8
21	Retailers – hardware, tools, materials	41	70.0	117.6	23.3
22	Retailers – furniture	59	268.6	1545.5	89.5
23	Retailers – book shops	115	121.2	273.4	40.4
24	Retailers – non sedentary/outdoor	3	97.0	37.2	32.3
25	Retailers – other	543	66.2	220.5	22.1
26	Others	218	57.7	113.3	19.2
27	Tertiary – offices	350	91.7	803.0	30.6
28	Tertiary – services	154	39.6	63.6	13.2
29	Public administration	118	105.8	245.6	35.3
30	Public education	55	42.8	68.5	14.3
31	Hospitals	142	88.1	303.8	29.4
32	End-consumers	142	136.1	1605.6	45.4
33	Associations	7	754.3	1733.8	251.4
34	Warehouses	2	14.5	10.5	4.8
35	Generalist department stores	89	218.4	417.5	72.8
36	Consolidation and cross-docking platforms	37	928.4	3017.3	309.5

City logistics through the canals? A simulation study on freight waterborne transport in the inner-city of Amsterdam

J.H.R. van Duin, R. Kortmann and S.L. van den Boogaard

Faculty of Technology, Policy and Management, Delft University of Technology, Delft, The Netherlands

This study investigates whether distributing goods across the water to the city of Amsterdam can be a potential future solution considering the busy traffic of the pleasure crafts and touring boats on the canals. A simulation model was developed to analyse the logistics performances and traffic influences for different fleet size configurations. The simulation tests have shown that four vessels are needed to guarantee the requested delivery times, a sufficient loading rate (82%) was generated for each ship, and no significant delays will happen due to interaction with other water traffic. Conclusion of this study is that a waterborne city logistics concept through the canals of Amsterdam has demonstrated the capability to reduce congestion in the inner-city and is able to satisfy the delivery requirements of the shopkeepers without significant interference with other waterborne traffic.

1. Introduction

Freight transport is a major cause of congestion on the narrow roads along the canals of Amsterdam (Department of Infrastructure, Traffic and Transport, 2010). Currently, there are daily 20,000 freight trips on their way to 40,000 delivery points in the city centre of Amsterdam (City of Amsterdam, 2010). DHV Research (2007) showed that 80% of the loading and unloading activities actually take place on the road due to lack of space. An average stop to load and unload quickly takes 20 minutes and during that time, passing of other traffic is impossible. Therefore, other traffic seems severely affected by the freight distribution. In addition, shopkeepers are affected by the unreliable trip times (i.e. congestion) and local residents have nuisance from emissions and noise (City of Amsterdam, 2010). Therefore, the idea has emerged to reuse the canals again as a 'new' freight distribution system for the city of Amsterdam.

Several companies, such as TNT and Mokum Mariteam, have picked up this idea and started delivering goods across the canals in the centre of Amsterdam. Currently, Mokum Mariteam operates on a small scale with clean and quiet electric vessels in the canals of Amsterdam. Many entrepreneurs and companies want to follow this new idea. Cooperation of the municipality of Amsterdam is a necessary condition to create appropriate and workable unloading bays (Ploos van Amstel, 2013). However, contrary to the attitude of the entrepreneurs, the municipality uses no incentives to stimulate the use of the canals for freight transport like other cities such as Venice in Italy and Utrecht in the Netherlands. The concept of distributing goods through the canals with electric, silent vessels seems to be a promising alternative. The question is whether a change to this renewed transport concept originated from the seventeenth century is easy to implement. The canals are currently being used extensively by pleasure crafts, houseboats and touring boats, therefore scarce capacity might be left for freight transport (Klein, 2012). A concern of the municipality is extra nuisance at the canals which is reflected in longer transit times (i.e. congestion on the canals), emissions and noise hindrance according to the municipality (Zindel, 2010). However, the use of electric, silent vessels will overcome the problems of emissions and noise, still the risk of longer transit times exists. The purpose of this study was to determine whether a city logistics concept via water will be a serious alternative if it will be exploited at a large scale in the inner-city of Amsterdam. Therefore, the research question to be answered is: 'To what extent is it possible to distribute goods at city- level to shops and restaurants via the canals without causing inconvenience for the other users of the canals and meanwhile satisfying meeting the logistics requirements of the shopkeepers?'

This article follows the modelling paradigm of Sargent (2010, p. 170) which shows the processes of developing system theories and simulation models, and relates verification and validation to both of these processes. First, Section 2 explores the literature on simulation of city logistics (waterborne transport) followed by the description of the first process step of the paradigm concerning the demarcation and definition of the conceptual model. Section 3 presents the second step of the paradigm, the specification and validation of the simulation model. Section 4 describes the last step of the paradigm showing the results of the experiments with different fleet sizes. Section 5 ends with some conclusions and recommendations.

2. Towards a conceptual model of the canals in Amsterdam

This section gives a brief overview on simulation of city logistics using waterborne transport, the demarcation of the problem, the description of the objects and processes and the performance indicators related to the stakeholders' importance.

2.1. *Simulation of city logistics using waterborne transport*

Simulation approaches in city logistics have become an important discipline providing a clear insight to the performances of new city logistics concepts or policy-related measures (Ambrosini, Gonzalez-Feliu, & Tolier, 2013; Ambrosini & Routhier, 2004; Boussier, Cucu, Ion, & Breuil, 2011; Ehmke & Campbell, 2014; Marcucci, Gatta, Valeri, & Stathopoulos, 2013; Polimeni, Russo, & Vitetta, 2010; Routhier & Toilier, 2007; Russo & Comi, 2010; Russo, Musolino, & Trecozzi, 2013). All these scientific contributions deal mainly with vehicles and roads instead of vessels and canals. Besides one contribution on noise performance at terminals (van Duin & van der Heijden, 2012), our literature search found no other contributions with respect to simulating a city logistics concept based on canals and vessels. However, literature contributions of discrete event simulation can be found with respect to the modelling inland navigation and barge operations for freight transport. Caris, Macharis, and Janssens (2011) use discrete event simulation to analyse the impact on waiting times and capacity utilization at potential hubs and at sea terminals. Although Caris et al. (2011) applied this model at a more national scale, that is, connecting the main port with the hinterland connections, some similarities can be observed in terms of waiting times and capacity utilization. There is a lot of literature available coping with the complexity of the terminal operations. In these studies (see, for instance, Liu, Jula, & Ioannou, 2002; Rijsenbrij & Saanen, 2007; Saanen, 2004), (micro-)simulation models are used to evaluate the performances. The micro-simulation models break down to the smallest sensible connected components (Roadknight, Aickelin, & Sherman, 2011) and can be applied to any scenario involving complex vehicle interactions. They have been used to model roads, rail, air and sea ports (see, for instance, Campbell, Smith, Sweeny, Mundy, & Nauss, 2007; Dobson, 2007; Smith, Sweeney, Campbell, & Nauss, 2008). In general, it can be concluded that in case of urban freight transport the on-time deliveries of the orders have the highest priority meanwhile the cost should be reduced as good as it can. These perspectives, unique for city logistics, are not found in the other discrete event models. Therefore, the focus in our model is (1) to guarantee the on-time deliveries to the shopkeepers and restaurants and (2) to maximize the usage of the fleet seize (and therefore reducing the cost of delivery). The occupation of the vessels is more important than the terminal occupation, that is, the fleet size of the vessels needs to be determined based on an on-time delivery to the shops. The developed model of the vessel concept is based on the discrete event modelling, since the transport and loading operations can be represented as a chronological sequence of (sometimes parallel) events. The vessels are using common shared infrastructure such as canals and loading zones. The operations at the canals and loading zones can be interpreted as a discrete queuing systems. There are several reasons for selecting simulation modelling. The most important ones are (Verbraeck, 2010):

- The mathematical part of the problem can be treated as a stochastic queuing system.
- The problem is complex in such a way that the outcomes are not simple and one-sided.
- The new concept we want to study does not exist yet and it is too expensive, and too time-consuming to experiment with a 'real world' model.
- Not all information required to describe the problem situations is available.
- There is no simple, analytical solution to the mathematical models of the system.

To model the discrete event system, in particular, the dynamic interactions between the ordering, delivering and (un)loading operations, stochastic simulation is chosen as the modelling technique. Stochastic simulation can improve the confidence of the modelling outcomes by replicative experiments.

2.2. *Demarcation*

The freight transport via the canals in the city centre of Amsterdam is modelled. The transport demand is derived from all the shops and restaurants located close to the canals the Singel, Herengracht, Keizersgracht and Prinsengracht. Offices are excluded in the model, as their amount of goods is negligible compared to shops and restaurants. Basically, the traffic on the water is modelled on these canals connected with a plurality of small canals. The precise geographical delimitation is shown in Figure 1.

The moment a ship arrives at the Amstel River, the ship will enter the model. It is modelled from the moment a ship starts sailing on the canal. All ships can sail on the canals from the Amstel River due to their connectivity. For bridges across the canals, it implies that only one ship at a time can pass due to the width of the vessels. All processes, waiting for enough orders, loading, sailing and unloading, are modelled. The final delivery to shop is not explicitly modelled, however it is considered in the loading and unloading times because normally service men on board bring the goods to the final destination. The reverse freight flows are also not explicitly modelled, however, they are also considered in the loading and unloading times.

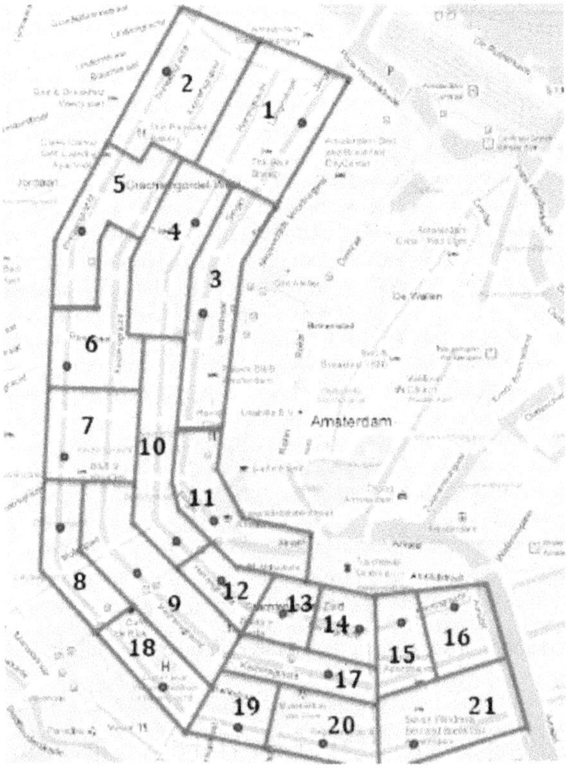

Figure 1. Geographical demarcation of the canals and zones in Amsterdam.

The model is based on the summer season. During this season, the canals by far the busiest, so there is the greatest risk of developing traffic bottlenecks. There are also strong differences during the days of the week. The simulation is based on a Friday, when most of the goods distribution occurs. The vessels are not restricted by the time-window constraints. However, most vessels start delivering goods in the morning and early in the afternoon due to desired time-windows of the shops and restaurants. Besides the freight vessels, other ships are also included in the model such as canal boats, houseboats and pleasure crafts.

2.3. *Objects and processes*

To model a system, objects and processes have to be defined. The first object in our model is an order. Each order consists of a demand of goods and has a specific destination and a specified volume. All goods are supplied in roll-containers. Based on their destination and their volume, the orders are assigned to a specific vessel. Second, the goods need to be handled by hydraulic cranes and hand trucks on board of the ship. These objects are needed to load and unload goods from a ship. As mentioned before, each ship can be specified as a goods vessel, a pleasure craft or a touring boat to move around the canals. Finally, the network bridges and canals are needed to facilitate the ships. Special notice is needed for the dropping points where the vessels can (un)load. If the dropping point is occupied by another vessels, the vessel has to wait for its turn.

The process starts with the arrival of orders. A vessel is only loaded when the fullest possible charge is available. Therefore, it is important that the destination of the goods

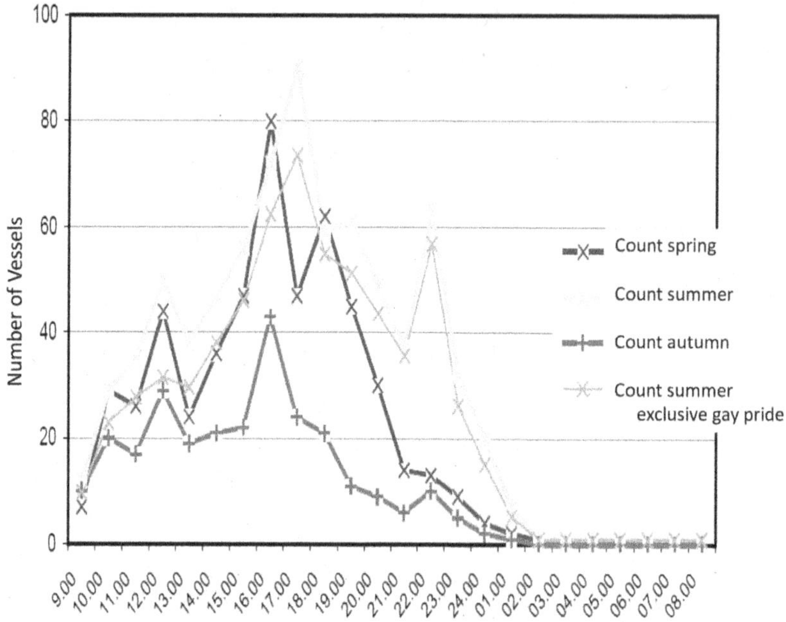

Figure 2. Average number of vessels per day at the Prinsengracht (Jakobs & Klein Wolt, 2004).

is known to prepare a logistic route. There are 21 different final destinations (= zones) divided into four areas. After the vessel is loaded, it departs to one of the four areas by sailing through the canals on the Amstel. The route chosen will depend on the destination of the goods and the congestion at the canals. The vessel selects the quickest (in time!) route. The route is based on the shortest-path algorithm of Dijkstra. Once the vessel arrives at a dropping point, the vessel dissolves a (part of) the cargo using the hydraulic crane and the hand truck on board. After the (un)loading, the vessel continues to its next dropping point. Once the vessel has unloaded all its goods, the vessel takes back the empty containers and sails back at the river Amstel to the original destination waiting for new orders. Again the quickest route is applied.

Besides the process of distributing goods, there are two other processes within the system, that is, the processes of sailing touring boats and pleasure vessels. In the summer, many touring boats are sailing through the canals to bring the tourists along all the highlights of Amsterdam. Also many pleasure vessels sail around to enjoy the inner-city of Amsterdam. Based on the counting of vessels (Jakobs & Klein Wolt, 2004), 24% is a touring vessel and 76% is a pleasure vessel. Figure 2 illustrates the business of vessels on an average day during the different seasons.

2.4. *Performance indicators*

The performance of the system is based on five performance indicators (PIs). These PIs give a complete picture of the potential quality of the concept and their impact to its users:

1. *Average waiting time to be loaded*
   This is closely related to the number of ships available. The average waiting time is counted for each order.

2. *Lead time of an order arriving at a shop/restaurant*
   The quality of the goods distribution is largely determined by how long it takes before the goods arrive at their destination. It is very important for shopkeepers/restaurants that goods arrive on time and the transport times remain reliable. The time until an order arrives at the company is determined by taking the difference between the time of order-entry and the time the order is unloaded at their destination.
3. *Average load factor of a cargo vessel*
   To keep the delivery of an order as soon as possible, the vessels frequently sail to the shopkeepers. This can result in poorly loaded vessels. On the other hand, for the economic viability, it is necessary that the capacity offered should be used, otherwise this leads to unnecessary costs (Buurgaard Nielsen & Van Essen, 2005). In our study, the load factor of a cargo ship is measured by the amount of roll containers to be transported at the departure of the vessels divided by the maximum capacity of the vessel, that is, 65 roll-containers.
4. *Average transit time in the network for touring boats*
   If the average transit time in the system increases by the introduction of one or more freight vessels, this is an indicator that congestion arises in the network. Both the average time and the number of entities are measured in the network of canals.
5. *Average transit time in the network for pleasure crafts*
   This indicator is determined in the same manner as for the touring boats.

3. Specification and validation

3.1. *Specification*

The conceptual model described in Section 2 was specified and augmented with data using the Arena platform for discrete-event simulation (Kelton, Sadowski, & Swets, 2010). The resulting simulation model consisted of three interacting components – one for each type of vessels on the canals (touring boats, pleasure crafts and freight vessels). The simulation model and its input and output variables are shown schematically in Figure 3.

In each traffic simulation component in the figure above, three types of transporters are created and added to a shared simulated traffic network. Touring boat and pleasure craft entities are assigned itineraries which are realized by the simulator. In the freight vessel traffic component, freight order entities are created in a station called 'Amstel' and assigned a final destination (one of the canals). For each freight order entity, it is checked whether the order fits within the available vessel capacity (Figure 4).

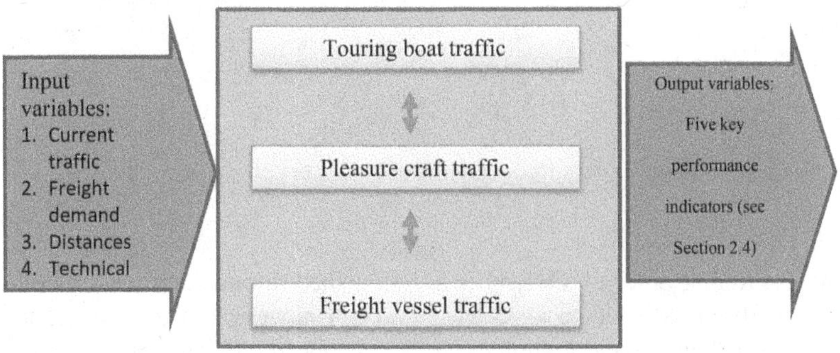

Figure 3. Schematic view of the simulation model with input and output variables.

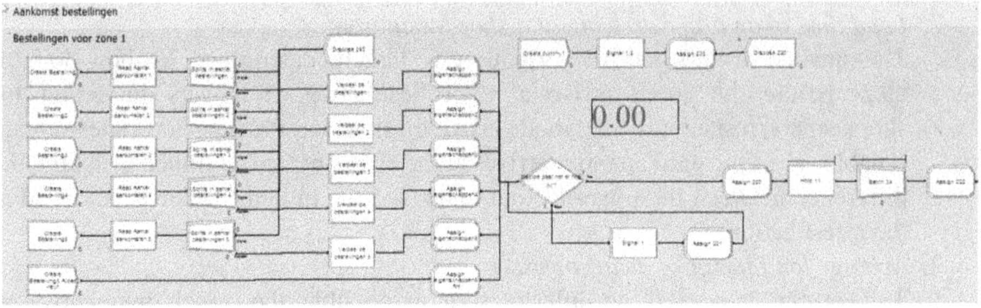

Figure 4. Arrival and assignment of the orders for destination zone 1(including vessel capacity check (= decide-module)).

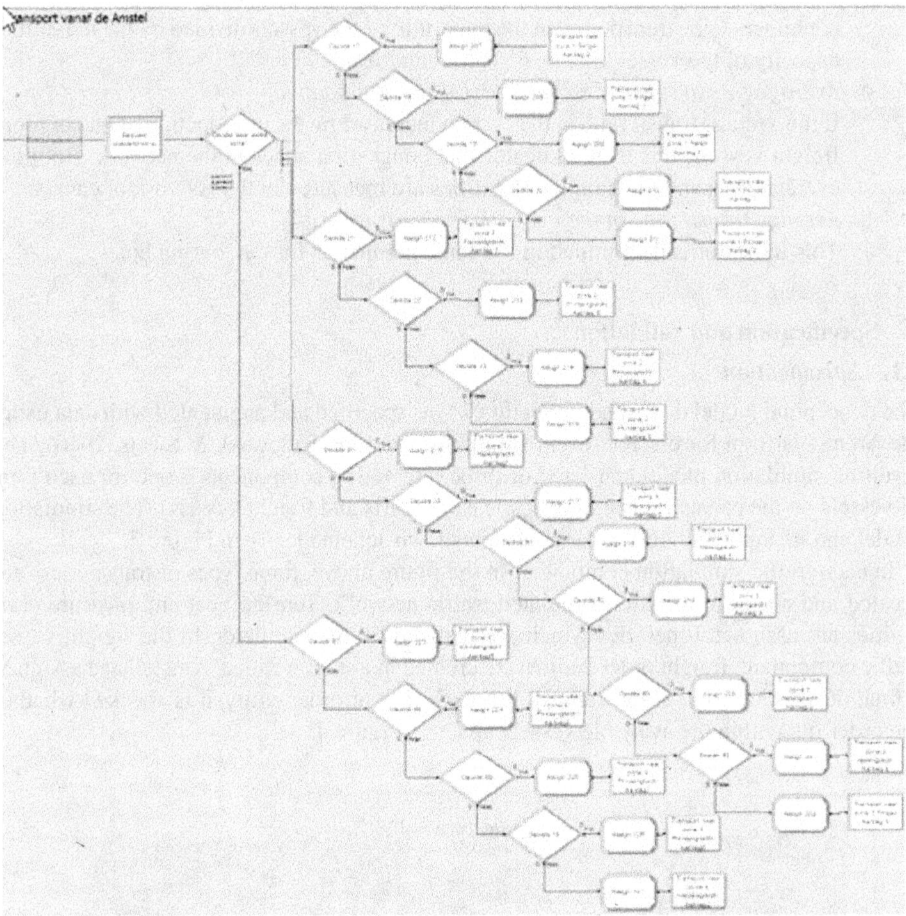

Figure 5. Departure of the vessels from the Amstel.

Assigning a freight order to a vessel is accomplished through a request-module. After the loads have been assigned to a vessel, the vessel moves from the Amstel to its first destination. A number of decide-modules check whether freight deliveries are on board for each destination and thus control the vessel's routing (Figure 5).

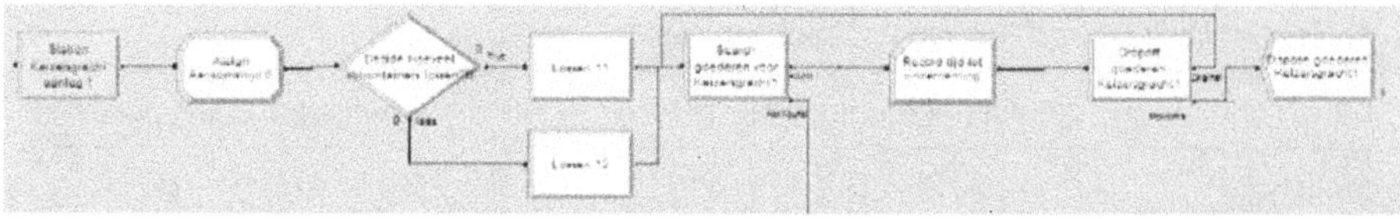

Figure 6. The unloading process of a vessel.

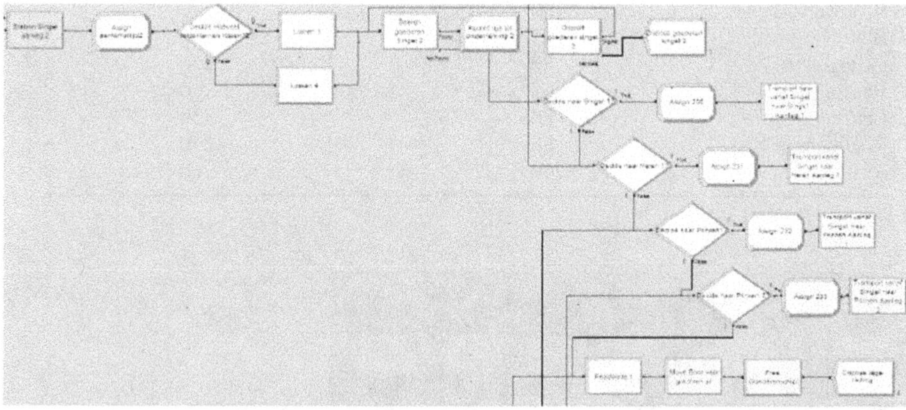

Figure 7. Route continuation of a vessel.

Once arrived at the destination (station-module), the vessel starts unloading. The duration of the unloading process depends on the number of freight loads to be delivered. The search- and drop-off module decides which freight loads have to be unloaded. The duration of the process is recorded by the record-module (Figure 6).

When all required freight loads have been unloaded at a particular destination, the vessel continues to its next destination. Again a check (decide-module) is made whether freight loads need to be unloaded for this new location. In case there are no loads available, it continues to the following destination. Once the vessel is empty (decide-module), the vessel will return through the canals to its starting station Amstel (Figure 7).

In the simulated traffic network, we modelled canal and ship widths and the options for overtaking to study the formation of queues on the canals. The touring boats and pleasure crafts enter the model as entities (according to the arrival pattern given in Table 1). These vessels do not make roundtrips, instead they just move in one canal from the beginning to the end and vice versa. By implementing the source in this way, the exact number of vessels (and vessel-types) can be brought into the network. For each vessel, it is decided which direction the vessel came from (North or South). The vessel starts requesting a channel and waits until the channel has enough capacity. The vessel makes its tour and at the end of the tour, the entity will leave the models and increase the capacity of the channel by one. The source of the module is shown in Figure 8(a) and 8(b) for one canal (Prinsengracht). The touring boat traffic on other canals follows the same source specification.

3.2. *Collection of data*

The data used to build the model were derived from a range of sources. First, data on the current shipping traffic on the canals were obtained from the City of Amsterdam, Research and Statistics Department (Jakobs & Klein Wolt, 2004; Jakobs & Laan, 2012). The municipality of Amsterdam had only vessel traffic data from the Singel, Brouwersgracht, Prinsengracht

Table 1. Data on current shipping traffic on canals.

Canal	Number of touring boats per day	Number of pleasure crafts per day
Singel	192	610
Herengracht	110	350
Keizersgracht	100	350
Prinsengracht	170	440
Brouwersgracht	180	570
Blauwburgwal	65	200
Leliegracht	80	250
Beulingssloot	65	200
Leidsegracht	80	250
Reguliersgracht	80	250
Amstel	240	760

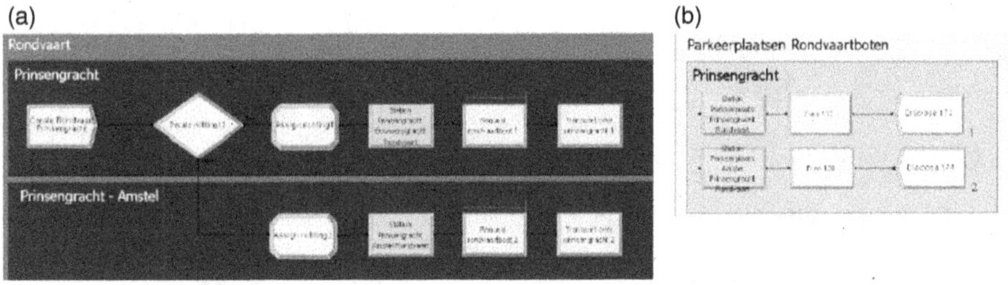

Figure 8. (a) and (b) Touring boats at the Prinsengracht.

and the Amstel River. Based on the width and length of the canals, quantitative traffic data were estimated for the remaining canals (Table 1).

Second, from field research an inventory of the existing catering facilities and shops was produced to estimate the demand for freight transport (see result in Table 2).

The data in Tables 1 and 2 were used to simulate the creation processes of the three vessel types (inter-arrival times were drawn from exponential distributions that were fitted to yield the reported vessel intensities). Third, Google Map was used to estimate the distances between different points in the network (Table 3).

Fourth and finally, Willem Post, the manager of Mokum Mariteam, was interviewed to obtain the necessary technical and logistic data on the delivery vessels (22 May 2013). These and other vessel data are shown in Table 4.

3.3. *Verification and validation*

Before conducting experiments, various verification tests are performed to determine the correctness of the model: an input test (see, for example, Table 5), a structure test and a test to verify if all of the entities in the model leave the model before the end of the simulation run. Our model passed all of these tests.

Moreover, the model was operationally validated (Sargent, 2009). We used the following experimental treatment: a simulation run lasted 24 hours. The system that was modelled was considered finite and, therefore, a warm-up time is not needed (we are interested in both the transient and steady-state phase of the simulation). We used the method by Pegden, Sadowski, and Shannon (1995) to calculate the required number of replications of the experiment (209) to yield a sufficiently narrow 95% confidence interval. We compared

Table 2. Order demand pattern for each zone in rolling containers (van den Boogaard, 2013).

Zone	Café/restaurant	Shop	Hotel	Total
1	4	3	12	20.5/day
2	18	7	3	31.5/day
3	8	7	3	21.5/day
4	7	2	10	20/day
5	16	4 + AH	2	26/day + AH
6	13	17	6	44.5/day
7	10	8	5	27/day
8	12	11	2	30.5/day
9	5	13	3	27.5/day
10	5	2	2	10/day
11	6	1	4	11.5/day
12	1	3	0	5.5/day
13	2	1	2	5.5/day
14	3	0	3	6/day
15	11	0 + AH	6	17/day + AH
16	4	2	0	10/day
17	2	1	1	4.5/day
18	9	4	2	23/day
19	4	2	0	10/day
20	4	1 + AH	2	7.5/day +

Note: AH = Big grocery Albert Heijn wants to be delivered three times a day: 7.00 am, 1.00 pm and 7.00 pm.

Table 3. Distances between the canals.

Canal	Distance in model (m)
Singel	1215
Herengracht	2335
Keizersgracht	2960
Prinsengracht	3240
Brouwersgracht	410
Blauwburgwal	90
Leliegracht	250
Beulingssloot	100
Leidsegracht	290
Reguliersgracht	285
Amstel	335

Table 4. Main system parameters.

Parameter	Value
Length freight vessel	20 m
Capacity freight vessel	65 rolling containers
Length of touring boat	20 m
Length pleasure craft	6 m
Speed of vessels	6 km/hour
Order size/frequency restaurant	1 rolling container/day
Order size/frequency shop	1.5 rolling container/day
Time for loading	1–4 rolling containers: UNIFORM (5, 10) minutes 5 or more rolling containers: UNIFORM (10, 20) minutes

Table 5. Input test: number of entering pleasure crafts.

Canal	Number of vessels in the model per day	Real number of vessels per day (Jakobs & Laan, 2012)
Singel	611.46	610
Herengracht	347.10	350
Keizersgracht	346.81	350
Prinsengracht	446.22	440
Brouwersgracht	568.34	570
Blauwburgwal	205.25	200
Leliegracht	246.11	250
Beulingssloot	204.75	200
Leidsegracht	246.97	250
Reguliersgracht	253.57	250
Amstel	761.88	760

durations of travel in the model with those estimated from the actual distances and travelling speeds of different types of vessels. No significant differences were found between them. Therefore, we consider our model a valid representation of the target system. More detailed information on verification and validation is available in van den Boogaard (2013).

4. Experiments

Actually the experiments are based on five specific situations: one experiment without cargo vessels (the baseline) and the other experiments are situations with freight distribution based on 1, 2, 3 and 4 vessels. First, this section provides an overview of the logistics performances of the new concept, and then the traffic consequences for the other vessel types are shown.

4.1. *Logistic performances of the vessel concept*

As mentioned before, the logistics performances are based on the following indicators: average waiting time to be loaded, lead time of an order arriving at a shop/restaurant and the average load factor the cargo vessels. From the experiments with a different fleet-size-mix, it can be deduced that the average time until the goods arrive strongly decreases if more ships sail. By comparing the experiments (one-way analysis of variance test) for the average waiting time to be loaded and lead time of an order arriving at a shop/restaurant, the tests showed significant differences. At the maximum order-lead time to shop, it turns out significant differences everywhere except (10.36 down to 7.28) at between the experiments with three and four vessels. In general, it can be concluded that the load factor does not differ significantly between the different experiments due to that fact that a ships leaves when the fullest possible charge is available (considering the time-windows of the shopkeepers). The results are summarized in the Tables 6 and 7.

4.2. *Impact on transit times for touring boats and pleasure crafts*

As mentioned before, other users of the canals, touring boats and pleasure crafts might be hindered due to presence of the freight vessels. This seems to be an important argument for the municipality and, therefore, the transit times without the new system are compared with the transit times with the new system implemented. To observe the strongest influence, the comparison is based on Experiment 5 with four freight vessels in operation. The values

Table 6. Lead times to shop (Experiments 1, 2, 3 and 4 vessels).

Experiments (number of vessels)	Order lead time to shop (hours)	95% Confidence interval (hours)	p-value between experiments	Maximum order lead time to shop (hours)	95% Confidence interval (hours)	p-value between experiments
1	0.46	0.44–0.47		10.36	9.82–10.90	
2	0.38	0.36–0.39	.00	9.07	8.56–9.58	.00
3	0.33	0.31–0.35	.00	8.10	7.57–8.61	.03
4	0.27	0.26–0.29	.01	7.28	6.77–7.79	.09

Table 7. Waiting times to be loaded and load factors (Experiments 1, 2, 3 and 4 vessels).

Experiments (number of vessels)	Waiting time to be loaded (hours)	95% Confidence interval (hours)	p-value between experiments	Load factor vessel (%)	95% Confidence interval (hours)	p-value between experiments
1	2.6181	2.47–2.76		83.32	79.53–87.12	
2	0.9506	0.90–1.00	.00	83.30	79.51–87.09	1.00
3	0.4030	0.38–0.43	.00	82.00	78.06–85.83	1.00
4	0.2244	0.20–0.25	.00	82.00	78.15–85.85	1.00

Table 8. Transit times pleasure crafts and touring boats.

Canal	Transit times without new system (hours)	95% Confidence interval (hours)	Transit times with new system (hours)	95% Confidence interval (hours)	Absolute difference (hours)	p-value
Pleasure crafts						
Singel	0.37	0.34–0.40	0.40	0.37–0.44	0.03	.87
Herengracht	0.56	0.52–0.60	0.55	0.50–0.60	−0.01	.48
Keizersgracht	0.71	0.68–0.74	0.75	0.70–0.79	0.04	.06
Prinsengracht	0.55	0.52–0.58	0.59	0.55–0.64	0.04	.20
Brouwersgracht	0.32	0.29–0.35	0.32	0.29–0.34	0.00	.95
Blauwburgwal	0.29	0.26–0.32	0.28	0.25–0.31	−0.01	.42
Leliegracht	0.37	0.34–0.40	0.39	0.36–0.42	0.02	.72
Beulingssloot	0.21	0.19–0.23	0.21	0.19–0.23	0.00	.42
Leidsegracht	0.32	0.30–0.34	0.36	0.33–0.39	0.04	.06
Reguliersgracht	0.34	0.32–0.36	0.39	0.35–0.43	0.05	.59
Amstel	0.31	0.29–0.34	0.37	0.32–0.42	0.06	.86
Touring boats						
Singel	0.37	0.34–0.40	0.40	0.37–0.44	0.03	.87
Herengracht	0.56	0.52–0.60	0.55	0.50–0.60	−0.01	.48
Keizersgracht	0.71	0.68–0.74	0.75	0.70–0.79	0.04	.06
Prinsengracht	0.55	0.52–0.58	0.59	0.55–0.64	0.04	.20
Brouwersgracht	0.32	0.29–0.35	0.32	0.29–0.34	0.00	.95
Blauwburgwal	0.29	0.26–0.32	0.28	0.25–0.31	−0.01	.42
Leliegracht	0.37	0.34–0.40	0.39	0.36–0.42	0.02	.72
Beulingssloot	0.21	0.19–0.23	0.21	0.19–0.23	0.00	.42
Leidsegracht	0.32	0.30–0.34	0.36	0.33–0.39	0.04	.06
Reguliersgracht	0.34	0.32–0.36	0.39	0.35–0.43	0.05	.59
Amstel	0.31	0.29–0.34	0.37	0.32–0.42	0.06	.86

without the new concept are compared with the values with the new concept by application of an independent t-test between the two samples. Table 8 shows that there exits significant time differences for touring boats and pleasure crafts. However, the maximum absolute time difference is 0.06 hour, that is, 3.6 minutes at the Amstel. For the pleasure crafts and touring boats, this might not lead to a big issue due to the leisure character of their activities.

5. Conclusions and recommendations

Based on our simulation study, it can be concluded that in case of Amsterdam, it can be a serious alternative to transfer freight from road transport to waterborne transport, especially when the vessels used are electric driven. In the literature, no empirical studies were found concerning waterborne (city-)freight concepts analysed by simulation. In the case of Amsterdam, the supportive role of simulation has been explained to the stakes of the actors involved, that is, the shopkeepers, the logistics service provider who operates the concept and the municipality. Other actors are not considered in this study since the focus of this study is just on the operational feasibility and the related waterborne traffic interaction. The related logistics performances give a clear insight in the (order-)lead times, the waiting times before loading and the load-factors of the vessels. For the municipality, the traffic interferences with pleasure crafts and touring boats are shown. It can be concluded that simulation has made the whole new concept transparent to all the actors involved.

Case-specifically, it can be concluded (if the freight demand is well estimated) that one operating vessel will not be sufficient to meet the demanded logistical performances of the shopkeepers and cafes. However, operating with four ships vessel reduces the waiting time with 92% and the (order-) lead time drops with 53%. Still the load factor does not drop significantly by deploying more vessels (2%). So no extra costs (besides the investment costs) arise due to a lower load-factor in the deployment of four ships. Also the traffic interference with the pleasure crafts and touring boats shows no significant changes in their transit times. Based on these first simulation results, it can be concluded that a fleet size of four freight vessels has potential to be a good solution. Additional research is needed to analyse the economic viability and to estimate the reduction of emissions of air pollutants, greenhouse gasses and noise, especially when construction products are also likely to be transported by waterborne transport (Ploos van Amstel, 2013).

In future, reconsideration of canal-usages might be an interesting sustainable option for many other European cities having canals in their city centres. Based on our study, it is an almost forgotten opportunity to improve both the distribution network and the environmental quality of the inner cities by the usage of canals.

References

Ambrosini, C., Gonzalez-Feliu, J., & Tolier, F. (2013). A design methodology for scenario – Analysis in urban freight modeling. *European Transport – Trasporti Europei, 54*(7), 1–21.

Ambrosini, C., & Routhier, J. L. (2004). Objectives, methods and results of surveys carried out in the field of urban freight transport: an international comparison. *Transport Reviews, 24*(1), 57–77.

van den Boogaard, S. L. (2013). *Kan vracht door de gracht?* (Bachelor thesis). Delft University of Technology, Technology, Policy & Management, Delft, The Netherlands.

Boussier, J. M., Cucu, T., Ion, L., & Breuil, D. (2011). Simulation of goods delivery process. *International Journal of Physical Distribution and Logistics Management, 41*(9), 913–930.

Buurgaard Nielsen, J., & Van Essen, H. P. (2005). *Beladingsgraden – Ruimte voor verbetering (Loadfactors – Space for improvement)*. Delft: CE Delft.

Campbell, J. F., Smith, L. D., Sweeny, II, D. C. S., Mundy, R., & Nauss, R. M. (2007). Decision tools for reducing congestion at locks on the upper mississippi river. In R. Sprague (Ed.), *HICSS '07:*

Proceedings of the 40th annual Hawaii international conference on system sciences, paper 56a, (pp. 1–10). Washington, DC: IEEE Computer Society.

Caris, A., Macharis, C., & Janssens, G. K. (2011). Network analysis of container barge transport in the port of Antwerp by means of simulation. *Journal of Transport Geography, 19*(11), 125–133.

City of Amsterdam. (2010). *Actionplan smart and clean urban distribution Amsterdam.* (in Dutch). Retrieved February 15, 2013, from http://www.amsterdam.nl/gemeente/organisatie-diensten/ivv/publicaties/nota%27-uitgaven/

Department of Infrastructure, Traffic and Transport. (2010). *Mobility in and around Amsterdam – A future vision from a historical perspective.* (in Dutch). Retrieved February 15, 2013, from http://www.amsterdam.nl/gemeente/organisatie-diensten/ivv/publicaties/nota%27-uitgaven/

DHV. (2007). Vision on supply – Research of urban freight distribution in Amsterdam. Retrieved February 15, 2013, from http://www.tramgroningen.nl/documenten/Bevoorradingsprofiel20507.pdf

Dobson, I. (2007). Complex interacting infrastructure systems. In R. Sprague (Ed.), *HICSS '07: Proceedings of the 40th annual Hawaii international conference on system sciences, paper 111* (pp. 1–10). Washington, DC: IEEE Computer Society.

van Duin, J. H. R., & van der Heijden, R. E. C. M. (2012). A new barge terminal in a residential area; using simulation modeling to support governance of noise. *Journal of Computational Science, 3*(4), 216–227.

Ehmke, J. F., & Campbell, A. M. (2014). Customer acceptance for home deliveries in metropolitan areas. *European Journal of Operational Research, 233* (1), 193–207.

Jakobs, E., & Klein Wolt, K. (2004). *Drukte op het water?* (in Dutch). Amsterdam: Research and Statistics Department City of Amsterdam.

Jakobs, E., & Laan, N. (2012). *Overlast op het water* (*Nuisance at the water*). Amsterdam: Dienst Onderzoek en Statistiek Gemeente Amsterdam.

Kelton, W. D., Sadowski, R. P., & Swets, N. B. (2010) *Simulation with arena* (5th ed.). Boston, MA: McGraw-Hill.

Klein, M. (2012). Dat drukke stadverkeer kan best door de gracht. *NRC Handelsblad.* Retrieved February 10, 2013 from, http://archief.nrc.nl/index.php/2012/December/27/Overig/NH_NL01_014/Dat+drukke+stadsverkeer+kan+best+door+de+gracht/identify=Y

Liu, C. I., Jula, H., & Ioannou, P. A. (2002). Design, simulation, evaluation of automated container terminals. *IEEE Transactions on Intelligent Transportation Systems, 3*(1), 12–26.

Marcucci, E., Gatta, V., Valeri, E., & Stathopoulos, A. (2013). *Urban freight transport modelling: An agent specific approach.* Milano, Italy: Franco Angeli.

Pegden, D. C., Sadowski, R. P., & Shannon, R. E. (1995). *Introduction to simulation using SIMAN.* New York, NY: McGraw-Hill.

Ploos van Amstel, W. (2013). *Wispelturige bestuurders belemmeren stedelijke distributie* (*Inconsistent management hinders the urban freight distribution*). Retrieved July 31, 2013, from http://www.logistiek.nl/Distributie/duurzaam-transport/2013/6/Wispelturige-bestuurders-belemmeren-stedelijke-distributie-1282732W/?goback=.gde_2172568_member_249477628

Polimeni, A., Russo, F., & Vitetta, A. (2010). Demand and routing models for urban goods movement simulation. *European Transport – Trasporti Europei,* (46), 3–23.

Rijsenbrij, J. C., & Saanen, Y. (2007). *Design of systems and operations in container terminals* (*Revision 10*). Rotterdam, The Netherlands: Center for Maritime Economics and Logistics, Erasmus University Rotterdam.

Roadknight, C., Aickelin, U., & Sherman, G. (2011). Validation of a micro simulation of the Port of Dover. *Journal of Computational Science, 3*(1–2), 56–66.

Routhier, J. L., & Toilier, F. (2007). FRETURB V3, a policy oriented software of modelling urban goods movement. In *Proceedings of the 11th world conference on transport research,* Berkeley, CA: WCTR. Retrieved from, http://trid.trb.org/view.aspx?id=876773

Russo, F., & Comi, A. (2010). A modelling system to simulate goods movements at an urban scale. *Transportation, 37* (6), 987–1009.

Russo, F., Musolino, G., & Trecozzi, M. R. (2013). A system of models for the assessment of an urban distribution center in a city logistic plan (conference paper). In *19th international conference on urban transport and the environment,* UT (Vol. 130, 799–810). Southampton, UK: WIT Transactions on the Built Environment.

Saanen, Y. (2004). *An approach for designing robotised maritime container terminals* (Doctoral dissertation). Delft University of Technology, Delft, The Netherlands.

Sargent, R. G. (2009). Verification and validation of simulation models. In M. D. Rossetti, R. R. Hill, B. Johansson, A. Dunkin, & R. G. Ingalls, (Eds.), *Proceedings of the 2009 winter simulation conference* (Vol. 37, pp. 162–176). Austin, TX: IEEE. doi:10.1109/EMR.2009.5235461

Sargent, R. G. (2010). Verification and validation of simulation models. In B. Johansson, S. Jain, J. Montoya-Torres, J. Hugan, & E. Yücesan (Eds.), *Proceedings of the 2010 winter simulation conference* (pp. 166–183). Piscataway, NJ: IEEE.

Smith, L. D., Sweeney, D. C., Campbell, J. F., & Nauss, R. M. (2008). Simulation of operating procedures and infrastructure changes in the upper Mississippi navigation system. In H. Rajaei (Ed.), *Proceedings of the 2008 spring simulation multiconference* (pp. 231–238). San Diego, CA: Society for Computer Simulation International.

Verbraeck, A. (2010). *Discrete modellen deel 2*. Delft: Faculteit Techniek, Bestuur en Management.

Zindel, K. (2010). *Stedelijke distributie over grenzen* (*City Logistics beyond frontiers*). Den Haag: Ambassadeur Stedelijke Distributie.

City logistics long-term planning: simulation of shopping mobility and goods restocking and related support systems

Agostino Nuzzolo[a], Antonio Comi[a] and Luca Rosati[b]

[a]*Department of Enterprise Engineering, Tor Vergata University of Rome, Rome, Italy;* [b]*Department of Civil Engineering and Computer Science, Tor Vergata University of Rome, Rome, Italy*

The growing necessity to improve city sustainability and liveability has pushed local administrators to look also at medium/long-term city logistics measures, such as land-use governance policies. In order to assess long-term scenarios, it is necessary to have models and methods able to take into account the effects on shopping mobility and goods restocking, generated by these classes of measures (e.g. relocation of shopping zones). Besides, we have to consider that modifications of shopping attitudes, deriving from changes of demographic and socio-economic characteristics of end consumers, can impact on purchasing behaviour and hence on restocking mobility. This paper discusses a number of issues related to the simulation of medium/long-term scenarios and presents a system of models that consider shopping mobility and restocking jointly. The presented shopping demand models, in combination with urban restocking models, are implemented within a simulation support system named City Logistics Analysis and Simulation Support System and are used to assess the effects on the freight restocking due to demographic and socio-economic variations including some hypotheses on new land-use development governance measures in a medium-size urban area. The main results confirm the modelling goodness and, at the same time, demonstrate that changes in demographic and socio-economic characteristics could cause relevant effects, in particular increasing car use in shopping mobility. The growing e-shopping could limit the negative effects of these changes, but the impacts of home deliveries have to be considered. The relocation of commercial and logistics centres, closer to the residential distribution, could drive a different restocking pattern with a consequent reduction in freight vehicle mobility. Anyway, this reduction is not very relevant and therefore further city logistics measures have to be implemented.

1. Introduction

In the last years, in the field of city logistics planning, two innovative approaches, among others, have been developed. The first innovative approach considers freight distribution and shopping mobility jointly (Comi & Nuzzolo, 2014; Oppenheim, 1994; Russo & Comi, 2004, 2006). In fact, shopping-related activity is the second main scope of travelling within urban areas and some surveys showed that purchasing activities account for about twice the veh-kms of deliveries and pick-up activities. Each person consumes about 3 kg of products daily and the average distance travelled per inhabitant is less than 2 km, against 0.8 km due to deliveries and urban management flows (Guzzo & Mazzulla, 2006; Lindholm, 2013; Schoemaker, Allen, Huschebek, & Monigl, 2006). Besides, end consumers prefer cars for shopping trips and the result is more cars, hence more congestion and pollutant emissions. Besides, end-consumer's choices in relation to the type of retail outlets undoubtedly impact on freight distribution flows. End consumers undertake their trips to satisfy their needs, they buy at a shop and hence their shopping choices influence the restocking flows. Therefore, shopping demand represents the input of restocking, and subsequently modifications occurring on shopping have indubitable effects on the restocking. In fact, end-consumer choices in relation to the type of retail outlet influence the freight distribution flows for restocking shops. The characteristics of the restocking process, in terms of delivery size, delivery frequency, freight vehicle type and so on, are strictly related to the size of commercial activities to be restocked. Since end-consumer choices depend on their characteristics, such as age, gender and type of employment, which change over time in an urban area, changes in such characteristics impact upon the nature of freight restocking. Nevertheless, the changes in economic activity locations (e.g. residences and shops) have to be pointed out, especially when medium/long-term measures are implemented.

The second innovative approach is relative to the type of city logistics measures to be implemented (Browne, Allen, Nemoto, Patier, & Visser, 2012; Dablanc, 2007; Muñuzuri & Gonzalez-Feliu, 2013; Nuzzolo & Comi, 2014a; Russo & Comi, 2010a). The city administrators mainly managed operational actions in order to reduce interferences with other vehicles and inhabitants (e.g. using Limited Freight Traffic Zones) and the pollutant emissions (e.g. using constraints based on Euro emission standards and new urban distribution centres). Recently, local administrators are also looking at other classes of measures of medium/long-term type, such as urban land-use development governance: allotment of retail area among small, medium and large retail activities; location of retail activities with respect to warehouses and distribution centres.

The proper choice of a set of city logistics measures (city logistics scenario) to be implemented has to be based on the simulations of the specified scenario (i.e. using a 'what if approach'; Cascetta, 2009; Ortuzar & Willumsen, 2001), computing some effect indicators able to quantify the expected results in terms of internal and external, direct and indirect costs (Nuzzolo & Comi, 2014b). Generally, these indicators are obtained from the road network performances and impacts, forecasted using the procedure reported in Figure 1. Such a procedure requires as input the shopping car and the freight vehicle origin–destination (O–D) matrices. These matrices are assigned to the road network, obtaining link flows, which in turn are used as inputs of the other models that, for example, allow determination of pollution emissions, energy consumption, road accidents (Russo & Comi, 2013) and so on.

The shopping car O–D matrices and the restocking freight vehicle O–D matrices are obtained using the freight demand models reported in the following sections. In order to obtain the shopping vehicle O–D matrices for medium/long-term scenarios, demand models, able to take into account the changes of shopping mobility due to demographic and socio-economic characteristics, are necessary.

In this context, the paper aims to analyse and apply simulation models that can be used for the assessment of the effects on urban freight transport system of medium/long-term city logistics scenarios, considering the demographic, socio-economic and activity location changes. In particular, the paper focuses on the factors that mainly influence shopping trip generation. Some new models calibrated for simulating shopping trip generation are hence presented. The models were obtained using some surveys carried out in Rome, where more than 900 end consumers (more than 300 families) were interviewed.

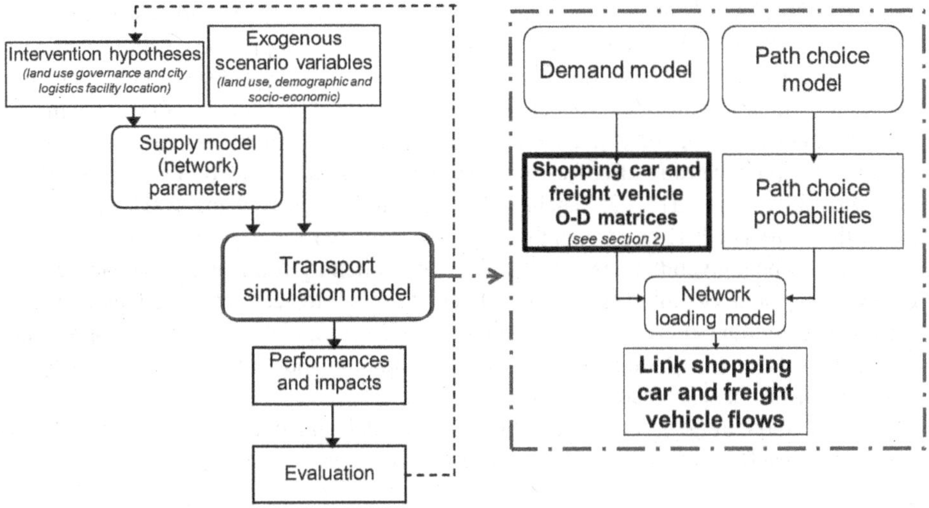

Figure 1. Simulation of medium/long-term city logistics scenarios (Nuzzolo & Comi, 2013).

Besides, the complexity of these methods and models has pushed researchers to develop decision support systems (DSSs) for the analysis and simulation of the effects of city logistics measures and the effects of exogenous scenario changes, as land-use, demographic and socio-economic characteristics (Comi, Donnelly, & Russo, 2014; Muñuzuri & Gonzelez-Feliu, 2013; Taniguchi, Thompson, & Yamada, 2012). In fact, today, there is a growing interest to support systems able to support decision-makers to understand and simulate the structure of freight urban system and to compute some indicators that compared with target and benchmarking values allow to identify its level of service (Browne et al., 2012; Stathopoulos, Valeri, & Marcucci, 2012). A DSS of this type, named City Logistics Analysis and Simulation Support System (CLASS), has been developed by the authors and is described in Section 2. The presented shopping demand models, in combination with urban restocking models, were implemented within CLASS and were used to assess the effects on the freight restocking due to demographic and socio-economic variations including some hypotheses on new land-use development governance measures in a medium-size urban area (Section 3). The results obtained are reported and discussed in Section 4. Finally, some conclusions and further developments of this study are given in Section 5.

2. Background

The section reviews the demand modelling and DSSs developed in the field of urban freight transport and aims to identify areas in which further research would be beneficial.

2.1. *Joint shopping and restocking demand modelling*

Although several urban freight demand models have been proposed (see for a state of art Ambrosini, Meimbresse, Routhier, & Sonntag, 2008; Anand, Quak, Van Duin, & Tavasszy, 2012; Gonzalez-Feliu & Routhier, 2012; Nuzzolo, Coppola, & Comi, 2013), they sometimes neglect to point out the relationships between restocking and shopping mobility. Few studies have proposed joint modelling frameworks that explicitly consider restocking flows as being generated to satisfy end-consumer demand (Barone, Crocco, & Mongelli, 2014a; Crocco,

De Marco, Iaquinta, & Mongelli, 2010; Gonzalez-Feliu, Ambrosini, Pluvinet, Toilier, & Routhier, 2012; Gonzalez-Feliu, Toilier, & Routhier, 2010; Oppenheim, 1994; Russo & Comi, 2010b). Besides, few of them have analysed shopping mobility as a component of freight mobility and considered that changes in shopping attitudes or actions impacting on purchasing behaviour of end consumers (e.g. location of shopping zone and transport mode to use for shopping) can also affect restocking mobility (Barone, Crocco, & Mongelli, 2014b; Miodonski & Kawamura, 2012; Sanchez-Diaz, Holguin-Veras, & Wang, 2013). This shows that further work needs to be done in this field, especially when long-term scenarios have to be assessed. Then, given the desirability of a joint modelling framework, the paper recalls a modelling system (Comi & Nuzzolo, 2014) that takes into account some factors of end-consumer behaviour (such as the choice of retail outlet type and links between shopping and shop restocking mobility) and new models for simulating shopping trip generation, when socio-economic changes occur, are presented.

The used modelling system is a multi-stage model and considers a discrete choice approach for each decisional level. It consists of two main steps (Figure 2):

- shopping model sub-system: it allows us to simulate end-consumer behaviour for shopping and to estimate quantity bought by end consumers in order to satisfy their needs and hence to identify the freight flows attracted by each traffic zone;
- restocking model sub-system: given the quantity attracted by each traffic zone, it allows us to estimate the restocking quantity O–D matrices characterized by freight types and type of vehicle used.

The shopping model sub-system allows us to point out the effects arising from the implementation of medium/long-term actions on the location of retail outlets and places of residence and due to changes in the characteristics of the population (e.g. demographic and socio-economic changes).

The restocking sub-system includes models for the simulation of the freight distribution process from the freight centres to the retail zone and can be also used to determine the medium/long-term effects arising from implementation of actions on the location of logistic establishments (e.g. warehouses and distribution centres).

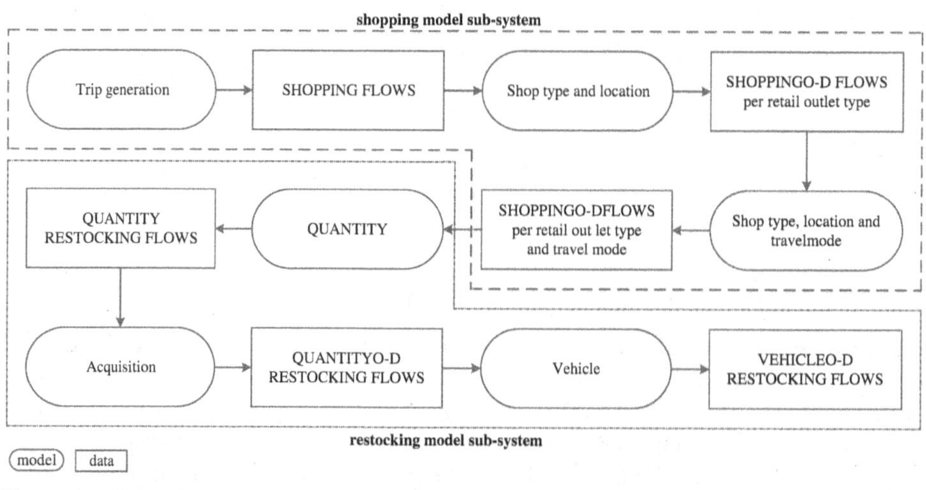

Figure 2. Urban freight modelling structure.

2.2. *DSSs for city logistics*

As reported in Section 1, the complexity of the simulation methods and models has pushed researchers and practitioners to develop DSSs for the analysis of city logistics systems and the simulation of the effects of city logistics measures (Ambrosini, Gonzalez-Feliu, & Toilier, 2013; Crainic, 2008; Taniguchi, Thompson, & Yamada, 2001).

In Germany, Sonntag (1985) proposed the WIVER that allows to simulate vehicle trip O–D for restocking activities. Following the approach of WIVER, Lohse (2004) developed the tool Viseva-W that allows to consider in the simulation both the restocking and passenger flows. However, the two segments of mobility are managed independently without considering that restocking flows can be also generated by the requests of end consumers who move for shopping.

To improve the simulation of restocking, in France the delivery approach was proposed and implemented within the support system named Freturb (Routhier & Toilier, 2007). The implemented models consist of a sequence of statistic-descriptive models that give as output the freight characterized in terms of transport service, vehicle and journey types (i.e. round or trip chain).

Based on the Freturb approach, CityGoods was developed by Gentile and Vigo (2013). On the basis of some surveys (carried out within City Port Project; City Ports, 2005) among transporters, shippers and establishments, they proposed a specific approach for the generation of total number of movements as a function of the NACE (European Classification of Economic Activities) code and the number of employees at each establishment.

Focusing mainly on logistics chains and on the main assumptions that liveability and accessibility of urban areas are influenced by freight traffic resulting from logistical choices in the supply chain, like warehouse location, delivery frequencies, vehicle type and routing, Boerkamps, van Binsbergen, and Bovy (2000) proposed a general framework implemented in GoodTrip. The developed models simulate these choices and their effects, in current and future situations, through some identified empirical relationships. GoodTrip allows the estimation of goods' flows (in terms of quantity), urban freight traffic and its impacts, such as vehicle mileage, network loads, emissions and, finally, energy use of urban freight distribution.

From the above literature analysis, it emerges that some DSSs were developed but many of them are based on empirical relations that well describe the current state of the system but they could have some limits when new city logistics scenarios (before implementation) are simulated and assessed. Based on this statement, a new DSS, called CLASS, was proposed by Comi and Rosati (2013). It will be briefly described in the following section.

2.3. *CLASS: the proposed DSS*

In order to manage the relationships of urban goods movements (i.e. shopping and restocking) in a demographic, socio-economic and land-use scenario, the above presented system of models was implemented within a DSS (namely CLASS; Comi & Rosati, 2013). The earlier version of CLASS is mainly devoted to the identification of critical stages and the simulation of city logistics scenarios. Then, some advancements were implemented in order to link shopping and restocking mobility, including the new shopping models described in Section 3 that allow to point out that shop restocking is mainly to satisfy the demand of end consumers who buy at shops.

The logical architecture of CLASS consists of: input database, road network module, demand module, assignment module and output module (Figure 3). Below, for the sake of

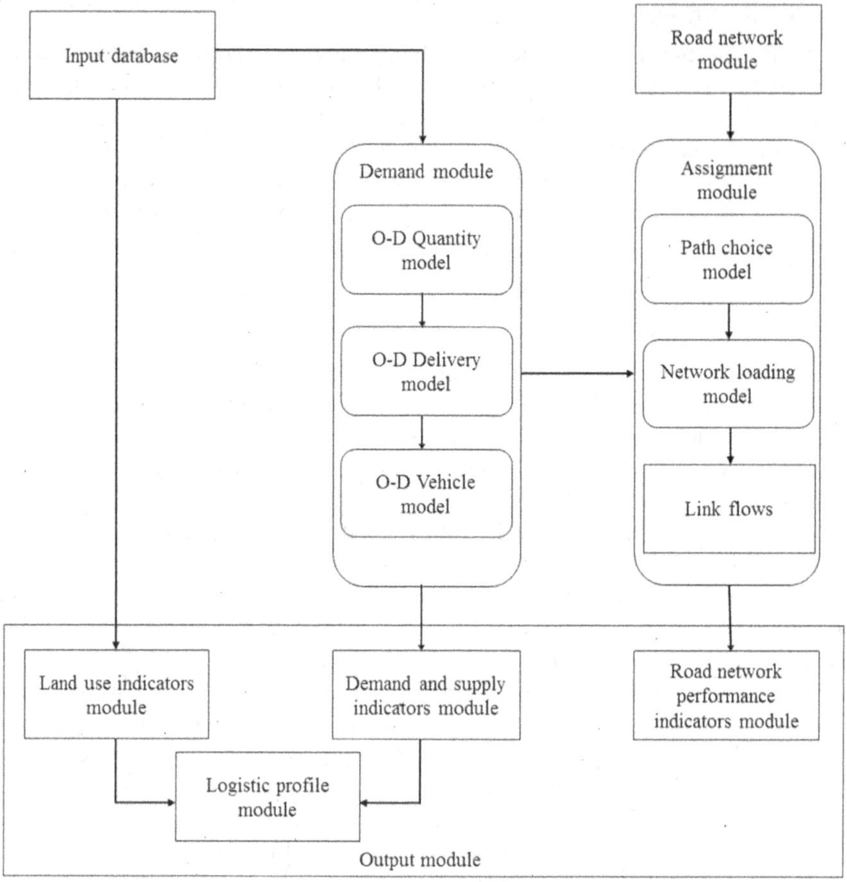

Figure 3. CLASS framework (Comi & Rosati, 2013).

readability, the main characteristics of DSS will be summarized. For more details, refer to Comi and Rosati (2013).

The *input database* contains information on exogenous variables of the scenario, presence and number of logistic infrastructures, and information about freight vehicle road accidents.

The *road network* module comprises the graph of the main road network and relative link cost functions specific to both passenger and freight vehicles. The module simulates the relevant aspects of travel demand and includes the demand models that give the O–D matrices, which are the input for the subsequent assignment sub-system.

The *assignment* module includes path choice models and network loading models for both passenger and freight vehicles. The network loading model simulates how O–D vehicle flows load the paths and the links of the road network and estimates the link flows, i.e. the number of cars and freight vehicles on each network link.

The *output* module allows to estimate, using data and results of above modules, the city logistics scenario indicators. It includes four sub-modules: land-use indicators, demand and supply, logistic profile and road network performances.

3. Used shopping–restocking modelling framework

In this section the used and implemented shopping–restocking modelling framework is synthetized. Then, the advancement in shopping trip generation modelling is reported.

3.1. *The shopping model sub-system*

Assuming that the decision-maker (i.e. end consumer) is in zone o, the choice dimensions involved are: the number of trips (x) for shopping, the type of shop (k; e.g. small, medium and large) and destination (d) and the transport mode (or sequence of modes; m). According to survey results (Comi & Nuzzolo, 2014), the simulation period h is the week and for simplicity of notation, it will be omitted. Besides, in order to point out seasonal trends, different models can be estimated with similar functional forms. The global demand function can be decomposed into the product of sub-models, each of which relates to one or more choice dimensions. The sequence used is the following:

$$D^i_{od}[skm] = D^i_{o.}[s] \cdot p^i[dk/so] \cdot p^i[m/dkso], \tag{1}$$

where

- $D^i_{od}[skm]$ is the weekly average number of trips with origin in zone o undertaken by the end consumer belonging to category i (e.g. families with one or more components) for purchasing goods of type s (e.g. foodstuffs) in the type of retail outlet k (e.g. small, medium and large retail outlets) located in zone d by using transport mode m;
- $D^i_{o.}[s]$ is the weekly average number of trips undertaken by end consumers belonging to category i for purchasing goods of type s with origin in zone o, obtained by a *trip generation model*;
- $p^i[dk/so]$ is the probability that users, undertaking a trip from o, travel to destination zone d for purchasing at shop type k, obtained by a *shop type and location choice* model;
- $p^i[m/dkso]$ is the probability that users, travelling between o and d for shopping in shop type k, use transport mode m, obtained by a *mode choice* model.

Finally, the quantities required by each zone to satisfy end-consumer needs can be obtained by introducing a *quantity purchase* model (Russo & Comi, 2010b). This model gives us the probability that the end consumer, arriving in a given zone, purchases something of a certain size. Therefore, the total quantity of goods of type s attracted by retail outlet k in zone d, $QT_d[sk]$, can be calculated as

$$\begin{aligned} QT_d[sk] &= \sum_i Q^i_d[sk] + QE^i_d[sk] \\ &= \sum_i \sum_{o,m,dim} D^i_{od}[skm] \cdot p^i[dim/mks] \cdot dim + QE^i_d[sk], \end{aligned} \tag{2}$$

where

- $Q^i_d[sk]$ is the goods quantity bought/sold in retail outlet k in zone d given by the demand of end consumers belonging to category i living in a zone *within* the study area;
- $QE^i_d[sk]$ is the goods quantity bought/sold in retail outlet k in d given by the demand of end consumers belonging to category i living in a zone *external* to the study area;

- *dim* is the dimension of purchases, e.g. expressed in kg;
- $p^i[dim/mks]$ is the probability that a trip concludes with a purchase of dimension *dim* conditional upon undertaking a trip from zone *o* to retail outlet *k* for a purchase of goods of type *s* using the transport mode *m*.

In the following, we consider the study area as a closed system and then assume that the goods quantity bought by end consumers living in a zone external to the study area can be neglected ($QE^i_d[sk] = 0$).

A complete description of the above models is reported in Nuzzolo and Comi (2014b, 2014c). In the following a new trip generation model, calibrated using some surveys carried out in the city of Rome, is reported.

3.1.1. *New shopping trip generation model*

Although the number of shopping trips is also related to the characteristics of the zone of residence, as a first approximation we can express them only in relation to the main demographic and socio-economic characteristics of the end consumers (e.g. age, gender, number of household members and type of employment) that can be easily obtained from the Italian Statistics database (ISTAT). Besides, the current trip generation models estimate the average shopping trip index (i.e. average number of trips undertaken by end consumers) through two types of models: aggregate ones, in which the explanatory variables corresponding to the zone of origin (e.g. population, employees related to retail activities, number of shops; Gonzalez-Feliu et al., 2012; Holguin-Veras et al., 2011; Sanchez-Diaz et al., 2013) or disaggregate ones, in which the explanatory variables refer to single user (Comi & Conte, 2011; Comi & Nuzzolo, 2014). Then, according to the recalled modelling framework and to the aim of this study new individual shopping models were developed in order to express the end-consumers' choices as a function of their characteristics, i.e. age, gender and employment status.

The shopping models were developed using the results of some surveys carried out in the city of Rome where more than 900 end consumers (more than 300 households) were interviewed (Comi & Nuzzolo, 2014). Of the sampled households, 74% had more than three members. Only 3% made a trip chain (i.e. visit to more than one zone during the same shopping trip); 22% stated that they made further shopping trips during the week (average of 1.34 weekly trips) without buying anything (even if they were left to spend more than €30). Mainly, the shopping trips start from home, with higher percentages for foodstuffs. Only the 2% of purchase trips are undertaken by end consumers younger than 19 years, and then they were not considered in the following. The models estimated and reported in the following refer to trips undertaken by end consumers older than 20 years, for purchasing in a shop, spending more than €30 in order to avoid to include trips for which shopping was not the main scope of the journey. Furthermore, collected data showed that possible interdependences among trips for purchasing products belonging to different freight types can be neglected.

We identified four main classes of goods: foodstuffs, hygiene and household products, clothing and other. According to this classification, 36% of weekly shopping trips were undertaken for foodstuffs, 19% for hygiene and household products, 27% for clothing products and the remaining 18% for other products. Most trips (77%) were undertaken to buy only one type of goods, 17% for two types and 6% for more than three. Given the data described above, the weekly average number of trips undertaken by end consumers for purchasing goods of type *s* with origin in zone *o*, $D_o[s]$, is expressed as

$$D_{o.}[s] = ns[o] \cdot ms[o] = ns[o] \cdot \sum_j \beta_j \cdot X_{jo}, \tag{3}$$

where

- $ns[o]$ is the number of inhabitants over 20 years old residing in traffic zone o;
- $ms[o]$ is the average number of weekly trips undertaken by inhabitants older than 20; it is expressed as a linear function in the coefficients β_j of attributes X_{jo}.

The considered attributes X_{jo} are the values of demographic and socio-economic variables, such as the number of household members, number of car per households, and dummy variable specified according to age, gender and type of employment. The individual estimated parameters for the four goods types are reported in Table 1. We can see that the parameters are statistically significant as demonstrated by t-st values. As confirmed by survey statistics, parameter analysis shows that housewives undertake more trips than those in other types of employment, while young people travel less than elders, and men mainly for other types of goods.

3.2. *Restocking model sub-system*

Once the quantity of goods bought/sold in retail outlet k in zone d, $QT_d[sk]$, has been estimated by the above model sub-system, the restocking quantity flows characterized for

Table 1. Average number of weekly shopping trips made by residents (older than 20 years): parameter estimation.

		Freight type			
Attributes	Type of variable	Foodstuffs	Hygiene and household products	Clothing	Other
Number of household components		−0.05 (−3.49)	−0.03 (−2.09)	−0.04 (−1.97)	
Average number of car per family	no. cars on no. of household members	0.12 (1.70)	0.07 (1.33)		0.13 (2.48)
Employees	0/1	0.11 (2.42)		0.24 (2.42)	0.06 (1.67)
Independent worker	0/1			0.19 (1.78)	0.17 (3.36)
Other type of employment	0/1			0.24 (2.64)	
Student	0/1				0.13 (3.07)
Age between 20 and 44 years	0/1	0.18 (2.80)	0.12 (2.42)	0.18 (3.01)	0.08 (1.88)
Age between 45 and 64 years	0/1	0.50 (7.37)	0.33 (6.72)	0.24 (3.60)	0.12 (2.76)
Over 65	0/1	0.65 (6.59)	0.19 (2.51)		0.19 (2.61)
Housewife	0/1	0.26 (3.55)			
Female	0/1	0.18 (4.68)	0.08 (2.69)	0.12 (3.43)	−0.17 (−6.24)
R^2		0.40	0.23	0.28	0.21

Note: (−) t-st value.

vehicle type v, QV_{od}, departing from zone o can be obtained as follows:

$$QV_{od}[skv] = QT_d[sk] \cdot p[o/dks] \cdot p[v/dk], \tag{4}$$

where

- $QV_{od}[skv]$ is the freight quantity of type s bought/sold in retail outlet k in zone d transported on pair od by vehicle type v;
- $p[o/dks]$ is the probability that the freight attracted by outlet type k located in zone d comes from warehouse zone o, obtained by an *acquisition model*;
- $p[v/dk]$ is the probability that the freight attracted by outlet type k located in zone d and coming from zone o is transported by vehicle type v, obtained by a *vehicle choice model*.

These models are not the primary focus of this paper and for details refer to Nuzzolo and Comi (2013, 2014d). The focus here is on the application of a joint modelling framework to an urban transportation network when demographic, socio-economic and economic activity location changes occur, a topic for which the literature is quite sparse (Kawamura and Sriraj, 2012; Sanchez-Diaz et al., 2013).

4. Application test to a medium-size urban area

The recalled modelling framework, implemented within CLASS, was tested studying the effects on freight mobility due to changes in demographic and socio-economic characteristics and in e-shopping attitudes, expected for the year 2025. Furthermore, the simulation models were also tested to forecast the effects of land-use governance policies as warehouse and shop relocations.

The test area comprises the Municipality of the medium-size urban area of Padua in northern Italy and 13 small neighbouring municipalities (Figure 4). The total population in 2011 was about 370,000, mainly concentrated in the centre of Padua where residential density is over 18 inh./ha. In the study area, the total number of shops is 6761 with 23,144 retail employees that are mainly located in the historical city centre and in the small touristic town of Abano Terme, in the south of the study area. There were 4750 warehouses with 17,016 warehouse employees, mainly located west of the city centre, near the boundary with Noventa Padovana, where a large warehouse centre is located (Padua City Porto).

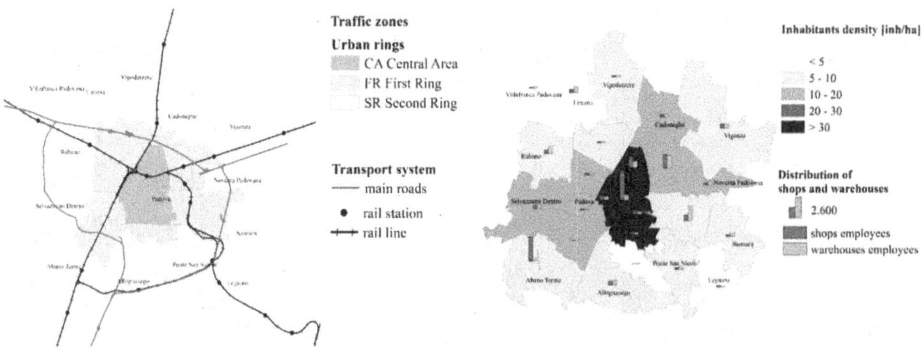

Figure 4. The study area and distribution of shops and warehouses and inhabitant density in the 25 traffic zones.

The study area was split into 25 traffic zones. This area was chosen as test because it is an example of an urban area, which already has a well-balanced distribution of freight activity location. Padua's city council has long sought to deal with the problems of urban freight transport, as shown by the successful Cityporto logistics scheme. This scheme entails urban freight consolidation and distribution in the freight village known as 'Interporto Padova' and has been operative since 2004 (Gonzalez-Feliu & Morana, 2010; Vaghi & Percoco, 2011). Furthermore, its well-defined commercial supply suggests that it may be considered a closed system, validating the assumptions that the goods quantity bought by end consumers living in zones external to the study area can be neglected.

4.1. *Scenario definition*

In our test, the current scenario (CS) and the following future scenarios for the year 2025 are simulated and compared:

- trend scenario (TS), which includes the simulation of the effects of the changes in shopping activity due to changes in demographic and socio-economic characteristics (TSA) and in e-shopping attitudes (TSB);
- design scenario (DS), with some land-use governance measures relative to the relocation of logistics and retailing activities.

4.1.1. *Trend scenario*

In the *TS*, the effects of demographic and socio-economic changes on end-consumer choices, such as where to shop and how to get there, are analysed. In particular, we suppose to keep the main demographic and socio-economic trends revealed in the last 10 years. In order to emphasize the above effects, in the following we assume that no modifications occur on total population and residence locations.

In the last 10 years, there is a different trend according to age: the class of inhabitants between 20 and 44 years has decreased, while the percentage in the upper two age groups (over 45) has increased. As regards socio-economic status, the class of employees has increased, while the percentages of independent workers and other types of employment have decrease. Age, employment status and number of cars per household distributions change according to the estimated trends, as pictured in Figure 5.

Further, in the TS, it is necessary to take into account the effects due to changes in e-shopping, too. In fact, the growth in the home deliveries and the increase in services offered by retailers (such as click & collect) all lead to changes in the pattern of urban freight flows and vehicle movements in cities. The changes can be influenced by wider factors such as demographic change and the adoption of new consumer technologies. In our survey, the shares of e-purchases made by interviewees according to the three identified age classes are reported in Table 2. Youngers purchase more than elders, especially other products. In order to take into account the growth of e-shopping, based on the revealed shares (Table 2) and the current trends revealed in some worldwide countries (Visser, Nemoto, & Browne, 2014), the possibility of making this type of purchase was considered, pointing out the inclination to make e-shopping changes with age and freight type.

4.1.2. *Design scenario*

The *DS* can be considered a medium/long-term result of some different land-use governance measures that local administrators could promote in order to improve the sustainability of the

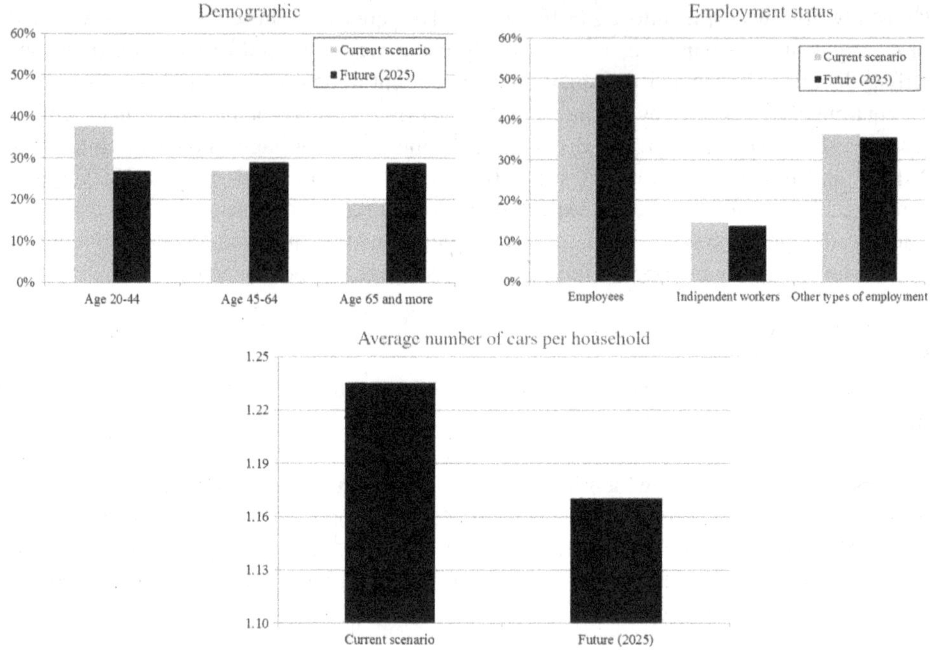

Figure 5. Future scenario: demographic and socio-economic composition of investigated population classes.

Table 2. Current revealed average percentage of weekly e-purchases made by residents (older than 20 years).

Age	Foodstuffs	Hygiene and household products	Clothing	Other	Average
Age between 20 and 44 years	0.0%	14.5%	10.3%	46.0%	21.3%
Age between 45 and 64 years	0.4%	4.1%	4.7%	25.0%	6.3%
Older than 65 years	0.0%	0.0%	0.0%	0.0%	0.0%
Average	0.3%	6.6%	7.2%	35.7%	11.6%
Employees	0.6%	7.4%	6.0%	33.0%	9.5%
Independent workers	0.0%	3.8%	5.7%	31.0%	12.8%
Other types of job	0.0%	6.7%	8.5%	39.8%	13.1%
Average	0.3%	6.6%	7.2%	35.7%	11.6%
Housewives	0.0%	0.0%	4.8%	28.6%	2.5%

city, reducing internal and external transportation costs. The *DS* is based on the statements that the costs of freight distribution and shopping trips depend on the locations in the urban area of end consumers, warehouses, distribution centres and retail outlets. From the freight distribution point of view, the location outside residential or central zones of warehouses and distribution centres increases restocking costs by increasing the distances between retailers and distribution facilities. The location of large retail businesses outside residential or central zones reduces restocking costs by reducing the distances between retailers and restocking activities and increasing the average transported quantity and vehicle size. As regards the impact of shopping mobility, the location of large retail businesses outside the residential or

Table 3. DS definition: shares of retail and warehouse employees with respect to the total number.

	CS		Future (2025)	
	RE	WHE	RE	WHE
D% Central area (CA)	37%	18%	37%	14%
D% First ring (FR)	20%	35%	29%	48%
D% Second ring (SR)	43%	48%	34%	38%
Total	100%	100%	100%	100%

Note: Future scenario (2025): increase in warehousing and distribution centre density in the first ring and an increase in medium-size retail businesses in the first ring; RE: retail employees; WHE: warehouse employees.

Table 4. Synopsis of future scenario definition.

Future scenario (2025)	Demographic and socio-economic changes	E-shopping increase	Shop and warehouse relocation
Trend scenario A (TSA)	X		
Trend scenario B (TSB)	X	X	
DS	X	X	X

central zones reduces the number of shopping trips (trip frequency) but increases shopping trip lengths and car use, while reducing the attractiveness of city centres.

Land-use scenario was defined hypothesizing to shift both retail and warehouse employees among three identified urban spaces (i.e. centre, the first and the second rings; see Figure 4). Scenario definition was made in terms of percentages of retail and warehouse employees with respect to the total number and the CS (status quo). Then, the future land-use scenario was defined moving the retail employees from the second ring to the first ring and the warehouse employees from the centre and the second ring to the first ring (Table 3). According to the general strategies, the retail employees of the central area were not moved in order not to modify the attraction of city centre, while the medium and large retail outlets and the warehouses are located in high accessible areas, along major roads and junctions. Therefore, based on the above assumptions three scenarios were simulated (Table 4) and the main obtained results are described in the following section.

4.2. *Simulation results and discussion*

The number of future daily store shopping trips in scenario TSA is about 56,000 with an average increase of 9.8% with respect to the CS, with different percentages according to age and freight types, as reported in Tables 5 and 6. When the development of e-shopping is also considered (Scenario TSB), we observe a smaller increase of only the 3.9%. In particular, we observe that trips for foodstuffs purchases increase more than others because of ageing and the few impacts of e-shopping. In fact, as expected the elders tend to make more trips because of considerable time is available and they tend to buy in small or medium retail outlets, generally located close to the residential areas. It is different for other products, which are mainly bought at medium–large retail outlets. In fact, in the future scenario TSA we observe an increase of 31.2%, while in scenarios TSB and DS a decrease in daily trips of about 18%. This result is justified by the inclination to make e-shopping and of elders to buy in small and medium shops.

Table 5. Scenario comparison: variation of store shopping trips according to freight types and age.

Age	Foodstuffs	Hygiene and household products	Clothing	Other products	Average
TSA					
20–44	−20.3%	−24.9%	−26.5%	−7.0%	−22.6%
45–64	19.8%	13.0%	11.0%	39.3%	16.6%
65 and more	67.7%	58.9%	57.0%	94.0%	63.9%
Average	12.8%	6.4%	4.5%	31.2%	9.8%
TSB and DS					
20—44	−21.9%	−29.8%	−29.6%	−42.1%	−26.7%
45—64	17.5%	5.6%	6.4%	−13.2%	10.4%
65 and more	64.4%	48.6%	50.5%	20.8%	55.1%
Average	10.6%	−0.5%	0.2%	−18.3%	3.9%

Table 6. Scenario comparison: variation of store shopping trips according to freight types and type of retail outlets.

Freight type	Small retail outlets	Medium retail outlet	Large retail outlet	Average
TSA				
Foodstuffs	10.7%	26.9%	2.2%	12.8%
Hygiene and household products	62.0%	−21.2%	10.0%	6.4%
Clothing	5.9%	−21.5%	53.6%	4.5%
Other products	31.5%	−1.0%	94.0%	31.2%
Average	16.3%	−3.8%	20.3%	9.8%
TSB and DS				
Foodstuffs	8.6%	24.4%	0.2%	10.6%
Hygiene and household products	2.4%	9.6%	−16.5%	−0.5%
Clothing	34.4%	−12.8%	−20.5%	0.2%
Other products	8.5%	−28.5%	−34.8%	−18.3%
Average	15.5%	4.3%	−10.0%	3.9%

Table 7. Scenario comparison: trip variations with respect to scenario CS.

	TSA				TSB and design scenario (DSA)			
	Small retail	Medium retail	Large retail	Average	Small retail	Medium retail	Large retail	Average
On foot	12.6%	6.0%	−5.6%	11.9%	6.6%	0.0%	−11.1%	6.0%
Private car	23.5%	10.6%	−5.5%	9.9%	16.9%	4.3%	10.0%	4.0%
Transit	22.3%	10.2%	−5.5%	6.3%	15.8%	4.0%	10.0%	0.8%
Average	22.0%	10.5%	5.5%	9.8%	15.5%	4.3%	10.0%	3.9%

In relation to the mode used, shopping trips increase mainly on car and on foot (Table 7), due mainly to the increase in trips undertaken by elders who travel more on these modes.

The results of simulations are reported as variations of some indicators of the future scenarios compared with the current one (CS). As many outcome indicators are a function of vehicle-kms, in the first instance, the total distance covered by car and commercial

Table 8. Scenario comparison: variations of veh-kms with respect to scenario CS.

Scenario	Private cars	Light goods vehicles	Medium goods vehicles	Heavy goods vehicles	Average[a]
TSA	8.4%	9.4%	12.1%	17.6%	8.5%
TSB	2.6%	0.3%	2.8%	8.2%	2.5%
DS	2.6%	−3.1%	−2.3%	−0.4%	2.3%

[a]Equivalent veh-kms.

vehicles has been considered as main indicator (Table 8). In particular, the equivalent veh-kms are computed, with specific weights for cars and light, medium and heavy goods vehicles. Focusing on the scenario DS, which has the same demographic and socio-economic characteristics of scenario TSB and the same incidence of e-shopping, the total equivalent veh-kms increase of 2.3% (Table 8), but with good results in restocking trips. We observe a steady value for heavy goods veh-kms and a decrease in light and medium goods veh-kms of 2.3% and 3.1%, respectively.

5. Conclusions and further developments

This paper presents a modelling framework that can be used in order to forecast urban freight transport flows in medium/long-term scenarios and the results of its application to a medium-size town are reported. The main results confirm the modelling goodness and at the same time demonstrate that changes in demographic and socio-economic characteristics could cause relevant effects, in particular increasing car use in shopping mobility. The e-shopping could limit the negative effects of these changes, decreasing shopping trip production, but the pattern of home deliveries has to be investigated. The expectation is that Internet shopping development could cause more deliveries and more freight vehicles in residential areas. Then, new actions have to be investigated in order to promote consolidation for making home deliveries more efficient.

The relocation of commercial and logistics centres, with a distribution in the urban area more close to the residential distribution, could drive a different restocking pattern with a consequent reduction in freight vehicle mobility. Anyway, this reduction is not very relevant and therefore further city logistics measures have to be implemented.

Further analyses are also in progress to improve these first results, developing other models, such as shopping mode choice models, and including zonal and level-of-service attributes (e.g. accessibility) in shopping trip generation, distribution and restocking models.

Acknowledgements

The authors thank the anonymous reviewers for their suggestions, which were most useful in revising this paper.

References

Ambrosini, C., Gonzalez-Feliu, J., & Toilier, F. (2013). A design methodology for scenario-analysis in urban freight modeling. *European Transport/Trasporti Europei*, *54*, paper no. 7.

Ambrosini, C., Meimbresse, B., Routhier, J. L., & Sonntag, H. (2008). Urban freight modeling: A review. In E. Taniguchi & R. G. Thompson (Eds.), *Innovations for city logistics* (pp. 197–212). Hauppauge, NY: Nova Science Publishing.

Anand, N., Quak, H., Van Duin, R., & Tavasszy, L. (2012). City logistics modeling efforts: Trends and gaps – A review. *Procedia – Social and Behavioral Sciences, 39*, 101–115.

Barone, V., Crocco, F., & Mongelli, D. W. (2014a). Freight transport demand models for applications in urban areas. *Applied Mechanics and Materials, 442*, 634–644.

Barone, V., Crocco, F., & Mongelli, D.W.E. (2014b). Models of choice between shopping and e-shopping. *Applied Mechanics and Materials, 442*, 607–616.

Boerkamps, J. H. K., van Binsbergen, A. J., & Bovy, P. H. L. (2000). Modeling behavioral aspects of urban freight movement in supply chains. *Transportation Research Record, 1725*, 17–25.

Browne, M., Allen, J., Nemoto, T., Patier, D., & Visser, J. (2012). Reducing social and environmental impacts of urban freight transport: A review of some major cities. *Procedia – Social and Behavioral Sciences, 39*, 19–33.

Cascetta, E. (2009). *Transportation systems analysis: Models and applications*. New York: Springer Science + Business Media.

City Ports. (2005). *City Ports – project interim report*. Emilia-Romagna Region.

Comi, A., & Conte, E. (2011). A modelling system for estimating freight quantities attracted by cities. In A. Pratelli & C. A. Brebbia (Eds.), *Urban transport XVII: Urban transport and the environment in the 21st century* (pp. 423–434). Southampton: WIT press. doi:10.2495/UT110361

Comi, A., Donnelly, R., & Russo, F. (2014). Urban freight models (chapter 8). In L. Tavasszy & J. De Jong (Eds.), *Modelling freight transport* (pp. 163–200). London: Elsevier. doi:10.1016/B978-0-12-410400-6.00008-2

Comi, A., & Nuzzolo, A. (2014). Simulating urban freight flows with combined shopping and restocking demand models. *Procedia – Social and Behavioral Sciences, 125*, 49–61. doi:10.1016/j.sbspro.2014.01.1455.

Comi, A., & Rosati, L. (2013). CLASS: A city logistics analysis and simulation support system. *Procedia – Social and Behavioral Sciences, 87*, 321–337. doi:10.1016/j.sbspro.2013.10.613

Crainic, T. G. (2008). City logistics. In Z. L. Chen & S. Raghavan (Eds.), *Tutorials in operations research 2008. State-of-the-art decision making tools in the information-intensive age* (pp. 181–212). Hanover, NH: INFORMS, e-book.

Crocco, F., De Marco, S., Iaquinta, P., & Mongelli, D. W. (2010). Freight transport in urban areas: An integrated system of models to simulate freight demand and passengers demand for purchase trips. *International Journal of Mathematical Models and Methods in Applied Sciences, 4*(4), 265–273.

Dablanc, L. (2007). Goods transport in large European cities: Difficult to organize, difficult to modernize. *Transportation Research Part A: Policy and Practice, 41*(3), 280–285.

Gentile, G., & Vigo, D. (2013). Movement generation and trip distribution for freight demand modelling applied to city logistics. *European Transport/Trasporti Europei, 54*, paper n° 6.

Gonzalez-Feliu, J., Ambrosini, C., Pluvinet, P., Toilier, F., & Routhier, J. L. (2012). A simulation framework for evaluating the impacts of urban goods transport in terms of road occupancy. *Journal of Computational Science, 3*(4), 206–215.

Gonzalez-Feliu, J., & Morana, J. (2010). Are city logistics solutions sustainable? The cityporto case. *TeMA. Journal of Land Use, Mobility and Environment, 3*(2), 55–64.

Gonzalez-Feliu, J., & Routhier J. (2012). Modeling urban goods movement: How to be oriented with so many approaches? *Procedia – Social and Behavioral Sciences, 39*, 89–100.

Gonzalez-Feliu, J., Toilier, F., & Routhier, J. L. (2010). End consumer goods movement generation in French medium urban areas. *Procedia – Social and Behavioral Sciences, 2*(3), 6189–6204.

Guzzo, R., & Mazzulla, G. (2006). La distribuzione urbana delle merci: Proposta di modelli per la stima delle quantità movimentate. In A. Nuzzolo & P. O. Coppola (Eds.), *Limiti e Prospettive di Sviluppo del Trasporto Ferroviario delle Merci* (pp. 408–421). Milan: Franco Angeli.

Holguín-Veras, J., Jaller, M., Destro, L., Ban, X. J., Lawson, C., & Levinson, H. S. (2011). Freight generation, freight trip generation, and perils of using constant trip rates. *Transportation Research Record: Journal of the Transportation Research Board, 2224*(1), 68–81.

Kawamura, H., & Sriraj, P. S. (2012). *Effect of the built environment on urban freight movement and operations*. Proceeding of the 91st Transportation Research Board Annual Meeting, Washington, DC, USA.

Lindholm, M. (2013). Urban freight transport from a local authority perspective – A literature review. *European Transport/Trasporti Europei, 54*, paper n° 3.

Lohse, D. (2004). *Travel demand modelling with model EVA – simultaneous model for trip generation, trip distribution and mode choice*. Working paper, TU Dresden.

Miodonski, D., & Kawamura, K. (2012). Effects of built environment on freight consumption. *Procedia – Social and Behavioral Sciences, 39*, 74–88.

Muñuzuri, J., & Gonzalez-Feliu, J. (2013). Decision-making tools and procedures for city logistics. An introduction to the special issue on decision support for urban logistics. In *European Transport/Trasporti Europei, 54*, paper n° 1.

Nuzzolo, A., & Comi, A. (2013). Tactical and operational city logistics: Freight vehicle flow modeling (chapter 21). In M. B. Akiva, H. Meersman & E. Van de Voorde (Eds.), *Freight transport modelling* (chapter 21, pp. 433–451). Bingley: Emerald Group Publishing.

Nuzzolo, A., & Comi, A. (2014a). Urban freight transport policies in Rome: Lessons learned and the road ahead. *Journal of Urbanism: International Research on Placemaking and Urban Sustainability*. doi:10.1080/17549175.2014.884976

Nuzzolo, A., & Comi, A. (2014b). City logistics planning: Demand modelling requirements for direct effect forecasting. *Procedia – Social and Behavioral Sciences, 125*, 239–250. doi:10.1016/j.sbspro.2014.01.1470.

Nuzzolo, A., & Comi, A. (2014c). Direct effects of city logistics measures and urban freight demand models. In J. Gonzalez-Feliu, F. Semet, & J. L. Routhier (Eds.), *Sustainable urban logistics: Concepts, methods and information systems* (pp. 211–226). Berlin: Springer-Verlag.

Nuzzolo, A., & Comi, A. (2014d). Urban freight demand forecasting: A mixed quantity/delivery/vehicle-based model. *Transportation Research Part E: Logistics and Transportation Review, 65*, 84–98. doi:10.1016/j.tre.2013.12.014.

Nuzzolo, A., Coppola, P., & Comi, A. (2013). Freight transport modeling: Review and future challenges. *International Journal of Transport Economics, XL*(2), 151–181.

Oppenheim, N. (1994). *Urban travel demand modeling*. New York: John Wiley & Son.

Ortuzar, J. de D., & Willumsen, L. (2001). *Modelling transport*. Chichester: John Wiley & Sons.

Routhier, J. L., & Toilier, F. (2007). *FRETURB V3, a policy oriented software of modelling urban goods movement*. Proceedings of the 11th world conference on transport research, Berkeley, CA.

Russo, F., & Comi, A. (2004). *A state of the art on urban freight distribution at European scale*. Proceedings of the European conference on mobility management, Lyon, France.

Russo, F., & Comi, A. (2006). Demand models for city logistics: A state of the art and a proposed integrated system. In R. G. Thompson & E. Taniguchi (Eds.), *Recent advances in city logistics* (pp. 91–105). Amsterdam: Elsevier.

Russo, F., & Comi, A. (2010a). A classification of city logistics measures and connected impacts. *Procedia – Social and Behavioral Sciences, 2*(3), 6355–6365. doi:10.1016/j.sbspro.2010.04.044

Russo, F., & Comi, A. (2010b). A modelling system to simulate goods movements at an urban scale. *Transportation, 37*(6), 987–1009. doi:10.1007/s11116-010-9276-y

Russo, F., & Comi, A. (2013). Impacts of accidents involving shopping and restocking vehicles on an urban road network. *WIT Transactions on the Built Environment, 134*, 517–528. doi:10.2495/SAFE130461

Sanchez-Diaz, I., Holguin-Veras, J., & Wang, C. (2013). *Assessing the role of land-use, network characteristics and spatial effects on freight trip attraction*. Proceedings of the 92nd TRB annual meeting, Transportation Research Board of the National Academies, Washington, DC, USA.

Schoemaker, J., Allen, J., Huschebek, M., & Monigl, J. (2006). "Quantification of urban freight transport effects I." BESTUFS Consortium. Retrieved from www.bestufs.net

Sonntag, H. (1985). A computer model of urban commercial traffic. *Transport, Policy and Decision Making, 3*(2), 171–180.

Stathopoulos, A., Valeri, E., & Marcucci, E. (2012). Stakeholder reactions to urban freight policy innovation. *Journal of Transport Geography, 22*, 34–45.

Taniguchi, E., Thompson, R. G., & Yamada, T. (2001). *City logistics: Network modelling and intelligent transport systems*. Amsterdam: Pergamon.

Taniguchi, E., Thompson, R. G., & Yamada, T. (2012). Emerging techniques for enhancing the practical application of city logistics models. *Procedia – Social and Behavioral Sciences, 39*, 3–18.

Vaghi, C., & Percoco, M. (2011). City logistics in Italy: Success factors and environmental performance. In C. Macharis & S. Melo (Eds.), *City distribution and urban freight transport: Multiple perspectives* (chapter 7, 151–175). Bingley: Emerald.

Visser, J., Nemoto, T., & Browne, M. (2014). Home deliveries and the impacts on urban freight transport: A review. *Procedia – Social and Behavioral Sciences, 125*, 15–27.

Model of debris collection operation after disasters and its application in urban area

Andie Pramudita and Eiichi Taniguchi

Department of Urban Management, Kyoto University, Kyotodaigaku-Katsura, Kyoto, Japan

Management of debris is a concern after any major disaster. In particular, debris removal after a disaster presents challenges unique to that disaster. Often, the debris removal process takes months or even years to finish. It is likely to be a concern for some time to come since there exists many factors that make it such a costly and complex operation. The cost is mostly arising from the cost of collection and transportation to the disposal sites. The debris collection and transportation routing problem is the subject of this study. The debris collection operation after disasters is a new capacitated arc routing problem (CARP). The uniqueness of this problem is due to the limited access from one section to the other, as a result of the blocked access by debris. Therefore a new constraint, which is developed in this study as access possibility constraint, has been added to the classical CARP. A tabu search meta-heuristics is also proposed to solve the augmented CARP formulation for the debris collection operation problem. Case studies on a test network as well as on realistic instances based on estimates of debris due to likely large-scale natural disaster in the Tokyo Metropolitan Area have also been reported at the end under various scenarios such as with or without intermediate depot as well as single vs. multiple vehicles (groups) operation.

1. Introduction

Management of debris is a concern after any major disaster. In particular, debris removal after a disaster presents challenges unique to that disaster. Often, the debris removal process takes months or even years to finish. As an illustration to allow one to imagine how large the amounts of debris, Luther (2008) reported that a total of about 113.5 million cubic yards of debris was leftover in Alabama, Mississippi and Louisiana, as an aftermath of Hurricane Katrina; Federal Emergency Management Agency (FEMA) an estimated debris removal cost of over US$4 billion as federal funding. It is likely to be a concern for some time to come since there exists many factors that make it such a costly and complex operation. The cost is mostly arising from the cost of collection and transportation to the disposal sites. Technical factors which form the cost of this process are first limited space to establish appropriate temporary or final disposal sites. The second factor is the cost of providing necessary heavy vehicles and tools to execute the debris collection operation. The third factor is the transportation cost of debris disposal that depends on vehicle's route choice to transport the debris to the temporary or final disposal sites. The debris collection and transportation routing problem will be the subject of this study.

The routing problem becomes one of the important issues in cost efficiency considering that vehicle's route choice greatly affect total travel cost that is incurred in the debris collection operation. In the context of routing problem, the following research questions can arise: What is the correlation between travel cost and routing? How to formulate this kind of problem with appropriate mathematical models? How to solve such mathematical models? (i.e. which solution algorithm shall be used to obtain the optimum cost?)

In this study, the disaster is assumed to be catastrophic that leaves large scale of debris scattered on almost whole affected area including existing access road. This assumption will lead to disruption of road accessibility or even blocked off entirely. Debris removal operation even though with limited information of the road accessibility is necessary. The information of road network accessibility can be determined by managing vehicles route choice, related to the sequence in opening blocked road. Therefore at this stage, the debris collection operation can be considered as an operation to remove the debris that blocks roads in order to rebuild the access connectivity in such area. To address these research questions, a variant of the undirected capacitated arc routing problem (CARP) was chosen. The problem in this study is motivated from debris collection operation after disasters; for that a modification in classical CARP is required. In this new CARP variant, roads are treated as a set of arcs. A set of required arcs consists of arcs that are covered by debris, thus they have demands to service. The objective function of the CARP is to service all required arcs in the graph at least cost with feasible vehicle routes.

In the debris collection problem, the sequences in visiting and servicing arcs are very important since one section may block other sections. Initially, only adjacent arcs can be connected with each other, while for distant arcs, there may be no way to be connected before removing the blocked access first. Another matter that should be paid attention to is that routes also can only be operated in a particular sequence, considering that one completed route will affect the access possibility for the other routes. This constraint was developed in this study as a binary matrix termed as the access possibility matrix, where an entry is equal to 1 if a vehicle can possibly move from one arc to another; 0 otherwise.

To better understand the problem, let us see a problem illustration in Figure 1. At stage 1, the access possibility from 0 to 1 is equal to 1 (i.e. $p_{01} = 1$); and $p_{02} = 0$ because the access is still blocked. In stage 2 after arc no. 1 has been serviced, p_{02} becomes 1. It means that vehicle should service arc no. 1 first, before being allowed to service arc no. 2 through the shortest path. The access possibility from one point to other always changes every time a single arc has been serviced by a vehicle.

Similar to the various CARP-related researches (as mentioned in detail in next section), the underlying CARP to our debris collection operation in this study was transformed into the capacitated vehicle routing problem (CVRP). Both the CARP and the CVRP are in fact closely related, the main difference being that in the CARP customers are set of arcs while in the CVRP customers are set of nodes. The resulting model formulation was applied to solve a realistic problem based on disasters debris estimation data resulting from large-scale earthquake and flood disasters scenarios in the Tokyo Metropolitan Area by Hirayama, Shimaoka, Fujiwara, Okayama, and Kawata (2010). In addition to that, spatial and statistical data of the Tokyo Metropolitan Area were also used based on Japanese Standard Grid Square and Grid Square Code used for the Statistics (Announcement No. 143 by the Administrative Management Agency Japan, on 12 July 1973).

The remaining paper is organized as follows. Literature review of the undirected CARP similar to our debris collection operation problem is first introduced in Section 2. Then,

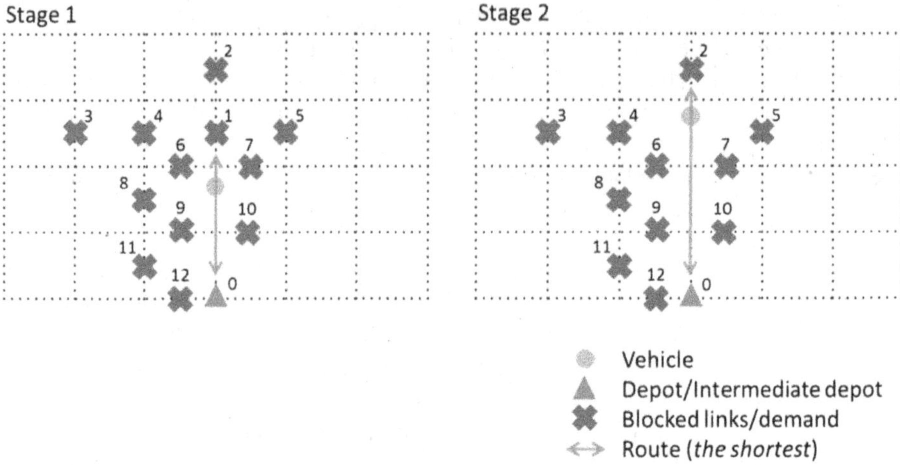

Figure 1. Problem illustration.

mathematical formulation of the problem is presented in Section 3. Meta-heuristics solution technique and problem instances are reported in Section 4. Application of model formulation to a realistic case study of the Tokyo Metropolitan Area disasters debris problem is presented in Section 5. Finally, the conclusion follows in Section 6.

2. Literature review

A vast literature is available on the routing problem in disaster management. Some of the topics discussed in the literature are dynamic vehicle routing with anticipation in disaster relief by Wohlgemuth, Oloruntoba, and Clausen (2012); an emergency logistics distribution approach for quick response to urgent relief demand in disasters by Sheu (2007); ant colony optimization for disaster relief operations by Yi and Kumar (2007); and a dynamic logistics coordination model for evacuation and support in disaster response activities by Yi and Odamar (2007). The research on debris collection operation after disasters is relatively new and very limited papers are available on this topic. The debris collection operation actually is similar to reverse logistics, which is reviewed in detail in Cardoso, Barbosa-Povoa, and Relvas (2013) and Hu, Sheu, and Huang (2002), and which considers the process of moving goods from their typical final destination for the purpose of capturing value, or proper disposal. However, the debris collection problem discussed here has remarkable dissimilarities with the reverse logistics problem as well because the debris collection problem involves a continuously evolving road network with varying levels of interconnectivity between customers and thus it enforces a strong sequencing of the customers.

Arc routing problem consists of determining a least cost traversal of some specified arcs of a graph, subject to side constraints. Such problems are encountered in variety of practical situations such as road or street maintenance, winter gritting operation, waste collection, mail delivery, school bus routing, and utility metre reading. Many surveys can be found explaining many arc routing problem variants; however, the three main variants are Chinese postman problem in which it is required to traverse all arcs of a graph; rural postman problem in which only a subset of arcs must be traversed; and the CARP which is a capacity constrained version of the two earlier variants with multiple real-life applications, as reviewed in detail in Cordeau and Laporte (2002), Dror (2000), Eiselt, Gendreau, and Laporte (1995a, 1995b), and Assad and Golden (1995).

In CARP, vehicles with varying capacity, move out from depot, service some of the required arcs and return to depot at the end of their tour. Each vehicle is not allowed to take load exceeding its capacity, to continue its tour it must unload at a designated point first, which could be an intermediate depot. The idea of an intermediate depot came from Crevier, Cordeau, and Laporte (2007), where the interest arose from a real-life grocery distribution problem in the Montreal area. Several similar applications were encountered in the context where the route of a vehicle could be composed of multiple stops at intermediate depots in order for the vehicle to be replenished. When trucks and trailers were used, the replenishment could be done by a switch of trailers.

Angelelli and Speranza (2002) presented an application of a similar problem in the context of waste collection. The study was an extension of the periodic vehicle routing problem where the vehicles could renew their capacity at some intermediate facilities. The vehicles returned to the depot only when the work shifts were over. When the capacity limit was reached, the vehicles renew their capacity by unloading the waste at one of the treatment plants or the intermediate depots.

The CARP is NP-hard (non-deterministic polynomial-time hard). It was first addressed with relatively simple heuristics, such as the path-scanning in Golden, De Armmon, and Baker (1983), construct strike in Christofides (1973), and greedy heuristics in Costa, Hertz, and Mittaz (2002). The solution methodologies have been improved over time using meta-heuristics such as the tabu search as reviewed in detail in Gendreau (2003), Mastrolilli (2001), Cordeau, Laporte, and Mercier (2001), Hertz, Laporte, and Mittaz (2000), and Augerat, Belenguer, Benavent, Corberan, and Naddef (1998). In this study as well, a tabu search meta-heuristics method is developed as a solution technique to solve the CARP related to the debris collection problem.

Solving CARP in this study begins with transforming the CARP graph into an equivalent CVRP graph. The transformation is performed to formulate the problem more easily in terms of mathematical algorithm since a vast literature exists for the CVRP topic as compared to the CARP. Such a graph transformation is common in operations research and such methods can be reviewed in detail in Baldacci and Maniezzo (2006), Longo, De Aragao, and Uchoa (2006), and Pearn, Assad, and Golden (1987).

To show the novelty of debris collection operation in this study, let us compare it with the winter gritting operation problem in Tagmouti, Gendreau, and Potvin (2007), which is similar with our problem. The fundamental difference between debris collection operation after disasters and winter gritting operation is described as follows. In winter gritting operation, the timing of the intervention is of prime importance. That is, if the intervention is too early or too late, the cost in material and time sharply increases. On the other hand, in debris collection operation after disasters, because some accesses are blocked by the debris, sequence in visiting and servicing arcs at the previous road network structure will affect aggregate accessibility at the next one. Besides studied by Tagmouti et al. (2007), many important publications of the past 10 years related to the winter gritting operation problem have been well summarized by Aguilar, Langevin, and Laporte (2012). The other publications related to disasters, particularly in the management of debris after disaster are also taken into consideration and as starting point in conducting this study such as reviewed by Ergun, Carbajal, Keskinocak, Stilp, and Villarreal (2010), Rafee, Karbassi, Nouri, Safari, and Mehrdadi (2008), and Altay and Green (2006).

Therefore, the uniqueness of this kind of CARP is due to the limited access from one section to the others, as a result of the blocked access by debris. A modification in classical

CARP is therefore, required to solve this kind of problem, i.e. by adding a new constraint, which is mentioned in this study as access possibility constraint. This constraint sets whether a vehicle can possibly move from one node to another in a particular network, or not.

At the final stage, the model formulation will be applied on the realistic case study of the Tokyo Metropolitan Area disaster debris maps. In a case study by Hirayama et al. (2010), the amount of disaster debris from earthquake and catastrophic flood disasters in the Tokyo Metropolitan Area was estimated according to hazard maps. Results from Hirayama et al. (2010) give the estimated amount of debris for a zone or area, therefore an additional estimation procedure was used (described in detail in Section 5) to get the amount of debris on the roads resulting from earthquake and flood disasters that is required to be collected and transported to disposal site(s).

3. Model formulation

The CARP can be defined on an undirected graph $G = (V, A)$, in which V is the set of nodes and A is the set of arcs. The set A is partitioned into a subset of required arcs $A1$, which must be serviced, and another subset of arcs $A2$ required to maintain connectivity. Each required arc $a \in A1$ is associated with a demand $z(a)$, a travel cost $\mathrm{tc}(a)$ which refers to travelled distance, and a service cost $\mathrm{sc}(a)$. The other arcs, in subset $A2$, have a travel cost $\mathrm{tc}(a)$ only. Usually, the service cost is greater than the travel cost because it takes more effort to service an arc than to only simply travel along it.

There exists a depot as a route starting point as well as a final destination point after all required arcs are completely serviced. In addition, intermediate depots can also be considered which serve as vehicles destination points to empty their loads. As soon as an arc or a road is serviced by the vehicle, it will open and can be used, without waiting until the vehicle which services it completes its route. In some practical cases, where roads are wide enough, the debris could be removed from the point to the road side. Considering that our objective is to collect the debris and open the blocked access, therefore the method whether to transport the debris to the intermediate depot or just remove it to the road side does not affect the progress. However, in this paper, the roads are assumed to be quite narrow and to respect the capacity of vehicle and labour, it is assumed as necessary to transport the debris to the intermediate depot. The fixed cost for establishing such an intermediate depot h is represented by G_h.

A set of identical vehicles, $K = \{1, \ldots, m\}$, is placed at the central depot node. Every vehicle has a fixed capacity Q_k and vehicle cost F_k which can be included in cost whenever the vehicle is used. Each vehicle serves a single route that must start and end at the depot. While doing so, vehicles can visit one of the intermediate depots whenever their loads exceed Q_k. As mentioned earlier, the vehicles are allowed to move from or to the adjacent arcs, whereas for distant arcs with blocked access, vehicles are not allowed to visit them before removing the blockage first (i.e. regulated by the access possibility constraint). This access possibility constraint belongs to the family of dynamic constraints, considering that the blocked access conditions in the entire network will immediately change every time a blockage is opened. The objective is to service all required arcs in the graph at least cost with feasible routes, where the cost is related to the number of vehicles used, the number of intermediate depots established, travel cost, and the service cost.

A transformation from CARP in graph $G = (V, A)$ into an equivalent CVRP in a transformed graph $G'' = (V', A')$ is performed. In a well-known transformation by Pearn et al. (1987), an arc $a \in A$ in CARP was represented by three nodes in the equivalent CVRP.

Since anticipating large instance of debris collection operation, the type of CARP transformation into CVRP with making two nodes for each required arc by Longo et al. (2006) will be used. In this transformation, an arc (i, j) in $A1$ is associated with two nodes s_{ij} and s_{ji}, thus the resulting CVRP instance is defined on a complete undirected graph $G' = (V', A')$, where

$$V' = \bigcup_{(i,j)\in A} \{s_{ij}, s_{ji}\} \cup \{o\}. \tag{1a}$$

Node o serves as the depot. The cost involved here is only travel cost (tc) since service cost (sc) is not considered. The arc costs (c) and the demands (z) are defined as follows:

$$c_{s_{ij}s_{kl}} = \begin{cases} 0 & \text{if } i = k \text{ and } j = l, \\ c_{ij} & \text{if } i = l \text{ and } j = k, \\ d(i,k) & \text{if } i \neq k \neq l \text{ or } j \neq l \neq k, \end{cases} \tag{1b}$$

$$c_{os_{ij}} = d(o, i).$$

Here $d(i, j)$ is the value of the shortest path from node i to node j in the CARP graph $G = (V, A)$. The new demands are

$$z_{s_{ij}} = z_{s_{ji}} = \tfrac{1}{2}z(i, j). \tag{1c}$$

To better understand the transformation process; let us see an illustration in Figures 2 and 3 which are taken from Longo et al. (2006). The transformation fixes the flow variable (x^k_{ij}) on all undirected arcs $\{(s_{ij}, s_{ji}) \in A' | (i, j) \in A$ to 1. It means that CVRP solutions are only feasible where pairs of nodes s_{ij} and s_{ji} are visited in sequence, either s_{ij} from or to s_{ji}. It could be said that the sum of z on s_{ij} and s_{ji} is a single quantity because they were obtained from the same single arc. As the impact, the vehicle must have sufficient load capacity to service pair of nodes s_{ij} and s_{ji} simultaneously, otherwise, vehicle must visit one of the intermediate depots to empty the load or look for other pair of nodes. After the above-mentioned transformation had been applied on debris collection operation problem, a CVRP with blocked access was obtained.

Notations used in this study are mostly the same as it was in Tagmouti et al. (2007), where $N' \subset V'$, is the set of required nodes that must be serviced. The depot is a single node; however, it is also duplicated into an origin depot o and a destination depot d in V'. In addition, there exists a set of potential intermediate depots $I = \{V'_{n+1\ldots}\}$, where $I \subset V'$ and n is the number of node that must be serviced. Even though the best location among a set of potential intermediate depots will be chosen, however, one of the intermediate depot is always established right at the depot location because of the efficiency reason. This situation is acceptable in condition where it is difficult to provide an empty space in a particular area to establish other intermediate depots. Therefore, the depot will be also duplicated into an intermediate depot V'_{n+1} in V'. Once load of vehicles exceed Q_k, vehicles can choose one of the intermediate depots to empty the load. At the last tour, when all required nodes have completely serviced, vehicles must return to the depot.

The operation of multiple vehicles will increase cost due to fixed cost (F_k) of every additional vehicle. Moreover, operating multiple vehicles may not decrease total travel cost (tc), considering that working in a network with blocked access imposes the condition that routes must be operated in a particular sequence. Technically, every time a vehicle completed service on one node, it will update information of the access possibility to all other vehicles. Therefore, operating multiple vehicles will still be tested in this study, because some vehicles

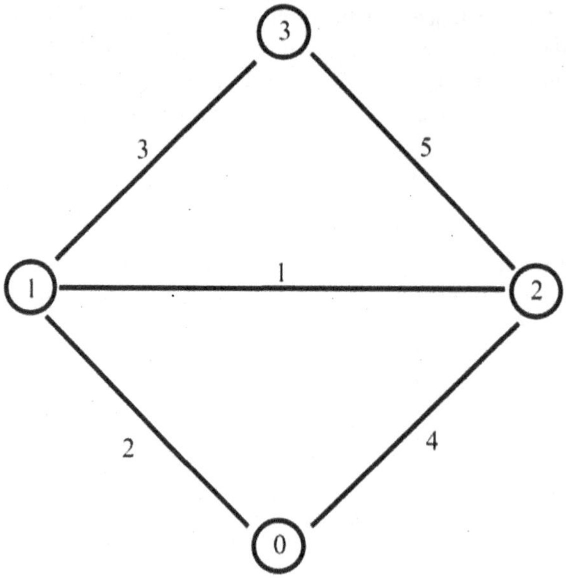

Figure 2. Original CARP Graph by Longo et al. (2006).

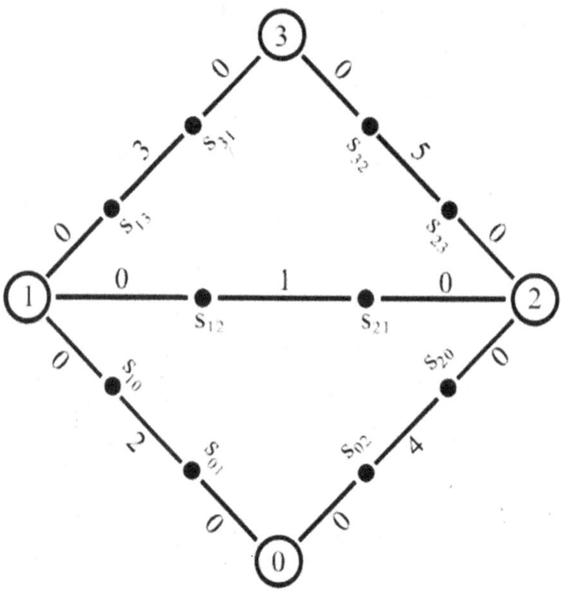

Figure 3. Transformed CVRP Graph Longo et al. (2006).

with varying routes which start simultaneously may decrease total required time (tt). Such an operation can be applied to solve the debris collection problem with time restriction, such as depot closing time or time windows at the demand nodes. It should be noted that the classical CVRP itself can be considered a single vehicle routing operation without any time constraints as demonstrated in detail in Yang, Mathur, and Ballou (2000).

As a new idea for the debris collection operation, an access possibility constraint is introduced on the nodes, which is represented by p_{ij}^k, $i \in V'$, $j \in V'$, $k \in K$, which is equal to 1 if vehicle k from node i can possibly visit or service node j, 0 otherwise. The access possibility matrix always changes from original or previous positions, every time a vehicle completed services a required node and the blockage is opened. Therefore, it can be classified as a dynamic constraint. The transformed CVRP's decision variables are as follows: (1) the binary flow variables on the arcs x_{ij}^k, $(i, j) \in A'$, $k \in K$, which are equal to 1 if vehicle k travels from node i to service node j, 0 otherwise; (2) The binary intermediate depot variables y_h, $h \in I$ which are equal to 1 if the intermediate depot h is established, 0 otherwise; and (3) the non-negative variables Q_i^k, $i \in V'$ which specify the remaining capacity of vehicle k just after servicing node i. Note that $Q_o^k = Q_k$, $k \in K$; $Q_h^k = Q_k$, $k \in K$, $h \in I$; the internodes travel cost (c_{ij}) is based on the shortest distance $d(i, j)$ of Equation (1b), which in turn depends on travel cost $\text{tc}(i, j)$ and service cost $\text{sc}(i, j)$ of arc (i, j). The demands at depot and intermediate depots are zero, i.e. $z_o = z_d = z_h = 0$, $h \in I$; the maximum number of vehicles is limited to number m; and g is the maximum number of intermediate depots, which can be established. The transformed CVRP can be formulated as follows:

$$\text{Min} \quad \sum_{k \in K} \sum_{(i,j) \in A'} c_{ij} x_{ij}^k + \sum_{h \in I} G_h y_h \tag{2a}$$

S.t.

$$\sum_{k \in K} \sum_{i \in N' \cup I \cup \{o\}} x_{ij}^k = 1, \quad j \in N', \tag{2b}$$

$$\sum_{k \in K} \sum_{j \in N'} x_{oj}^k \leq m, \tag{2c}$$

$$\sum_{h \in I} y_h \leq g, \tag{2d}$$

$$\sum_{j \in N' \cup \{d\}} x_{oj}^k = 1, \quad k \in K, \tag{2e}$$

$$\sum_{j \in N' \cup \{d\}} x_{ij}^k - \sum_{j \in N' \cup \{o\}} x_{ji}^k = 0, \quad k \in K, i \in N', \tag{2f}$$

$$\sum_{i \in N' \cup \{o\}} x_{id}^k = 1, \quad k \in K, \tag{2g}$$

$$x_{ij}^k (Q_i^k - z_j - Q_j^k) \geq 0, \quad (i, j) \in A', k \in K, \tag{2h}$$

$$x_{ij}^k - p_{ij}^k \leq 0, \quad i \in V', j \in V', k \in K, \tag{2i}$$

$$x_{jh}^k - y_h \leq 0, \quad h \in I, j \in N', k \in K, \tag{2j}$$

$$0 \leq Q_i^k \leq Q_k, \quad k \in K, i \in V', \tag{2k}$$

$$x_{ij}^k \in \{0, 1\}, \quad (i, j) \in A', k \in K, \tag{2l}$$

$$p_{ij}^k \in \{0, 1\}, \quad i \in V', j \in V', k \in K, \tag{2m}$$

$$y_h \in \{0, 1\}, \quad h \in I. \tag{2n}$$

To easily follow the formulation, main notations used will be rewritten briefly as sub-section of notation as follows.

- c_{ij} = cost (from i to node j),
- x_{ij}^k = flow variables (vehicle k travels from node i to service node j),
- y_h = intermediate depot variable (at node h),
- Q_i^k = remaining capacity variable (vehicle k just after servicing node i),
- p_{ij}^k = access possibility constraint,
- G_h = fixed cost for an intermediate depot (at node h),
- F_k = fixed cost for vehicle k,
- Q_k = capacity of vehicle k,
- z_j = demand (at node j),
- K = a set of identical vehicles,
- A' = a set of arcs in the transformed CVRP graph,
- V' = a set of nodes in the transformed CVRP graph,
- N' = a set of required nodes,
- I = a set of intermediate depots,
- m = maximum number of vehicles,
- g = maximum number of intermediate depots.

The objective function (2a) minimizes the sum of travel cost (tc) which refers to travel distance; and the sum of cost of establishing intermediate depots. Instead of travel cost, travel time can also be considered in the objective function if one wants to minimize the sum of total travel and service time (i.e. the total operation time) instead of the total cost. The fixed vehicle cost (F_k) can also be added to all out going vehicles from depot $o \in V'$ if one wants to penalize the use of an additional vehicle. Constraint (2b) requires that each node in N' must be serviced once. Constraint (2c) is for maximum number of vehicles used. Constraint (2d) is for maximum number of intermediate depots established. Constraints (2e)–(2g) are the flow conservation constraints. Constraint (2h) ensures that vehicles are allowed to move from node i to node j only if the remaining capacity after servicing node i is still feasible to load demand in node j. Constraint (2i) ensures that vehicles are allowed to move from node i to node j only if the access between node i and node j is opened, i.e. $p_{ij}^k = 1$. Constraint (2j) ensures that vehicles are allowed to move from node i to intermediate depot h to dispose the debris only if intermediate depot h is already established, i.e. $y_h = 1$. Constraint (2k) ensures load values that do not exceed Q_k and are positive. Constraint (2l) is for binary values for the flow variables. Constraint (2m) is for binary values for access possibility. Constraint (2n) is for binary values for establishing intermediate depots.

4. Meta-heuristics solution technique

This section is concerned with the tabu search as a proposed meta-heuristics solution technique to solve the debris collection operation as well as the testing of the model formulation on small problem instances before applying it on the realistic case study.

4.1. *Tabu search algorithm*

In this study, a tabu search meta-heuristics is proposed to solve the underlying CVRP to our debris collection operation, as the tabu search or heuristics in general are practically more

$s = s \rightarrow k = 1$.
Generate initial solution
WHILE the stopping condition is not met **DO**
  Identify $N(s)$. (Neighborhood set)
  Identify $T(s,k)$. (Tabu set)
  Identify $As(s,k)$. (Aspiration set)
  Choose the best $s' \in N(s,k) = \{N(s) - T(s,k)\} + As(s,k)$.
  Memorize s' if it improves the previous best solution
  $s = s' \rightarrow k = k+1$.
END WHILE

Figure 4. Basic algorithm of Tabu search by Mastrolilli (2001).

appropriate and faster to solve large instances. The tabu search scheme that proposed here is well documented in the literature by Gendreau (2003), Mastrolilli (2001), Cordeau et al. (2001), Hertz et al. (2000), and Augerat et al. (1998). The method performs an exploration of the solution area in a subset of the neighbourhood $N(s)$ by moving from a solution s at iteration k to the best solution s' at iteration $k + 1$. Since s' at iteration $k + 1$ does not always have an improvement upon s at iteration k, a tabu mechanism is implemented to prevent the process from cycling over a sequence of solutions. The prohibited moves are kept in the list called as tabu list $T(s, k)$. Aspiration criterion As(s, k) is set as an exception, which says even though some moves are tabu, however, as long as there is an improvement in the solution, the tabu list can be violated. Figure 4 shows the basic algorithm of the tabu search that is reviewed in Mastrolilli (2001).

The application of the tabu search in our study is preceded by finding initial solution (with vehicle route) using simple heuristics, like greedy heuristics, which was also used in study by Costa et al. (2002). Greedy algorithm makes locally optimal choice at each stage, with the hope of finding a global optimum. This technique attempts to construct a feasible solution that is moving from the current point. The idea of performing local search in this study is fairly simple; starting from the depot, a vehicle chooses the closest demand node until all required nodes are visited. Then proceed with finding better solutions using the tabu search method, by changing vehicle route sequence until the best solution is obtained. Stopping criterion is performed using either a fixed amount of CPU time or a fixed number of consecutive iterations without an improvement in the best objective function value.

The important matter that should be paid attention to is: the changes of vehicle route combination using the tabu search technique are executed by swapping node pair that exists on the same arc (from the original CARP graph) with the other node pairs, instead of swapping a node with the other nodes. Due to every node (in the transformed CVRP graph) is not assumed as single node, however as node pair derived from single arc (from the original CARP graph).

4.2. *Performance validation of the algorithm*

In order to assess the accuracy of the tabu search algorithm more conclusively, we performed a computational experiment on a set of benchmark problems and compared the result with best-known solutions for the 25, 50 and 100 customer instances of Solomon's vehicle

Table 1. Tabu search's result vs. Solomon's best-known solution.

No	Problem	Average gap (%)	Average CPU time (s)
1	25 customers–C	0.57	120.31
2	25 customers–R	0.65	34.20
3	25 customers–RC	0.87	66.38
4	50 customers	2.85	549.99
5	100 customers	5.24	2993.76

routing problem with time windows (VRPTW) benchmark problems (Solomon, 1987). The algorithm described above was coded in MATLAB R2010b and compiled on a 2666 MHz Genuine Intel processor ×86 Family 6 Model 15 Stepping 11 with 2 GB of RAM under the Windows 7 Professional OS. Some modifications were needed in the proposed tabu search algorithm since Solomon's VRPTW problems are typically different from our problem, first by setting all p_{ij}^k to be 1 (i.e. all links were opened or no blocked access exists), and second by applying time windows. After solving Solomon's VRPTW problems using our tabu search, the obtained results were tabulated in Table 1; it gives the average performance of our tabu search meta-heuristics for various benchmark problems of Solomon's VRPTW problems.

Most of Solomon's VRPTW problems consisting of 25 customers were solved by the tabu search within reasonable time and with a relatively small optimality gap. The average optimality gap of problems type C tested was 0.57%, and for tested problems of type R and type RC the optimality gap was 0.65% and 0.87%, respectively, while the average optimality gap for all 25 customers' instances tested was about 0.70%. Some Solomon's VRPTW problems consisting of 50 and 100 customers were also solved by the tabu search. The average optimality gap for 50 customers' instances was 2.85% and for 100 customers' instances was 5.24%. In light of this computational experiment, it can be concluded that the designed tabu search heuristics has sufficient efficiency. As can be seen from Table 1, the performance of the tabu search seems deteriorate as the size of the problem grows, both in terms of quality of the solution as well as running times. Therefore, if the realistic problems are larger than the instances evaluated, the proper performance of heuristic is not guaranteed. To deal with such condition, solving realistic problem with large customers can be approached by performing region clustering. Then, the large of customer in each region is limited as much as the proposed tabu search can solve it. In this case study, the maximum expected size of the typical realistic debris removal problem that can be confidently solved by the proposed tabu search is 200 customers in every region.

This may also be noted that the tabu search meta-heuristics is designed for non-time windows. Therefore, even a better performance is expected for the debris collection operation. One of the reasons to use Solomon instances as a benchmark in assessing the tabu search algorithm performance is that the possibility of applying time windows in the debris collection operation problems in the future. Therefore, if the expected modification of the tabu search algorithm is actually performed, assessment of the new algorithm performance will still be valid using the same benchmark (Solomon's VRPTW problems). In addition, the proposed formulation in this study is mostly modified from the formulation used in Tagmouti et al. (2007), which took into consideration time windows constraints. This situation makes easier to assess the accuracy of the proposed tabu search also using Solomon's VRPTW instances.

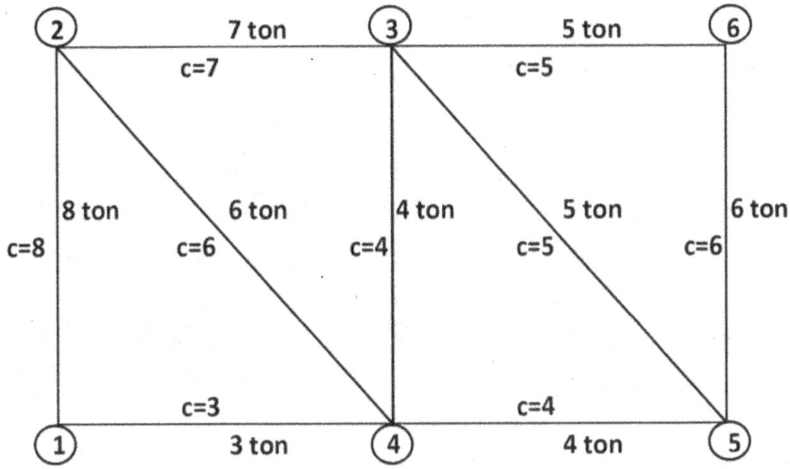

Figure 5. CARP test instance.

4.3. *Problem instances*

For a better and easier understanding of the algorithm, before applying on the realistic case study of the Tokyo Metropolitan Area, the model formulation (i.e. its underlying modified CVRP) is tested on a small problem instance, which was also reviewed in Pramudita, Taniguchi, and Qureshi (2012), see Figure 5.

A hypothetical test instance with six nodes (node no. 1 is a depot) and nine arcs (all are required arcs) was developed, where

- $V = \{1, 2, 3, 4, 5, 6\}$;
- $Q_k = 20$ ton;
- Travel cost $\mathrm{tc}(i, j)$: $\mathrm{tc}(1, 2) = 8, \mathrm{tc}(1, 4) = 3, \mathrm{tc}(2, 3) = 7, \mathrm{tc}(2, 4) = 6, \mathrm{tc}(3, 4) = 4$, $\mathrm{tc}(3, 5) = 5$, $\mathrm{tc}(3, 6) = 5$, $\mathrm{tc}(4, 5) = 4$, $\mathrm{tc}(5, 6) = 6$;
- Demand $z(i, j)$: $z(1, 2) = 8$ ton, $z(1, 4) = 3$ ton, $z(2, 3) = 7$ ton, $z(2, 4) = 6$ ton, $z(3, 4) = 4$ ton, $z(3, 5) = 5$ ton, $z(3, 6) = 5$ ton, $z(4, 5) = 4$ ton, $z(5, 6) = 6$ ton;
- $\mathrm{sc} = 0$ and $F_k = 0$, thus $c = \mathrm{tc}$.

In the test instance, the service cost (sc), the fixed vehicle cost (F_k) and also the cost of establishing an intermediate depot (G_h) have been assumed as 0, thus the cost involved is only the travel cost (tc) (i.e. $c_{ij} = \mathrm{tc}_{ij}$). The service cost can be taken into consideration by assuming that sc is included in tc. In our case, the objective is to service all required nodes, and due to the fact that the considered debris collection operation is not time constrained, therefore the amount of service cost is always fixed and it will not affect the optimization process. Similarly, as mentioned earlier, the fixed cost of a vehicle can be added to all outgoing arcs from the origin depot but for this particular test instance, just a single vehicle is considered.

Establishing intermediate depots in a real-life disaster problem is more likely classified in the area of politics, thus in the test instances, the intermediate depots are assumed to be pre-located at zero cost. However, G_h is still considered in the formulation. The existence of G_h aims to avoid perceptions that the intermediate depots could be established as many as possible, as well as to keep the general form of the formulation so it can also be applied

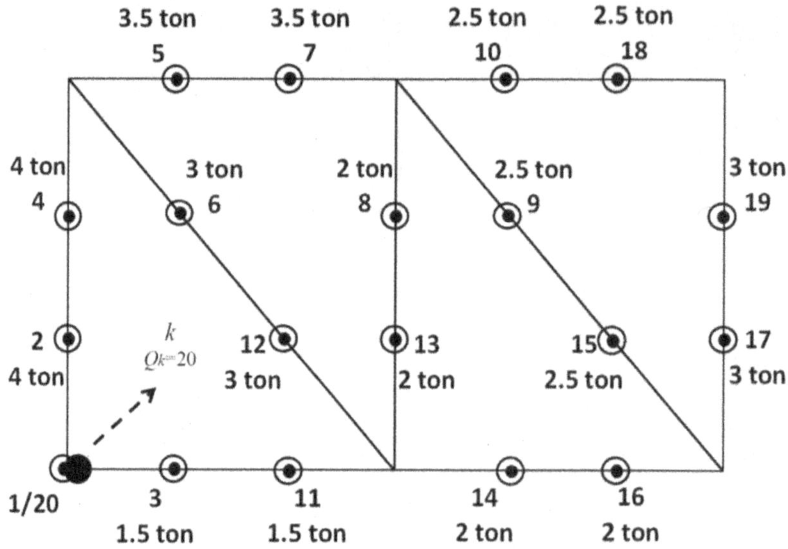

Figure 6. Transformed test instance in CVRP.

on the more complex problems in the future research. Another assumption taken in this case is that the shortest path from node i to node j in graph is the only path that exists for every node pair. Accordingly, the connection between i and j depends on whether $d(i, j)$ is blocked or not, however if j is depot or intermediate depot, the vehicle always can move from i to j through the shortest path.

The CARP graph of test instance in Figure 5 is transformed into the corresponding CVRP graph as shown in Figure 6, with number of nodes $V' = 2n + 1 + n'$; n is the number of arcs and n' is the number of an intermediate depot. After transformation, the graph turns into a CVRP with number of nodes $V' = 20$. Node no. 1 still serves as depot; as well as duplicated into node no. 20, which serves as the intermediate depot. The transformation introduces nodes s_{ij} and s_{ji} for all required arcs $(i, j) \in A$, where

- $V' = \{1, 2, 3, 4, 5, 6, 7, 8, 9, 10, 11, 12, 13, 14, 15, 16, 17, 18, 19, 20\}$;
- $Q_k = 20$ ton;
- As calculated by Equation (1c), new demands $z_i : z_2 = 4$ ton, $z_3 = 1.5$ ton, $z_4 = 4$ ton, $z_5 = 3.5$ ton, $z_6 = 3$ ton, $z_7 = 3.5$ ton, $z_8 = 2$ ton, $z_9 = 2.5$ ton, $z_{10} = 2.5$ ton, $z_{11} = 1.5$ ton, $z_{12} = 3$ ton, $z_{13} = 2$ ton, $z_{14} = 2$ ton, $z_{15} = 2.5$ ton, $z_{16} = 2$ ton, $z_{17} = 3$ ton, $z_{18} = 2.5$ ton, and $z_{19} = 3$ ton.

The final transformed instance, a constrained CVRP instance with 20 nodes, is defined over a complete graph where the travel cost c_{ij} between nodes is calculated by Equation (1b) and presented in Table 2.

The process starts by finding an initial solution using a greedy heuristics. Starting from the depot, a vehicle chooses the closest demand node until all required nodes are visited. The vehicle returns to the depot at the end of its tour; however, it may also visit one of the established intermediate depots, whenever its load exceeds the capacity. The objective value of total travel cost (tc) obtained is **93** with route **1-3-11-13-8-9-15-17-19- 20-2-4-6-12-14-16-20-7-5-10 -18-1**. Then, the tabu search was used to find a better solution than the

Table 2. Travel cost matrix of CVRP.

	1	2	3	4	5	6	7	8	9	10	11	12	13	14	15	16	17	18	19	20
1	0	0	0	8	8	8	7	7	7	7	3	3	3	3	7	7	7	12	12	0
2	0	0	0	8	8	8	7	7	7	7	3	3	3	3	7	7	7	12	12	0
3	0	0	0	8	8	8	7	7	7	7	3	3	3	3	7	7	7	12	12	0
4	8	8	8	0	0	0	7	7	7	7	6	6	6	6	10	10	10	12	12	8
5	8	8	8	0	0	0	7	7	7	7	6	6	6	6	10	10	10	12	12	8
6	8	8	8	0	0	0	7	7	7	7	6	6	6	6	10	10	10	12	12	8
7	7	7	7	7	7	7	0	0	0	0	4	4	4	4	5	5	5	5	5	7
8	7	7	7	7	7	7	0	0	0	0	4	4	4	4	5	5	5	5	5	7
9	7	7	7	7	7	7	0	0	0	0	4	4	4	4	5	5	5	5	5	7
10	7	7	7	7	7	7	0	0	0	0	4	4	4	4	5	5	5	5	5	7
11	3	3	3	6	6	6	4	4	4	4	0	0	0	0	4	4	4	9	9	3
12	3	3	3	6	6	6	4	4	4	4	0	0	0	0	4	4	4	9	9	3
13	3	3	3	6	6	6	4	4	4	4	0	0	0	0	4	4	4	9	9	3
14	3	3	3	6	6	6	4	4	4	4	0	0	0	0	4	4	4	9	9	3
15	7	7	7	10	10	10	5	5	5	5	4	4	4	4	0	0	0	6	6	7
16	7	7	7	10	10	10	5	5	5	5	4	4	4	4	0	0	0	6	6	7
17	7	7	7	10	10	10	5	5	5	5	4	4	4	4	0	0	0	6	6	7
18	12	12	12	12	12	12	5	5	5	5	9	9	9	9	6	6	6	0	0	12
19	12	12	12	12	12	12	5	5	5	5	9	9	9	9	6	6	6	0	0	12
20	0	0	0	8	8	8	7	7	7	7	3	3	3	3	7	7	7	12	12	0

initial solution and finally the best solution was found with a total travel cost (tc) of **69** and with route **1-3-11-13-8-10-18-19-17-20-2 -4-6-12-20-14-16-15-9-7-5-1**.

The new idea proposed in this study is an access possibility constraint represented by p_{ij}^k which controls whether the vehicle can possibly move from one node to another, or not. If vehicle k wants to move from i to j, node i and j must be either adjacent; or blocked nodes between node i and j must be serviced by vehicle k first or are already serviced by other vehicles. This constraint belongs to the family of dynamic constraints, considering that the blocked access structure in the entire network will immediately change every time a blockage is opened. To better understand how it works; let us see the access possibility matrix in Tables 3–5 at various stages of the solution.

In stage 1, when vehicle is still at node no. 1 or depot and its tour has not yet started, the access possibility conditions are as follows; (1) Only if i and j are adjacent nodes, the vehicle can move from i to j and vice versa, 1-1, 1-2, 1-3, etc., which is shown by $p_{ij}^k = 1$ which means that the accesses are opened; and (2) If j is an intermediate depot, the vehicle always can move from i to j through the shortest path. In stage 2, after vehicle moved from node 1 to node 3, the blocked access structure in the entire network is changed. It can be seen as the change of $p_{ij}^k = 1$ at 1-11, 2-11, etc. Then in stage 3, after vehicle moved from node 3 to node 11, the matrix of access possibility is changed again, which can be seen as the change of $p_{ij}^k = 1$ at 1-12, 1-13, 1-14, 2-12, 2-13, 2-14, 3-12, 3-13, 3-14, etc. This change process of the matrix of access possibility continues until the vehicle ends its tour and returns to the depot.

5. Application on Tokyo metropolitan area case study

An estimation procedure was established by Hirayama et al. (2010) to assess the amount of debris resulting from earthquake and flood disasters in the Tokyo Metropolitan Area.

Table 3. Access possibility matrix (stage 1).

	1/20	2	3	4	5	6	7	8	9	10	11	12	13	14	15	16	17	18	19
1/20	1	1	1	0	0	0	0	0	0	0	0	0	0	0	0	0	0	0	0
2	1	1	1	1	0	0	0	0	0	0	0	0	0	0	0	0	0	0	0
3	1	1	1	0	0	0	0	0	0	0	1	0	0	0	0	0	0	0	0
4	1	1	0	1	1	1	0	0	0	0	0	0	0	0	0	0	0	0	0
5	1	0	0	1	1	1	1	0	0	0	0	0	0	0	0	0	0	0	0
6	1	0	0	1	1	1	0	0	0	0	0	1	0	0	0	0	0	0	0
7	1	0	0	0	1	0	1	1	1	1	0	0	0	0	0	0	0	0	0
8	1	0	0	0	0	0	1	1	1	1	0	0	1	0	0	0	0	0	0
9	1	0	0	0	0	0	1	1	1	1	0	0	0	0	1	0	0	0	0
10	1	0	0	0	0	0	1	1	1	1	0	0	0	0	0	0	0	1	0
11	1	0	1	0	0	0	0	0	0	0	1	1	1	1	0	0	0	0	0
12	1	0	0	0	0	1	0	0	0	0	1	1	1	1	0	0	0	0	0
13	1	0	0	0	0	0	0	1	0	0	1	1	1	1	0	0	0	0	0
14	1	0	0	0	0	0	0	0	0	0	1	1	1	1	0	1	0	0	0
15	1	0	0	0	0	0	0	0	1	0	0	0	0	0	1	1	1	0	0
16	1	0	0	0	0	0	0	0	0	0	0	0	0	1	1	1	1	0	0
17	1	0	0	0	0	0	0	0	0	0	0	0	0	0	1	1	1	0	1
18	1	0	0	0	0	0	0	0	0	1	0	0	0	0	0	0	0	1	1
19	1	0	0	0	0	0	0	0	0	0	0	0	0	0	0	0	1	1	1

Table 4. Access possibility matrix (stage 2).

	1/20	2	3	4	5	6	7	8	9	10	11	12	13	14	15	16	17	18	19
1/20	1	1	1	0	0	0	0	0	0	0	1	0	0	0	0	0	0	0	0
2	1	1	1	1	0	0	0	0	0	0	1	0	0	0	0	0	0	0	0
3	1	1	1	0	0	0	0	0	0	0	1	0	0	0	0	0	0	0	0
4	1	1	0	1	1	1	0	0	0	0	0	0	0	0	0	0	0	0	0
5	1	0	0	1	1	1	1	0	0	0	0	0	0	0	0	0	0	0	0
6	1	0	0	1	1	1	0	0	0	0	0	1	0	0	0	0	0	0	0
7	1	0	0	0	1	0	1	1	1	1	0	0	0	0	0	0	0	0	0
8	1	0	0	0	0	0	1	1	1	1	0	0	1	0	0	0	0	0	0
9	1	0	0	0	0	0	1	1	1	1	0	0	0	0	1	0	0	0	0
10	1	0	0	0	0	0	1	1	1	1	0	0	0	0	0	0	0	1	0
11	1	1	1	0	0	0	0	0	0	0	1	1	1	1	0	0	0	0	0
12	1	0	0	0	0	1	0	0	0	0	1	1	1	1	0	0	0	0	0
13	1	0	0	0	0	0	0	1	0	0	1	1	1	1	0	0	0	0	0
14	1	0	0	0	0	0	0	0	0	0	1	1	1	1	0	1	0	0	0
15	1	0	0	0	0	0	0	0	1	0	0	0	0	0	1	1	1	0	0
16	1	0	0	0	0	0	0	0	0	0	0	0	0	1	1	1	1	0	0
17	1	0	0	0	0	0	0	0	0	0	0	0	0	0	1	1	1	0	1
18	1	0	0	0	0	0	0	0	0	1	0	0	0	0	0	0	0	1	1
19	1	0	0	0	0	0	0	0	0	0	0	0	0	0	0	0	1	1	1

It was shown that the procedure of disaster debris estimation in disaster management and operation systems could be established for not only emergency response in the aftermath, but it can also be used in pre-disaster planning. In that case study, the amount of debris from earthquake and catastrophic flood disasters in the Tokyo Metropolitan Area was estimated according to the hazard maps.

Table 5. Access possibility matrix (stage 3).

	1/20	2	3	4	5	6	7	8	9	10	11	12	13	14	15	16	17	18	19
1/20	1	1	1	0	0	0	0	0	0	0	1	1	1	1	0	0	0	0	0
2	1	1	1	1	0	0	0	0	0	0	1	1	1	1	0	0	0	0	0
3	1	1	1	0	0	0	0	0	0	0	1	1	1	1	0	0	0	0	0
4	1	1	0	1	1	1	0	0	0	0	0	0	0	0	0	0	0	0	0
5	1	0	0	1	1	1	1	0	0	0	0	0	0	0	0	0	0	0	0
6	1	0	0	1	1	1	0	0	0	0	0	1	0	0	0	0	0	0	0
7	1	0	0	0	1	0	1	1	1	1	0	0	0	0	0	0	0	0	0
8	1	0	0	0	0	0	1	1	1	1	0	0	1	0	0	0	0	0	0
9	1	0	0	0	0	0	1	1	1	1	0	0	0	0	1	0	0	0	0
10	1	0	0	0	0	0	1	1	1	1	0	0	0	0	0	0	0	1	0
11	1	0	1	0	0	0	0	0	0	0	1	1	1	1	0	0	0	0	0
12	1	1	1	0	0	1	0	0	0	0	1	1	1	1	0	0	0	0	0
13	1	1	1	0	0	0	0	1	0	0	1	1	1	1	0	0	0	0	0
14	1	1	1	0	0	0	0	0	0	0	1	1	1	1	0	1	0	0	0
15	1	0	0	0	0	0	0	0	1	0	0	0	0	0	1	1	1	0	0
16	1	0	0	0	0	0	0	0	0	0	0	0	0	1	1	1	1	0	0
17	1	0	0	0	0	0	0	0	0	0	0	0	0	0	1	1	1	0	1
18	1	0	0	0	0	0	0	0	0	1	0	0	0	0	0	0	0	1	1
19	1	0	0	0	0	0	0	0	0	0	0	0	0	0	0	0	1	1	1

In this section, the model formulation of the debris collection problem will be applied to solve the realistic case study which was assessed by Hirayama et al. (2010). Considering the large size of entire Tokyo Metropolitan Area, the model formulation will be tested in two spot locations only, representing eastern and western parts of Tokyo.

5.1. *Tokyo eastern area (location A)*

Location A, as shown in Figure 7, is an area of 6,537,657 square meters in eastern part of Tokyo (139°48′0″E–139°49′53″E and 35°40′45″N–35°42′0″N). It consists of 22 roads which are also treated as the required arcs in our model formulation. After developing the graph transformation using Equation (1a), location A area can also be treated as a CVRP graph. Now the transformed graph consists of 46 nodes, as shown in Figure 8.

Node no. 1 serves as depot, where vehicles start and end their tour; and the other nodes are debris collection points or the required nodes. The distances between these required nodes (c_{ij}) are calculated by Equation (1b). Besides serving as depot, node no. 1 is duplicated into node no. 46 which serves as the intermediate depot. Node no. 1 or no. 46 is designated as depot or intermediate depot since considering that there is a huge open space available (*to be named*) close to the location which could function as vehicle parking area as well as the disposal site. In this case study, depot or intermediate depot is pre-located and not included in the optimization process.

Based on the assessment of debris resulting from earthquake and flood disasters in the Tokyo Metropolitan Area by Hirayama et al. (2010), the amount of debris information was obtained. It was spread over 5 × 5 grid areas or 25 grid areas of 261,506 square meters each. Since the data result is not detailed, therefore the amount of debris which is spread on every road in each grid area needs to be calculated. In this paper, such calculation was performed by dividing the road area by the grid areas, and then multiplied by the sum of debris in corresponding grid area. In order to get data of road area, the road lengths are

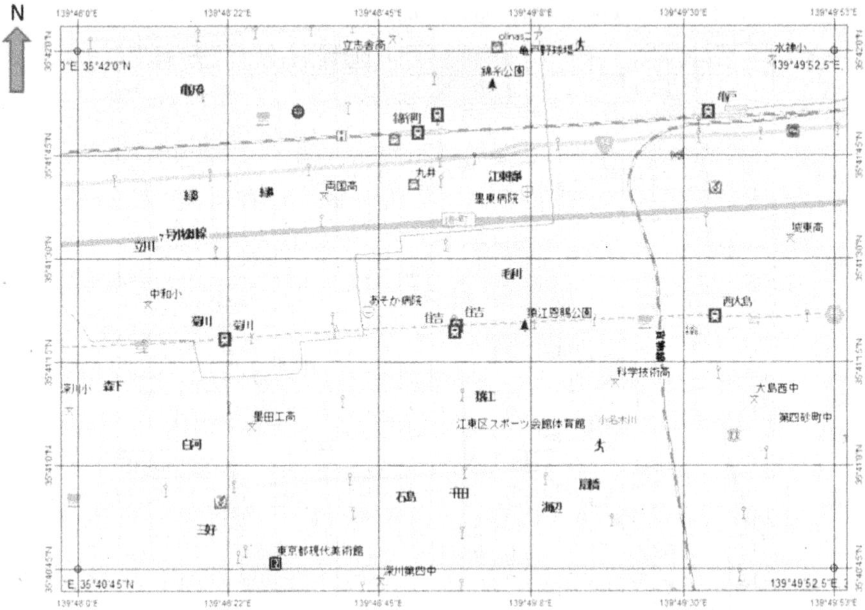

Figure 7. Tokyo eastern area (location A).

measured from existing Tokyo map; meanwhile the road widths are assumed as an average 3.25 m/lane and a total of 4 lanes were assumed for each road.

The objective function of this operation is opening the blockage; therefore the debris could be removed from the road to a near vacant space, such as near the road side. However in this case study, vehicles still need to load and transport some part of the debris to the disposal site due to the limited space and due to the assumption that some debris material cannot be left anyway in the public space. The assumption is that 50% of total amount of debris on the road needs to be loaded and transported to the disposal sites. It may be noted that the percentage figure (i.e. of 50%) is just an arbitrary assumption, since exact proportion may highly be dependent on specific site condition, the nature of debris and the urgency of debris removal operation.

In this case study, because of lack of available data, another assumption is taken that all considered arcs are blocked due to the debris; or every arc is treated as a required arc. Therefore, as mentioned earlier in the test problem instances, p_{ij}^k sets that only adjacent arcs can be connected with each other, while for distant arcs it was assumed that there may be no way to connect them before removing the blocked access first. On the other hand, considering that there may some other roads besides the main road, therefore the accessibility regarding the p_{ij}^k constraint could be relaxed. In such case, one may modify p_{ij}^k that does not exactly restrict the access only to adjacent arcs at the initial stage. Such modification, applied on p_{ij}^k constraint; would suggest that as long as there exist other paths from node i to node j, vehicle k still can possibly move from node i to node j even though without traversing the blocked shortest path; however, in that case the available open path may not be the shortest path connecting the node i to node j. However in this case study, the p_{ij}^k constraint is set to a maximum closed state due to the lack of available data and due the ease factor of such assumption.

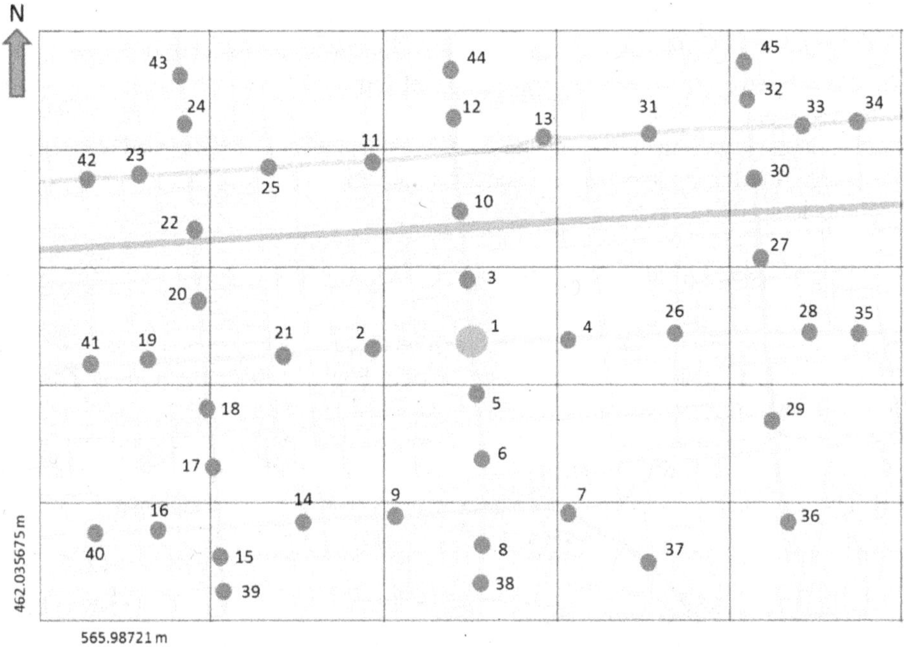

Figure 8. Application of CVRP in location A.

In the real-life situations, demands (i.e. the amount of debris to be removed) in some arcs could very possibly exceed the vehicle capacity, so was the case also in this case study of the Tokyo Metropolitan Area. Hence, in anticipating such situation, instead of a single vehicle some specified number of vehicles may be operated considering that they will work together in a group with the same route. Therefore, in this case study, it is assumed that there are eight standard dump truck vehicles involved in this debris collection operation with an individual capacity of 25 ton each. Furthermore, it is also assumed that those vehicles will be operated as one unit and thus will be treated as a single group of vehicles with unified capacity of 200 ton. In some cases, the number of vehicles could be reduced so that fixed vehicle cost may decrease. However as a consequence, the frequency of vehicles commuting to the disposal site to empty load as well as travel cost will increase. Even after assuming a reasonable size of a unit group of vehicles, still because of limited capacity, the group of vehicles may not necessarily be able to service a single arc completely without returning to intermediate depot to empty the load. This condition can give rise to additional costs, therefore, a fixed travel cost (tc′) is also considered, besides tc. Here tc′ is defined as the commuting cost of the group of vehicles from and to the nearest intermediate depot because of the limited capacity in servicing single required arc. If one wants to minimize the total travel time, tc′ can also be changed into tt′ (i.e. the total commuting travel time to and from an arc with a demand greater than the capacity of the group of vehicles), which will be referred as the fixed required time. The amount of tc′ before the transformation from arcs into nodes can be calculated with the following equation:

$$\mathrm{tc}' = \sum_{(i,j)\in A_1} \min\left(2c_{hj}\frac{z(i,j)}{Q_k}\right), \quad h \in I. \tag{3a}$$

By considering the tc′, it is assumed that the original demands ($z(i, j), (i, j) \in A_1$) can be reduced until the amount equal or less than the capacity of group of vehicles ($z'(i, j) \leq Q_k, (i, j) \in A_1$). Therefore, the model formulation is optimized by considering that the remaining demands ($z'(i, j), (i, j) \in A_1$) can be loaded by vehicle and then vehicle continues its tour to the other nodes without returning to intermediate depot if the capacity is still available. The amounts of remaining debris exist in each node or the remaining demands are presented in Appendix 1.

$$z'(i, j) = z(i, j) - Q_k \frac{z(i, j)}{Q_k}, \quad (i, j) \in A_1. \tag{3b}$$

Similar to the test instance and due to the reasons discussed in earlier section (§4.2) the service cost (sc) is assumed to be zero here as well. Some fixed costs can be determined before running the optimization process i.e. total fixed vehicle cost (F_k) as well as fixed travel cost (tc′) which was calculated as 641,338 distance units. Subsequently, the travel cost (tc) is calculated using proposed tabu search by applying the model formulation with the reduced demands as 45,933 distance units with route as shown in Appendix 2. The best total travel cost (tc + tc′) was obtained as 687,271 distance units.

5.2. *Tokyo western area (location B)*

Location B is an area of 6,537,657 square meters in the western part of Tokyo (139 °40′52″E–139 °42′45″E and 35 °40′45″N–35 °42′0″N). It has more complicated road network structures than the eastern part, in terms of larger number of existing arcs, i.e. 98 arcs, as shown in Figure 9. Location B area can also be treated as a graph. After developing the graph transformation using Equation (1a), now the final transformed CVRP graph consists of 198 nodes, as shown in Figure 10.

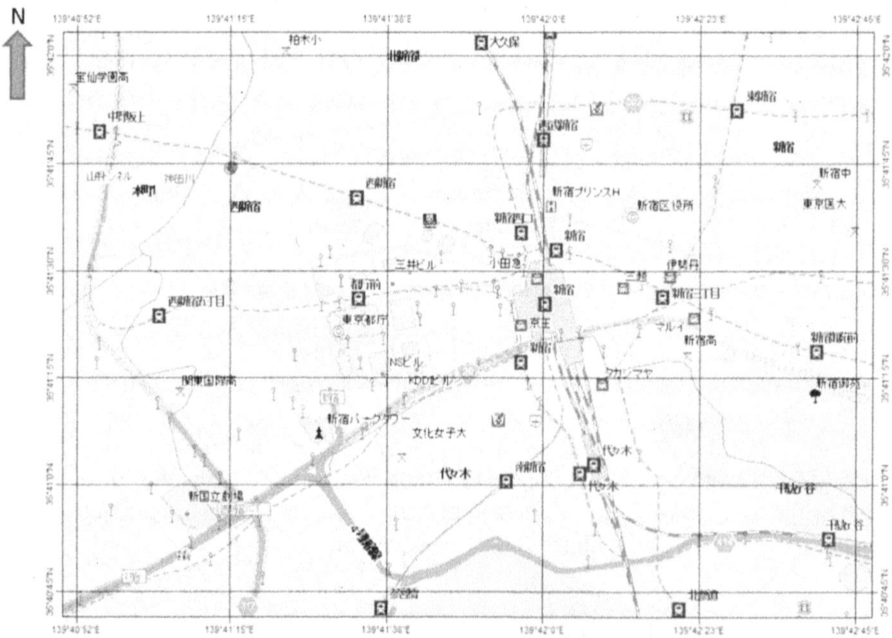

Figure 9. Tokyo western area (location B).

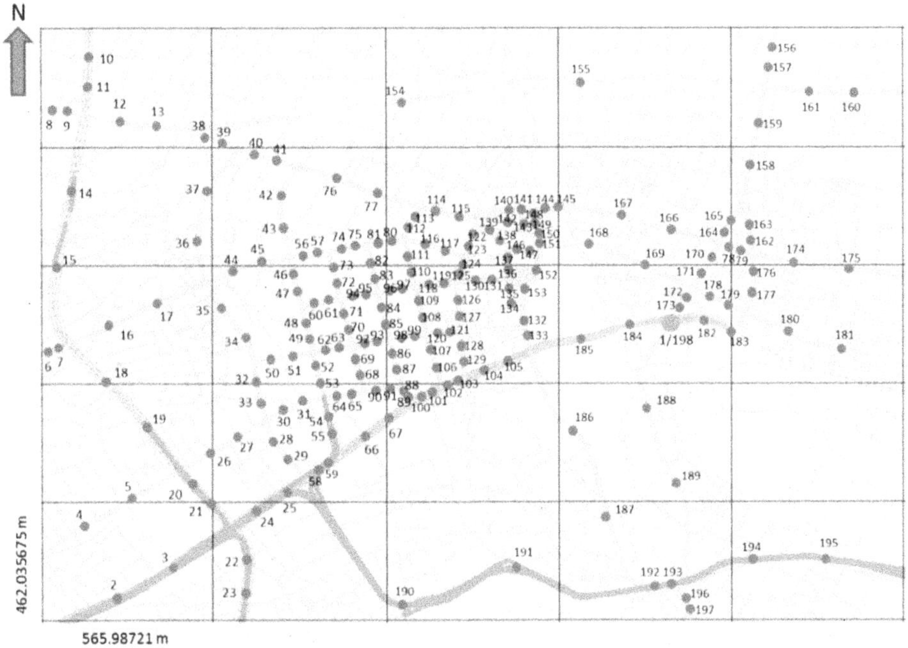

Figure 10. CVRP (single intermediate depot) in location B.

Node no. 1 serves as depot, and *in case 1*, it is duplicated into node no. 198 which serves as an intermediate depot. Node no. 1 or no. 198 is located as depot or intermediate depot considering the fact that there is a huge open space (*to be named*) available close to the location. Similar to location A, the amounts of remaining debris exist or the remaining demands in each node were calculated and are presented in Appendix 3. In this case also, it is assumed that there are eight standard dump truck vehicles involved in this operation with an individual capacity of 25 ton each working as a single group of vehicles with unified capacity of 200 ton. The fixed travel cost (tc′) was calculated as 5934 distance units before running the optimization process. Subsequently, the travel cost (tc) was calculated using proposed tabu search by applying the model formulation with the reduced demands as 93,036 distance units with route as shown in Appendix 4. The best total travel cost (tc + tc′) was obtained as 98,970 distance units.

Because of the complexity of the road network structure in location B, another strategy is evaluated *in case 2* for location B, i.e. with establishing a second intermediate depot. Besides at node no. 198, another intermediate depot was considered at node no. 199 which is also close to a huge open space (*to be named*), as shown in Figure 11.

The fixed travel cost (tc′) was reduced to 3398 distance units and the travel cost (tc) was also reduced to 57,970 distance units with route as shown in Appendix 5. The best total travel cost (tc + tc′) was obtained as 61,368 distance units. Therefore, availability of more intermediate depots (located strategically) would help in reducing the travel cost involved in debris collection operation. The presence of two intermediate depots would make more options of destination points available for a vehicle to empty its load. A brief description of the results is presented in Table 6. However, if their establishment requires an establishment cost (G_h), it must be evaluated that such a decrease in total travel cost is still overall a cost saving or not. It may be noted that the model formulation (2a–2n) is capable of handling this concern as well; the combination of debris collection operation and location of intermediate

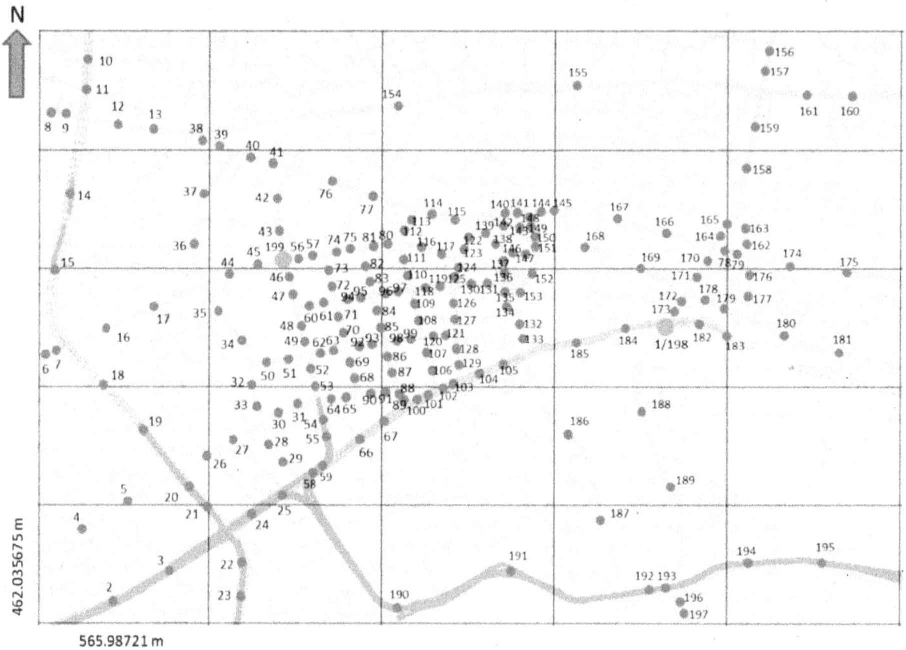

Figure 11. CVRP (two intermediate depots) in location B.

Table 6. Comparison of single and multiple intermediate depots.

No	Type of problem	Σ vehicle	*ID node	Σ travel cost (tc′ + tc) (distance units)
1	Single *ID	1 $Qk = 200$	198	98,970
2	Multiple *IDs	1 $Qk = 200$	198 & 199	61,368

∗ID = intermediate depot.

depot(s) will be considered in future research. Since only single group of vehicle used in the operation, the distance unit can be directly transformed into time unit. Then, the best total travel cost (tc) 61,368 distance units can also be used as an the best total required time (tt) as an input for the next case.

In case 3 along with the intermediate depots established at node nos 198 and 199, the problem is further modified by considering the operation of multiple groups of vehicles. It means that all vehicles may not move together as a single unit; however, it depends if the group is involved in debris collection from a specific node with large enough demand. It is assumed that there are four groups of vehicles with a capacity of 50 ton each and all may have varying routes in the operation. Since the capacity of vehicles is reduced, the remaining demands should be less than they were in the previous cases (cases 1 and 2) in Appendix 3. As mentioned earlier, that multiple vehicles operation has the objective function to find the best required time (tt); therefore, it has no effect to the number of vehicle used as well as the fixed vehicle cost (F_k) can also be ignored. The CVRP was optimized by considering the time of operation instead of travel distance. The fixed required time (tt′) was obtained as 20,899 time units and the required time (tt) was found as 32,924 time units using the

Table 7. Comparison of single and multiple groups of vehicles.

No	Type of problem	Σ vehicle	*ID node	Σ travel cost ($tc' + tc$) (distance units)	Σ required time ($tc' + tc$) (time units)
1	Single vehicle	1			
		$Qk = 200$	198 & 199	61,368	61,368
2	Multiple vehicles	4			
		@ $Qk = 50$	198 & 199	190,189	53,823

*ID = intermediate depot.

tabu search heuristics with routes for each vehicle group as shown in Appendix 6. The best total required time ($tt + tt'$) was obtained as 53,823 time units. A comparison between the effectiveness of the operation of single and multiple groups of vehicles was also performed.

As given in Table 7, the total travel cost by operating multiple vehicles seems not less than the total travel cost of the case using a single vehicle. Adding the number of vehicle will not necessarily reduce the total travel cost due to the fact that routes must be operated in a particular sequence in the debris collection problem with blocked accesses; therefore, the groups of vehicles still have limitation in their operation and must wait until one completes a particular part of operation. However, when minimization of total time was considered in the objective function instead of travel cost, there was a saving in the total travel time (tt) if the operation is performed by operating four groups of vehicles ($53,823 < 61,368$).

6. Conclusion

The debris collection operation after disasters is a new addition in the disaster management and CARP-related literature and not much research has been done in this topic. The uniqueness of this kind of CARP is due to the limited access from one section to the other, as a result of the blocked access by debris. Therefore, a modification in the classical CARP is required to model and solve this kind of problem. It is performed by adding a new dynamic constraint, which is developed in this study as access possibility constraint. This constraint sets whether a vehicle can possibly move from one node to another in a particular network, or not. Depending on the field conditions, p_{ij}^k constraint can be flexibly modified. In this case study, the p_{ij}^k was set to a maximum closed where only adjacent arcs can be connected with each other, while for distant arcs, it was assumed that there may be no way to connect them before removing the blocked access first. This situation particularly arises when considering a catastrophic disaster, severely affecting the whole study area and where the first priority is to re-establish the connectivity of the network. The access possibility matrix dynamically changes with servicing of each required arc or node of the problem, depicting the fact that the serviced arc may open up access to the other arcs.

In order to estimate feasibility of the formulation and its solution algorithm, a practical case study of the Tokyo Metropolitan Area was conducted. Dividing the area in location A and location B according to the complexity of the associated road network in terms of number of arcs, the case study was successfully solved. The optimized routes were improved significantly over the initial feasible solutions. It was shown that the problem formulation and the tabu search meta-heuristics algorithm can solve large-scale, realistic, and complicated instances within reasonable computation time.

Based on the realistic case study of the Tokyo Metropolitan Area tested in this research, it can be concluded that: (i) establishing multiple intermediate depots can effectively decrease total travel cost (tc); however, such a decrease shall be carefully analysed in case one need to include the establishment cost of the intermediate depot; (ii) operating multiple vehicles may not effectively decrease total travel cost (tc), considering that working in a network with blocked access imposes the conditions that routes must be operated in a particular sequence; and (iii) operating multiple vehicles can effectively decrease total required time (tt) which is appropriate in operations with time restrictions either at disposal site or at depot.

Considering that not much research has been done in the topic of disaster debris collection operation, we propose some topics that may be the future research. In addition, such proposed researches are expected to complement and enhance the results of our research. We recommend some topics which will improve the assumptions taken in our research, such as: (i) adding alternative shortest paths from node i to node j; (ii) adding value for access possibility constraint, i.e. $p_{ij}^k = 0$ (vehicles are not allowed to move from node i to node j); $p_{ij}^k = 1$ (allowed); and $p_{ij}^k = 2$ (allowed with penalty); (iii) adding information about the priority of road to serve in advance, as well as the urgency level of debris respect to the type and location.

Acknowledgements

We would like to thank the anonymous reviewers for the constructive comments and suggestions that have led to an improved paper. We also would like to thank Nagahisa Hirayama, Dr (Eng.), for providing us valuable data of the estimation of disaster debris from earthquake and catastrophic flood disasters in the Tokyo Metropolitan Area. These supports are gratefully acknowledged.

Funding

This work was partially supported by Department of Urban Management, Graduate School of Engineering, Kyoto University.

References

Aguilar, M. A. S., Langevin, A., & Laporte, G. (2012). Synchronized arc routing for snow plowing operations. *Journal of Computers & Operations Research, 39*, 1432–1440.

Altay, N., & Green, W. G. (2006). OR/MS research in disaster operations management. *European Journal of Operations Research, 175*(1), 475–493.

Angelelli, E., & Speranza, M. G. (2002). The periodic vehicle routing problem with intermediate facilities. *European Journal of Operational Research, 137*, 233–247.

Assad, A. A., & Golden, B. L. (1995). Chapter 5 arc routing methods and applications, handbooks in operations research and management science. *Journal of Network Routing, 8*, 375–483.

Augerat, P., Belenguer, J. M., Benavent, E., Corberan, A., & Naddef, D. (1998). Separating capacity constraints in the CVRP using tabu search. *European Journal of Operational Research, 106*, 546–557.

Baldacci, R., & Maniezzo, V. (2006). Exact methods based on node routing formulations for undirected arc routing problems. *Journal of Networks, 47*, 52–60.

Cardoso, S. R., Barbosa-Povoa, A. P. F. D., & Relvas, S. (2013). Design and planning of supply chains with integration of reverse logistics activities under demand uncertainty. *European Journal of Operational Research, 226*, 436–451.

Christofides, N. (1973). The optimum traversal of a graph. *Omega, 1*, 719–732.

Cordeau, J. F., & Laporte, G. (2002). *Modeling and optimization of vehicle routing and arc routing problems*. Les Cahiers du Gerard, G-2002-30, Montreal.

Cordeau, J. F., Laporte, G., & Mercier, A. (2001). A unified tabu search heuristic for vehicle routing problems with time windows. *Journal of the Operational Research Society, 52*, 928–936.

Costa, M. C., Hertz, A., & Mittaz, M. (2002). Bounds and heuristics for the shortest capacitated paths problem. *Journal of Heuristics, 8*, 449–465.

Crevier, B., Cordeau, J. F., & Laporte, G. (2007). The multi-depot vehicle routing problem with inter-depot routes. *European Journal of Operational Research, 176*, 756–773.
Dror, M. (2000). *Arc routing: Theory, solutions and applications*. Boston: Kluwer.
Eiselt, H. A., Gendreau, M., & Laporte, G. (1995a). Arc routing problems, Part I: The Chinese postman problem. *Journal of Operations Research, 43*, 231–242.
Eiselt, H. A., Gendreau, M., & Laporte, G. (1995b). Arc routing problems, Part II: The rural postman problem. *Journal of Operations Research, 43*, 399–414.
Ergun, Ö., Carbajal, J. A., Keskinocak, P., Stilp, M., & Villarreal, M. (2010). *Managing debris collection and disposal operations.* Proceedings of the seventh triennial symposium on transportation analysis (TRISTAN VII), Tromso, Norway, June 20–25.
Gendreau, M. (2003). An introduction to tabu search. In F. Glover & G. A. Kochenberger (Eds.), *Handbook of meta-heuristics* (pp. 37–54). Boston: Kluwer.
Golden, B. L., De Armmon, J. S., & Baker, E. K. (1983). Computational experiments with algorithms for a class of routing problems. *Computers and Operations Research, 10*, 47–52.
Hertz, A., Laporte, G., & Mittaz, M. (2000). A tabu search heuristics for the capacitated arc routing problem. *Journal of Operations Research, 48*, 129–135.
Hirayama, N., Shimaoka, T., Fujiwara, T., Okayama, T., & Kawata, T. (2010). *Establishment of disaster debris management based on quantitative estimation using natural hazard maps.* Waste management and the environment V. Tallinn, Estonia, WIT Press.
Hu, T. L., Sheu, J. B., & Huang, K. H. (2002). A reverse logistics cost minimization model for the treatment of hazardous wastes. *Journal of Transportation Research Part E, 38*, 457–473.
Longo, H., De Aragao, M. P., & Uchoa, E. (2006). Solving capacitated arc routing problems using a transformation to the CVRP. *Computers and Operations Research, 33*, 1823–1837.
Luther, L. (2008). *Disaster debris removal after hurricane Katrina: Status and associated issues, congressional research service.* CRS report for congress.
Mastrolilli, M. (2001). *Tabu search*, IDSIA –Dalle Molle Institute for Artificial Intelligence.
Pearn, W., Assad, A., & Golden, B. L. (1987). Transforming arc routing into node routing problems. *Computers and Operations Research, 14*, 285–288.
Pramudita, A., Taniguchi, E., & Qureshi, A. G. (2012). Undirected capacitated arc routing problem in debris collection operation after disaster. *Journal of Japan Society of Civil Engineers, Ser. D3 (Infrastructure Planning and Management), 68*(5), 805–813.
Rafee, N., Karbassi, A. R., Nouri, J., Safari, E., & Mehrdadi, M. (2008). Strategic management of municipal debris aftermath of an earthquake. *International Journal of Environmental Research, 2*(2), 205–214.
Sheu, J. B. (2007). An emergency logistics distribution approach for quick response to urgent relief demand in disasters. *Journal of Transportation Research Part E, 43*, 687–709.
Solomon, M. M. (1987). *VRPTW benchmark problems.* Retrieved from http://www.sintef.no/Project web/TOP/VRPTW/Solomon-benchmark/
Tagmouti, M., Gendreau, M., & Potvin, J. (2007). Arc routing problem with time dependent service costs. European *Journal of Operational Research, 181*, 30–39.
Wohlgemuth, S., Oloruntoba, R., & Clausen, U. (2012). Dynamic vehicle routing with anticipation in disaster relief. *Journal of Socio-Economic Planning Sciences, 46*, 261–271.
Yang, W. H., Mathur, K., & Ballou, R. H. (2000). Stochastic vehicle routing problem with restocking. *Journal of Transportation Science, 34*(1), 99–112.
Yi, W., & Kumar, A. (2007). Ant colony optimization for disaster relief operations. *Journal of Transportation Research Part E, 43*(6), 660–672.
Yi, W., & Odamar, L. (2007). A dynamic logistics coordination model for evacuation and support in disaster response activities. *European Journal of Operational Research, 179*(3), 1177–1193.

Appendix 1

The amount of debris in every node (in ton): 1/46 = 0; 2 = 81.1; 3 = 83.5; 4 = 21.1; 5 = 65.9; 6 = 65.9; 7 = 84.6; 8 = 1.8; 9 = 94.4; 10 = 83.5; 11 = 70.3; 12 = 49.2; 13 = 59.3; 14 = 94.4; 15 = 44.8; 16 = 91.6; 17 = 1.4; 18 = 1.4; 19 = 8.6; 20 = 99.6; 21 = 81.1; 22 = 99.6; 23 = 36.5; 24 = 79.2; 25 = 70.3; 26 = 21.1; 27 = 27.5; 28 = 44.6; 29 = 26.2; 30 = 27.5; 31 = 59.3; 32 = 98.5; 33 = 24.2; 34 = 24.2; 35 = 44.6; 36 = 26.2; 37 = 84.6; 38 = 1.8; 39 = 44.8; 40 = 91.6; 41 = 8.6; 42 = 36.5; 43 = 79.2; 44 = 49.2; 45 = 98.5.

Appendix 2

The best route of vehicles: 1-3-10-46-4-26-29-36-27-30-33-34-46-2-21-19-41-18-17-46-5-6-8-38-46-7-37 -46-9-14-46-11-25-46-12-44-28-35-46-13-31-46-20-22-46-23-42-15-39-46-16-40-46-24-43-46-32-45-1.

Appendix 3

The amount of debris in every node (in ton): 1/198/199 = 0; 2 = 23.7; 3 = 23.7; 4 = 30.7; 5 = 30.7; 6 = 11.3; 7 = 11.3; 8 = 18.4; 9 = 18.4; 10 = 42.1; 11 = 42.1; 12 = 46; 13 = 46; 14 = 92.2; 15 = 92.2; 16 = 60.8; 17 = 60.8; 18 = 64.8; 19 = 64.8; 20 = 21.1; 21 = 21.1; 22 = 20.9; 23 = 20.9; 24 = 21; 25 = 21; 26 = 29.3; 27 = 29.3; 28 = 23.7; 29 = 23.7; 30 = 18.6; 31 = 18.6; 32 = 22.1; 33 = 22.1; 34 = 41.5; 35 = 1.5; 36 = 55.2; 37 = 55.2; 38 = 21.7; 39 = 21.7; 40 = 23.6; 41 = 23.6; 42 = 46.3; 43 = 46.3; 44 = 35.7; 45 = 35.7; 46 = 22.9; 47 = 22.9; 48 = 21.6; 49 = 21.6; 50 = 23.7; 51 = 23.7; 52 = 20; 53 = 20; 54 = 21.4; 55 = 21.4; 56 = 15.5; 57 = 15.5; 58 = 10.1; 59 = 10.1; 60 = 15.4; 61 = 15.4; 62 = 16.3; 63 = 16.3; 64 = 11.3; 65 = 11.3; 66 = 31.3; 67 = 31.3; 68 = 19; 69 = 19; 70 = 23.4; 71 = 23.4; 72 = 22.7; 73 = 22.7; 74 = 14.6; 75 = 14.6; 76 = 40.9; 77 = 40.9; 78 = 9.4; 79 = 9.4; 80 = 12.3; 81 = 12.3; 82 = 21.7; 83 = 21.7; 84 = 22.8; 85 = 22.8; 86 = 14.5; 87 = 14.5; 88 = 9.4; 89 = 9.4; 90 = 11.9; 91 = 11.9; 92 = 15.1; 93 = 15.1; 94 = 14.6; 95 = 14.6; 96 = 12.3; 97 = 12.3; 98 = 9.7; 99 = 9.7; 100 = 11.8; 101 = 1.8; 102 = 7.3; 103 = 7.3; 104 = 19.6; 105 = 19.6; 106 = 17.2; 107 = 17.2; 108 = 14.9; 109 = 14.9; 110 = 13.8; 111 = 13.8; 112 = 8.7; 113 = 8.7; 114 = 12.9; 115 = 12.9; 116 = 13.8; 117 = 13.8; 118 = 10.8; 119 = 10.8; 120 = 8.1; 121 = 8.1; 122 = 8.7; 123 = 8.7; 124 = 6.8; 125 = 6.8; 126 = 15.7; 127 = 15.7; 128 = 14.7; 129 = 14.7; 130 = 12.9; 131 = 12.9; 132 = 14.9; 133 = 14.9; 134 = 11.1; 135 = 11.1; 136 = 7.5; 137 = 7.5; 138 = 10.7; 139 = 10.7; 140 = 12.6; 141 = 12.6; 142 = 9.3; 143 = 9.3; 144 = 7.8; 145 = 7.8; 146 = 6.8; 147 = 6.8; 148 = 5.1; 149 = 5.1; 150 = 6.9; 151 = 6.9; 152 = 18.8; 153 = 18.8; 154 = 9.5; 155 = 19.5; 156 = 16; 157 = 16; 158 = 38; 159 = 38; 160 = 31.1; 161 = 31.1; 162 = 23.1; 163 = 3.1; 164 = 17.7; 165 = 17.7; 166 = 43.6; 167 = 43.6; 168 = 41.1; 169 = 41.1; 170 = 15.5; 171 = 15.5; 172 = 8.8; 173 = 8.8; 174 = 53.7; 175 = 53.7; 176 = 24.7; 177 = 24.7; 178 = 15.9; 179 = 15.9; 180 = 6.6; 181 = 56.6; 182 = 19.1; 183 = 19.1; 184 = 34.9; 185 = 34.9; 186 = 77.7; 187 = 77.7; 188 = 67.5; 189 = 67.5; 190 = 94.3; 191 = 94.3; 192 = 6.3; 193 = 6.3; 194 = 39.6; 195 = 39.6; 196 = 7.3; 197 = 7.3.

Appendix 4

The best route of vehicles: 1-182-183-180-181-179-178-198-188-189-196-197-193-192-173- 172-198-184-185-105-104-103-102-129-128-121-120-99-98-198-169- 168-145-144-141-140-115-114-113-112-80-81-198-171-170-78-79-162- 163-158-159-148-149-150-151-198-177-176-174-175-164 -165-198-166- 167-143-142-139-138-137-136-131-130-119-118-198-186-187-101-100- 89-88-198-106-107-108-109-97-96-83-82-75-74-57-56-198-127-126- 125-124-117-116-111-110-84-85-86-87-91-90-198-67-66-55-54-31- 30-28-29-198-155-154-13-12-9-8-122-123-146-147-198-157-156- 161-160-152-153-132-133-134-135-198-194-195-25-24-3-2-58-59- 198-93-92-63-62-49-48-47-46-73-72-198-65-64-53-52-51-50-32-33- 68-69-198-77-76-41-40-39-38-198-191-190-198-70-71-61-60-94-95- 43-42-198-27-26-5-4-20-21-198-34-35-36-37-198-22-23-19-18-7-6-198-45-44-17-16-198-11-10-198-14-15-1.

Appendix 5

The best route of vehicles: 1-184-185-105-104-103-102-129-128-121-120-99-98-199-45- 44-17-16-199-46-47-60-61-71-70-63-62-49-48-199-43-42-41- 40-39-38-199-56-57-73-72-94-95-83-82-75-74

-173-172-198-188- 189-193-192-196-197-171-170-198-182-183-177-176-174-175-198- 169-168-145-144-141-140-142-143-149-148-150-151-147-146-137- 136-199-81-80-111-110-97-96-84-85-86-87-88-89-100-101-198-178- 179-180-181-79-78-164-165-198-166-167-152-153-132-133-134-135- 138-139-199-35-34-32-33-27-26-199-36-37-154-155-157-156-122-123- 199-51-50-52-53-31-30-28-29-58-59-199-112-113-77-76-13-12-199-116- 117-124-125-119-118-109-108-107-106-67-66-199-114-115-126-127-130- 131-93-92-69-68-65-64-90-91-199-54-55-25-24-3-2-21-20-7-6-199-15-14- 199-18-19-5-4-199-190-191-198-162-163-58-159-161-160-198-186-187-22- 23-199-9-8-11-10-199-194-195-1.

Appendix 6

The best route of vehicles.

Group_1 = 1-188-189-193-192-198-178-179-180-181-198-105-104-198-129-128-121- 120-199-43-42-199-48-49-199-74-75-122-123-199-71-70-199-62-63-124- 125-199-76-77-137-136-199-92-93-199-54-55-199-39-38-199-130-131- 135-134-199-15-14-199-190-191-198-194-195-1.

Group_2 = 1-173-172-169-168-198-177-176-198-166-167-198-158-159-161-160- 198-106-107-67-66-199-60-61-89-88-199-81-80-112-113-199-52- 53-199-116-117-139-138-199-114-115-146-147-199-31-30-27-26- 199-86-87-5-4-199-28-29-199-18-19-199-132-133-199-20-21-1.

Group_3 = 1-184-185-186-187-196-197-198-164-165-174-175-198-103- 102-101-100-199-46-47-199-56-57-36-37-199-35-34-150-151-199- 51-50-199-111-110-118-119-199-96-97-140-141-198-127-126-199- 64-65-90-91-199-13-12-199-7-6-199-25-24-199-9-8-199-3-2-1.

Group_4 = 1-182-183-198-171-170-78-79-198-162-163-198-145-144-148-149-143- 142-199-45-44-17-16-199-73-72-199-82-83-199-94-95-99-98-199-41-40- 199-84-85-199-69-68-199-109-108-59-58-199-32-33-199-154-155-198- 157-156-198-152-153-199-11-10-199-22-23-1.

London 2012: changing delivery patterns in response to the impact of the Games on traffic flows

Michael Browne[a], Julian Allen[a], Ian Wainwright[b], Andrew Palmer[c] and Ian Williams[d]

[a] *Faculty of Architecture and the Built Environment, Planning and Transport Department, University of Westminster, London, UK;* [b] *Transport for London, London, UK;* [c] *School of Management, Heriot Watt University, Edinburgh, UK;* [d] *Independent Consultant, UK*

The paper addresses road freight transport operations during the London Olympic and Paralympic Games in 2012. It presents work carried out prior to the Games to understand pre-Games patterns of freight deliveries in London (for both light and heavy goods vehicles) and the results of modelling work carried out to assess the likely impacts of the Games road restrictions on freight operations. The modelling results indicated that increases in total hours travelled carrying out collection and delivery work would range from 1.4% to 11.4% in the six sectors considered. The results suggested increases in hours travelled in excess of 3.5% in four of the six sectors modelled. The possible actions that could be taken by organizations to reduce these negative impacts were also modelled and the results indicated that such actions would help to mitigate the impact of the road restrictions imposed on operators during the Games. The actual impacts of the 2012 Games on transport both in general terms and specifically in terms of freight transport are also discussed, together with the success of the actions taken by Transport for London (TfL) to help the road freight industry. The potential freight transport legacy of the London 2012 Games in terms of achieving more sustainable urban freight transport is considered and the steps being taken by TfL to help ensure that such a legacy can be realized are discussed. Such steps include policy-makers continuing to collaborate closely with the freight industry through the 'London Freight Forum', and TfL's efforts to encourage and support companies revising their delivery and collection times to the off-peak; improving freight planning in the design and management of TfL-funded road schemes; electronic provision of traffic information by TfL to the freight industry, and the further development of freight journey planning tools.

1. Introduction

The London Olympic Games featured approximately 11,000 athletes from more than 200 nations competing in 26 sports consisting of 300 events. The Games ran for 16 days from 28 July to 12 August 2012. The London Paralympic Games commenced 18 days after the Olympic Games Closing Ceremony. This comprised 4200 athletes with a disability from 162 countries competing in 20 sports. The Paralympics ran for 11 days from 30 August to 9 September 2012.

In order for London to meet its commitment to an efficient transport service for athletes, officials, and others it required a number of transport measures will be put in place on the London road network. These measures included: the Olympic and Paralympic Route Networks (ORN/PRN) which linked competition and key non-competition venues; dedicated Games lanes on certain stretches of the ORN/PRN; and revised waiting and loadings restrictions on the ORN/PRN. There was a potential conflict between providing fast and reliable transport services to those visiting and participating in the London 2012 Games while at the same time ensuring that the Games-related traffic did not have a negative impact on freight deliveries in London.

Recent Olympic and Paralympic Games prior to London 2012 have required the implementation of road and non-road transport initiatives to help ensure that athletes, officials, sponsors, the media, spectators, and goods and services arrive at the venues as and when required. This has involved the development of new transport infrastructure and the imposition of road transport regulations (Bovy, 2001, 2004, 2009, 2010; Currie & Delbosc, 2011; Frantzeskakis & Frantzeskakis, 2006; Hensher & Brewer, 2002; Lui, Guo, & Sun, 2008; Minis & Tsamboulas, 2008; Zhou et al., 2010). However, before London 2012 the Games have not been subject to planning efforts to ensure that non-Olympics business could continue to operate efficiently during the Games period. In this sense, the London 2012 Games marked an important landmark, with substantial time and resources devoted to attempting to ensure that potentially negative transport and logistics impacts on businesses were avoided (London Assembly, 2010; Transport for London [TfL], 2011a).

The paper analyses pre-Games patterns of freight deliveries in London (for both vans and lorries) and presents the results of modelling work carried out to assess the likely impacts of the London 2012 Games road restrictions on freight operations, and the possible measures that could be taken by organizations to reduce these negative impacts. The actual transport impacts on the Games both in general terms and specifically in terms of freight transport are also discussed together with the potential freight transport legacy.

2. Road freight traffic in London

A starting point in the study was an assessment of pre-Games road freight traffic in London performed by light and heavy goods vehicles (LGVs and HGVs). In 2009, HGVs and LGVs travelled a total of 1.0 and 4.1 billion vehicle kilometres in London, respectively. HGV and LGV activity accounts for 16% of all vehicle kilometres on London's roads (Table 1).

An estimate of annual vehicle kilometres travelled by LGVs and HGVs was obtained based on data for annual vehicle kilometres travelled by LGVs and HGVs provided by the TfL Road Network Performance Team. Assumptions were then applied to the data to derive daily vehicle activity by trip purpose. In 2009, HGVs and LGVs travelled a total of 1.0 and

Table 1. Total vehicle kilometres travelled on roads in London in 2009 by vehicle type (billions and percentages).

	Vehicle kms (billion)	Proportion (%)
Cars and taxis	25.4	80
Two-wheeled motor vehicles	0.8	2
Buses and coaches	0.6	2
LGVs	4.1	13
HGVs	1.0	3
Total	31.9	100

Source: TfL (2011b).

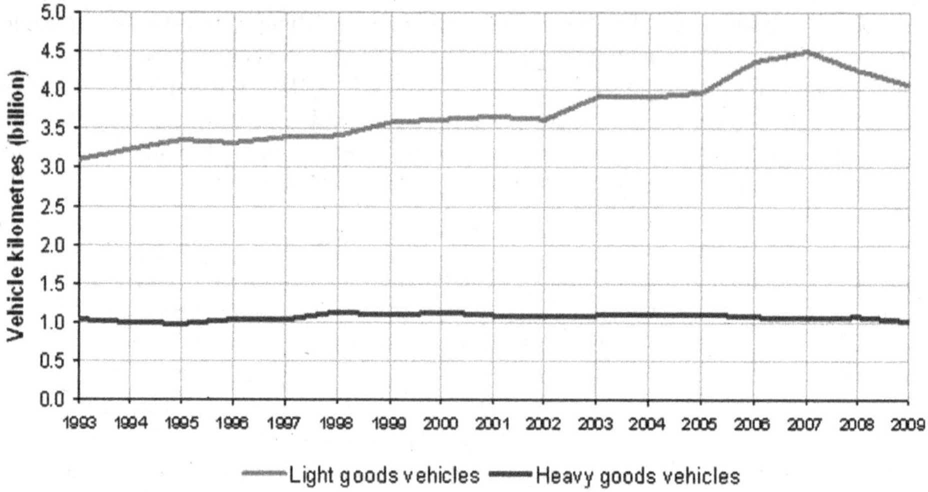

Figure 1. Vehicle kilometres performed by goods vehicles on all roads in London, 1993–2009. Source: TfL (2011b).

4.1 billion vehicle kilometres in London, respectively. HGV and LGV activity accounts for 16% of all vehicle kilometres on London's roads (Table 1). TfL data indicate that LGVs and HGVs performed 59% and 84%, respectively, of their total distance travelled in London on major roads (TfL, 2011a).

Figure 1 shows the annual vehicle kilometres travelled by HGVs and LGVs in London since 1993. This indicates that HGV traffic has remained relatively stable over the entire period, while LGV traffic rose between 1993 and 2007, and then fell to 2009, with the onset of the recession (TfL, 2011a).

In order to estimate LGV and HGV vehicle kilometres taking place in London on an average weekday by activity purpose it was necessary to take account of several factors and apply suitable assumptions to the annual activity data. First, not all LGV activity is associated with goods transport. In fact, data suggest that the majority of LGV activity is accounted for by other journey purposes (including the provision of services, commuting, and personal travel). Data from the Department for Transport (DfT) Company Van Survey 2003–2005 and Privately Owned Van Survey 2002–2003 indicate that at a national scale only approximately 30% of LGV vehicle kilometres are accounted for by goods transport, while servicing activity accounts for approximately 25% of vehicle kilometres and commuting and private activities account for approximately 45% of vehicle kilometres (DfT, 2004, 2008). It was assumed that all HGV activity was for the purpose of goods transport. Second, not all LGV and HGV activity associated with goods transport involves laden vehicles; some vehicle activity takes place with the vehicle running empty. The DfT Continuing Survey of Road Goods Transport estimates that between 2005 and 2009 approximately 30% of HGV kilometres were run empty on all journeys to, from, and within London (DfT, 2010). The DfT Company Van Survey 2003–2005 suggests that empty running among LGVs is approximately half the HGV rate (DfT, 2008).

Table 2 shows the estimate of the total number of LGV and HGV vehicle kilometres in London on a typical weekday by type of activity. LGV activity was subdivided into: goods transport activity, servicing activity, and commuting and private activity. Goods transport activity by LGVs and HGVs has been subdivided into laden and empty activity.

Table 2. Estimated LGV and HGV vehicle kilometres in London on a typical weekday in 2009.

Activity type	LGV vehicle km (million)	HGV vehicle km (million)	LGV + HGV vehicle km (million)
Goods transport (laden)	4.2 (26%)	2.8 (70%)	7.0 (34%)
Goods transport (unladen)	0.7 (5%)	1.2 (30%)	1.9 (10%)
Service provision	4.1 (25%)	0 (0%)	4.1 (20%)
Commuting and private	7.3 (45%)	0 (0%)	7.3 (36%)
Total	16.3 (100%)	4.0 (100%)	20.3 (100%)

Source: Estimated from data provided by TfL (2011b).

Table 3. Typical weekday 24-hour inbound vehicles crossing the London cordons (thousands and percentages).

	Boundary cordon		Inner cordon		Central cordon	
Time period	Number	Proportion (%)	Number	Proportion (%)	Number	Proportion (%)
Cars and taxis	1000	79	715	75	402	68
Two-wheeled motor vehicles	18	1	33	3	41	7
Buses and coaches	13	1	27	3	31	5
LGVs	168	13	142	15	87	15
HGCs	62	5	41	4	26	4
Total	1260	100	959	100	587	100

Source: TfL (2011b).

Cordon traffic count data also provide an insight into LGV and HGV activity in London. Analysing cordon traffic count data by time of day provided an insight into the times of day at which LGVs and HGVs carry out their activities in London. Locations of traffic counts for monitoring long-run trends in traffic flows in London are organized to form three cordons: (i) boundary cordon: roughly corresponding to the boundary of Greater London and entirely within the M25 orbital motorway, (ii) inner cordon: enclosing an area similar to the inner London boroughs, and (iii) central cordon: a cordon, enclosing central London, situated outside the Inner Ring Road and within a radius of 2.5–3 km from Aldwych.

These cordon data show that approximately 87,000 LGVs and 26,000 HGVs enter central London on a typical weekday (which accounts for 15% and 4%, respectively, of all motorized vehicles entering central London – see Table 3) (TfL, 2011b).

Table 4 shows the proportion of inbound LGVs and HGVs crossing each cordon by time period. This indicates that the vast majority of inbound vehicle movements for goods and service provision take place between 06:00 and 18:00 (approximately 80% of these inbound vehicle movements) (TfL, 2011b).

Various data sources were combined to estimate the types of goods vehicle activity underway during different periods of the day including the morning (AM) peak, the inter-peak, and the afternoon (PM) peak periods, further distinguishing for LGVs the type of activity being carried out (Table 5).

Important findings that can be drawn from this analysis in Table 5 include that for return commuting trips on LGVs, almost as many commence before 16.00 hours as after it; the latter are skewed towards the hour 16.00–17.00, with a declining percentage thereafter. For all other LGV trip purposes as well as for HGV movements, the proportion in the PM peak

Table 4. Proportion of inbound LGVs and HGVs crossing the London cordon counts by time period.

	Boundary cordon		Inner cordon		Central cordon	
Time period	LGV (%)	HGV (%)	LGV (%)	HGV (%)	LGV (%)	HGV (%)
00:00–05:59	4	8	5	9	8	11
06:00–11:59	46	46	51	50	46	48
12:00–17:59	36	35	32	33	34	31
18:00–23:59	14	11	12	9	12	10
24 hours	100	100	100	100	100	100

Notes: Cordon counts are based on 16-hour (06:00–22:00) manual classified counts using six minutes in 15 sample counts. Night-time flows are estimated based on a sample of sites which are counted for the full 24 hours. Boundary and central cordon data are based on 2004–2009 annual average and inner cordon data are based on 2005–2010 annual average.
Source: TfL (2011b).

Table 5. Proportion of LGVs by trip purpose and HGVs occurring by time period.

Weekday period		LGV				HGV
	Duration	Service (%)	Outbound commuting (%)	Return commuting (%)	Collection and delivery (%)	Collection and delivery (%)
Other	19.00–06.59	11	32	14	11	23
AM peak	07.00–09.59	22	48	4	23	25
Inter-peak	10.00–15.59	56	16	37	57	46
PM peak	16.00–18.59	10	4	45	9	6
24-hour		100	100	100	100	100

Source: Own estimation based on combining data from TfL Cordon counts, TfL CRISP RSI Surveys, and DfT's LGV Surveys of 2003–2005.

is much lower than that found earlier in the day. The reason for this is that on average goods vehicle usage starts earlier in the day than that of cars, so that a high number of goods vehicles are already on the road before 07:00. Because the goods vehicle drivers start early in the morning, they also tend to finish work in the afternoon, rather than later in the evening peak period.

This indicated that overlapping use of the road network by goods vehicle movements and Games traffic was likely to be most pronounced from the early morning (06:00) through the afternoon (to 17:00), by which time most service and delivery activity is scaling down, with the majority of goods vehicles returning to base rather than initiating new service or delivery activity. An important exception would be those vehicles picking up parcels, post, and courier items at the end of the business day.

In the early morning, the period of intense LGV and HGV activity would be likely to overlap with that of important Games movements. For example, the Olympic Stadium, would typically host two sessions per day; one in the morning, then another starting mid-afternoon, and lasting through the evening. The arrivals and the departures from the first session as well as the arrivals to the second session would all potentially occur during periods of high levels of goods vehicle activity. In other venues with a single session that did not commence too early in the morning, the highest level of LGV activity may already have passed by the main time of travel of Games participants and spectators.

In the PM peak it was predominantly the car traffic, rather than the goods vehicle traffic, that would potentially overlap with the Games traffic. The reduction in the goods vehicle traffic as the afternoon progresses would be more than compensated by the increase in car traffic such that total traffic would potentially be significantly higher in the PM than in the AM peak, leading in turn to slower speeds on average in the PM than in the AM peak for each of Central, Inner, and Outer London.

3. Road restrictions for the London 2012 Games and their likely impacts

In order to achieve the rapid transport of 80,000 athletes, officials, sponsors, and the media to the London 2012 sites (as well as goods and other equipment) an ORN/PRN was planned to be put in place across London's road network. The ORN/PRN was the series of roads around London and the UK that would link competition venues and key non-competition venues. The ORN would total 105 miles in London and 173 miles outside London and would be roadwork free and subject to measures such as traffic signal timing changes. The ORN would be in force from July to September 2012 on 2.6% of London's roads (Olympic Delivery Authority [ODA], 2010a). Almost 60 miles of the ORN in London would consist of dedicated lanes. Dedicated lanes to transport athletes, officials, sponsors, and the media to venues were also used at the Athens and Beijing Games (Currie & Delbosc, 2011).

Other measures to be used on the ORN/PRN included the prevention of right turns, side road closures, changes to traffic lights and pedestrian crossings, adjustments to bus and coach stops, and the temporary suspension of bus stops. There would also be additional parking restrictions and road closures around the sites and during on-street events (including the marathons, road cycling, triathlon, and race walks as well as cultural events). Stopping on the ORN/PRN was only to be permitted between midnight and 06:00, and journey times to central London businesses that were not on the ORN/PRN but were surrounded by it or which were close to event and non-event venues were likely to be longer than normal. Responsibility for the ORN/PRN was transferred from the ODA to TfL (2011a). These restrictions were considered to be potentially challenging to London businesses.

The ODA suggested in 2010 that the transport arrangements necessary for the Games would have a negative impact on deliveries and collections in the rest of London. It stated that the road restrictions put in place across London would affect goods and service provision at establishments and that businesses may not be able to receive goods and services at their usual times, with operations at some locations not being possible at all at certain times (ODA, 2010b). An investigation set up by the London Assembly Transport Committee into the transport arrangements for the Games also raised concerns about the potentially serious knock-on effects on traffic congestion and businesses in London (London Assembly, 2010). The Freight Transport Association (FTA) expected traffic restrictions being put in place for the Olympics to cause three types of disruption for non-Games road freight transport in London: (i) journey time unreliability arising from the reduction in road space and transfer of traffic onto other routes, (ii) difficulties accessing specific roads that are either closed or subject to banned right turns, and (iii) difficulty stopping on-street to load and unload as kerbside access would be affected by the restrictions (FTA, 2011). The impacts of the Games road restrictions would vary by sector, but two operational outcomes were likely:

- average journey lengths may increase, leading to an increase in total vehicle kilometres travelled and
- the average journey speeds and loading/unloading speeds may fall, leading to an increase in the total time taken to carry out freight operations and less predictable journey times.

Without pre-planning by businesses both of these outcomes could result in business continuity issues, empty shelves, and greater costs for companies; and if unconstrained, would lead to more freight vehicles on the road.

Analysis identified that the types of goods flow most likely to be affected by the Games road restrictions were: (i) time critical goods and service supply requirements, (ii) regular goods replenishment, (iii) products that have a short shelf life, and (iv) operations that involve many delivery legs (i.e. multi-stop) and require frequent kerbside access. This analysis suggested that sectors likely to be worst affected included: retail (food and non-food); restaurants, pubs and cafes; hotels; and hospitals and other health-care providers (especially in relation to medical emergencies). Logistics operators most likely to be affected were identified as: those specializing in fast-moving consumer goods (FMCG); fresh food; parcels, courier, and postal operators; cash and valuables-in-transit operators; and waste collection operators. The logistics industry contains some large companies but also many smaller firms. However influencing the resulting 'tail' of small and single owner-operator vans would be required as these are critical to supporting smaller firms. Service operators providing rapid response and emergency services (such as utility companies; and electrical/plumbing providers and individual contractors) were also identified as potentially being highly affected.

In terms of the geographical impact of the road restrictions for the Games, the analysis suggested that establishments located on or close to the ORN/PRN, Central London Zone, and venues were likely to be affected in terms of journey duration and journey time reliability, as well as experiencing difficulties in finding on-street stopping locations for loading/unloading/servicing activities.

Establishments not located close to the ORN/PRN, Central London Zone, and venues, may also experience journey time unreliability if they received visits from vehicles that needed to use roads on or near the ORN/PRN on the journey to them. In addition these areas could be seriously impacted by the active traffic management regime in controlling access onto and across the ORN/PRN. This was especially likely in the case of vehicles that make multi-stop journeys on or close to the ORN/PRN – such journeys could suffer delays that have repercussions for all establishment served on the journey regardless of their proximity to the ORN/PRN.

4. Modelling the impacts of road restrictions during the games

Modelling of the implications of the ORN on freight movements used a strategic logistics network planning model. The model is a single integrated application used specifically to address supply chain network problems. The model used has the ability to examine the different flows of goods, or distribution channels, from supply points through a network of storage and transhipment facilities to customer delivery locations. The techniques applied in this model have been used extensively by commercial organizations to minimize costs and maximize service levels and are now being used more frequently by researchers to assess the impacts of policy and sustainability measures on logistics networks. Supporting this software is a road network used for calculating times and distances between the various points such as depots and customers. In the London area, encompassing the region within the M25 motorway, this digitized road network comprises a set of nodes representing locations including motorway exits, junctions, roundabouts, traffic lights, and changes in road category, and a set of links which contains information about the stretch of road connecting the nodes. The journey speeds assigned to different roads can be modified in the model to reflect the prevailing conditions or restrictions that exist.

Data requirements for this type of modelling exercise include flow information with origin and destination locations, the frequency of movement and quantity moved between these two points, and the type of vehicle used. Transport operating parameters for each vehicle are also required, including vehicle capacity, operating hours, shifts, fixed and variable collection and delivery times, and typical fuel consumption.

Data for six different industrial sectors were used in the modelling: (i) the 'FMCG' sector based on data comprising the operations of six of the top eight supermarket retailers, plus wholesalers and major manufacturers in London, (ii) a major food service company that services thousands of local shops and restaurants in London and their delivery sizes are relatively smaller than the other companies in the FMCG data, (iii) transport movements into and out of the five London wholesale markets, (iv) household waste collection transport and volume by London borough, (v) home delivery of parcels in London from a major parcels carrier, and (vi) movements of large retail items (involving two-man delivery) in London from three major retailers. These data were obtained from the transport operators responsible for these collection and delivery services and their clients.

The model provides outputs that were expressed in terms of the total time taken to carry out the required goods collections and deliveries in a company's logistics network given the origins and destinations to be served, the frequency of these collections and deliveries, the assigned road speeds, and the vehicle types specified for use. This allowed various scenarios to be tested and their outcomes in terms of the total vehicle hours required to perform the required work in each of the sectors to be compared in order to analyse the effects of different road speeds, and company initiatives that could be used to mitigate against slower journey times. It must be noted there is not a direct translation from theoretical vehicle hours to the number of additional vehicles required, as drivers hours legislation comes into play in practice.

Road traffic modelling work carried out by TfL indicated that there would be substantial reductions in traffic speeds in and around the ORN/PRN if traffic volumes and timings in London remained the same during the Games as pre-Games levels given the road restrictions that were to be imposed. Given this traffic modelling work by TfL it was assumed in the logistics modelling that there would be a reduction of 20% in traffic speeds on and in the vicinity of the ORN/PRN if no action was taken to change to the pre-Games volume and timing of road traffic. Based on this assumption about traffic speeds, the logistics modelling results showed increases in total hours travelled carrying out collection and delivery work for all six sectors modelled, ranging from 1.4% (parcels – primarily home delivery, business to consumer movements) to 11.4% (wholesale markets – all business to business movements). The results suggested increases in hours travelled in excess of 3.5% in 4 of the 6 sectors modelled. An increase in the time taken to carry out collection and delivery work in London would result in additional labour and vehicle requirements and hence an increase in operating costs.

It was forecast that the UK will experience an additional £750 million consumer spending in the seven-week period of the Games; the vast majority of this additional spending will be made by international visitors and will occur in London (Visa Europe, 2011). The sectors likely to benefit most from this additional expenditure were retail and leisure (hotels, food and drink, entertainment, and travel) which would also lead to an increase in the demand for goods flows.

Modelling was therefore also carried out in which it was assumed that in addition to 20% lower vehicle speeds on and in the vicinity of the ORN there would also be a 10% increase in demand for retail goods and food and drink during the Games. The results indicated that in this scenario total vehicle hours would increase by 14–16% if the additional goods demand was met by operators making more deliveries (i.e. by increasing their delivery frequency).

5. Modelling of mitigations

The ODA and TfL produced guidance for London businesses informing them that they should consider altering their freight and logistics systems to avoid problems (ODA, 2010b). Their advice to businesses receiving, sending, and carrying out goods delivery and collection work and servicing activity was to consider the so-called 4Rs: namely reducing activity, re-timing activity, re-routeing activity, and revising the transport mode used where possible. Specific solutions put forward included: receiving and collecting goods at less busy times and on less busy days, assessing whether fewer goods could be received during the Games and reviewing which deliveries were essential; stockpiling non-perishable goods in advance of venue and on-street events, sharing resources and deliveries with other local businesses, changing the goods delivery point, considering whether there were alternative locations to receive deliveries, and planning alternative routes to avoid congestion hotspots. TfL worked closely with businesses and other organizations likely to be affected by the road restrictions during the Games to develop action plans to address these issues (TfL, 2012a). The actions that companies could take to mitigate the Games road restrictions mainly fell into two broad categories:

- Increasing the grouping of freight transport (through measures such as ordering less frequently, sharing deliveries with neighbouring businesses, using urban consolidation centres, etc.) and
- Changing the time at which freight transport activities take place to when the ORN restrictions are not in force.

Actions taken to increase the grouping of freight transport would be expected to increase vehicle load factors and reduce vehicle empty running, thereby leading to reductions in the vehicle hours and kilometres travelled. Actions taken to shift the times at which freight transport takes place to the off-peak/night would be expected to lead to faster vehicle speeds for these off-peak journeys, and hence also reduce total vehicle hours.

The modelling results indicated that both of these actions had the potential to play an important role in helping to minimize the consequences of the road restrictions imposed during the Games. It was calculated that if a transport operator could make use of out of hours deliveries (00:00–06:00 hours) this could lead to a reduction in total vehicle hours required of over 6%. Reducing the number of deliveries and collections made during the Games by grouping deliveries would also result in substantially lower total vehicle hours in 4 out of the 6 sectors modelled.

6. What actually happened during the London 2012 games

6.1. *Short-term economic effects of the Games*

Available data suggest that the London 2012 Games did help to contribute to UK economic growth. Office for National Statistics (ONS) data show that the UK economy grew 1% in the third quarter of 2012, emerging from recession in the three months from July to September. The ONS calculated that Olympic and Paralympic Games generated about £580 million in ticket sales and that this added 0.2% to the level of GDP in the third quarter of 2012 (ONS, 2012a).

The Games may not have had the hoped for effect on retail growth. British Retail Consortium data show retail sales in the UK were 4% lower in August 2012 than the same month in the previous year (BBC, 2012). Some retailers felt that warnings from the government and the Mayor of London to stay away from central London to avoid crowding had deterred shoppers (Alleyne & Ford Rojas, 2012).

Evidence on the effect of the Games on tourism has been mixed, with fewer people visiting Britain but those that do spending more on average. ONS figures show that the number of visits to the UK by overseas residents in August 2012 was 5% lower than the same month in 2011 (ONS, 2012b). The number of sea passengers arriving and departing at UK ports was 15% and 10%, respectively, lower in July and August 2012 than the same months in 2011 (DfT, 2012). There was also approximately 1–2% fewer arrivals and departures at UK airports in July and August 2012 compared to the same months in 2011 (DfT, 2012). International Passenger Survey data showed 4% fewer visits to the UK by overseas residents in July–September 2012 compared with the same period in the previous year. However, the average amount spent by Olympics visitors was approximately twice as much as the average spent by other visitors (ONS, 2012b). Some tourist sites reported fewer visitors during the Games than during the same period in 2011 (Smithers, 2012).

6.2. *General transport impacts of the games*

Using August 2011 as a representative baseline, road traffic reductions of between 6% and 7% in central London, 1–3% in inner London, and increases in 1–3% in outer London were experienced across both the Olympics and Transition period before the Paralympics (largely August 2012). Road traffic conditions during the Paralympics (in September 2012) were very close to 'business as usual' (TfL, 2012b).

A greater proportion of road traffic took place in the overnight hours compared to normal during the Olympics. In central London there was 13% more traffic in the period from midnight to 07:00, and in outer London there was 16% more. Morning peak (07:00–10:00) traffic in central London during the Olympics was 13% below the non-Games baseline, with inter-peak traffic 12% down and evening peak traffic down by 11%. During the Paralympics road traffic showed similar time shift patterns but were less marked than during the Olympics (TfL, 2012b).

Average traffic speeds at the Greater London level during the Olympics, transition and Paralympics period were

> close to what would otherwise have been expected given prevailing levels of traffic demand, and allowing for a degree of capacity removal from Games time traffic management measures. The same applies to journey time reliability for general traffic, with over 91 per cent of non-Games journeys completed reliably during the Olympics, and over 89 per cent during the Paralympics (compared to normal values of between 89 and 90 per cent). (TfL, 2012b)

Public transport was heavily used during the Games with the Underground carrying the majority of passengers. During the Games, Underground passengers were 28% higher than in the equivalent period in 2011. Tuesday 7 August was the busiest day in the Tube's history, with 4.57 million passengers carried. This demand was met by running more trains during normal service hours, particularly in the evening and late into the night to cope with returning spectators (TfL, 2012b).

London's transport network therefore functioned well during the period of the Olympic and Paralympic Games. However, it has been suggested that the communications campaign which advised people to avoid using public transport because of crowding was over-cautious (London Travel Watch, 2012).

6.3. *Freight industry actions and experiences during the games*

Large-scale telephone surveys with businesses and freight operators were carried out by TfL before and during the Games to establish its impact on business activity, the effectiveness of their plans to minimise disruption, and any long-term impacts. The results showed that 91% of businesses and 85% of freight operators said that they were ready for the Games. Fifty-eight per cent of freight operators and 57% of businesses made some sort of change to their operations as a result of the Games. Larger businesses were more likely to have changed with 72% of businesses with a turnover over £10m having made a change compared with 54% of those with under £10m turnover (TfL, 2012b).

Of the '4Rs' (i.e. reducing activity, re-timing activity, re-routeing activity, and revising the transport mode) that businesses were encouraged to consider implementing to cope with the Games, the survey work shows that 'reduce' and 're-time' options proved the most popular (with 45–50% of respondents taking initiatives in these areas), followed by 're-route' (with about 40% of freight operators and 25% of businesses adopting initiatives in this area), while the least popular were options around revising the mode of transport (with only 5% of businesses and freight operators changing the mode used) (Figure 2) (TfL, 2012b).

The most popular 'reduce' measures adopted by businesses and freight operators (in order of importance with the most adopted first) included: ensuring that deliveries were right first time, postponing non-essential deliveries, stockpiling, consolidating journeys, staff taking leave, staff working from home, sharing resources, and operating a temporary stockroom. The most popular 're-time' measures adopted (in order of importance

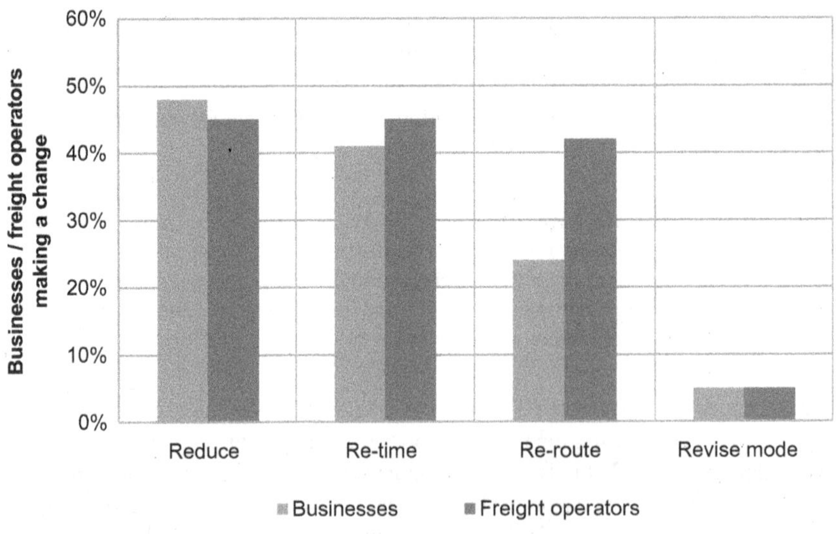

Figure 2. Proportion of businesses and freight operators who said that they made a change against each of the 4Rs.
Note: Based on 1000 freight operators and 1002 businesses.
Source: TfL (2012b).

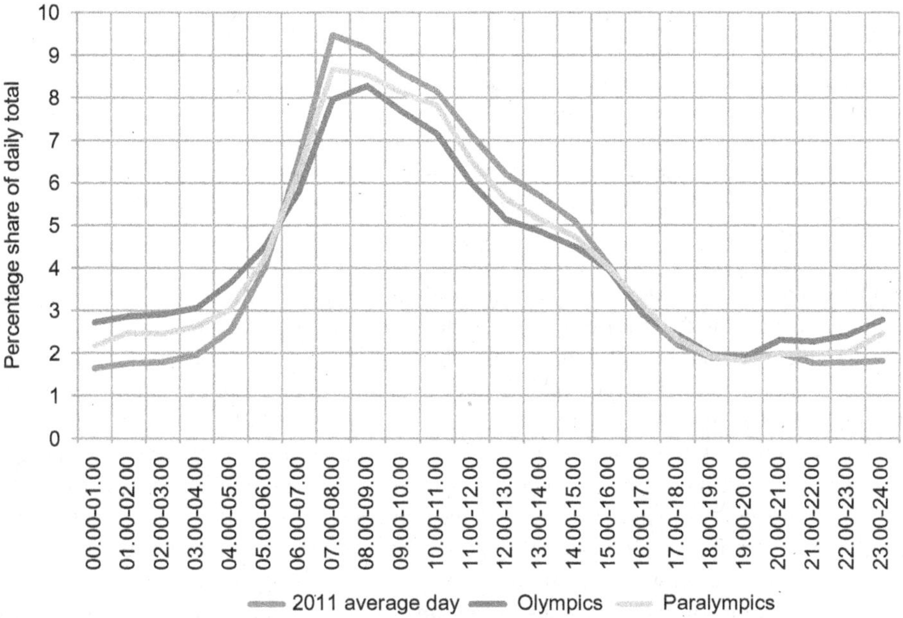

Figure 3. HGVs entering and leaving the Central London congestion charging zone.
Note: Each line sums to 100% = 100% of daily traffic.
Source: TfL (2012b).

with the most adopted first) included: and changing delivery and collection times, pre-ordering and pre-delivery of goods, changing staff starting times or shifts, and running out of hours operations. Figure 3 shows changes in the times of HGV operations in central London during the Games period compared with prior to it, indicating the shift to off-peak activity. 'Re-route' measures adopted (in order of importance with the most adopted first) included: avoiding congestion hotspots, avoiding traffic management restrictions, and the use of alternative locations. 'Revise mode' measures adopted (in order of importance with the most adopted first) included: walking, cycling, and river-based deliveries (TfL, 2012b).

Survey work carried out with freight operators and other businesses who were members of the Central London Freight Quality Partnership (CLFQP) following the end of the Games provided an insight into the actions taken by companies (CLFQP, 2012). Parcel carriers reported taking actions including starting delivery rounds earlier; out of hour deliveries including early morning, evening, and nights; re-planning of delivery rounds; relaxing of time guarantees; double-manning of vehicles; use of motorcycles and walkers; transfer of some product to other depots; and depots staffed for longer periods than normal to cope with early starts and late finishes. Other freight operators and receivers reported taking actions including: utilization of dedicated planning tools that incorporated all Games-related restrictions; risk assessment by matching of customer locations with restricted postcodes to identify possible road-related problems; evening and night deliveries to locations close to and on the ORN; delivery rounds commencing up to 3 hours earlier than normal; work reallocated to other depots; additional staffing and vehicles on-standby if required; planning of changed delivery times in advance with customers; and daily conference calls with customers.

A survey by the London Chamber of Commerce found that 51% of respondents made changes to their usual freight transport arrangements to help avoid delivery disruptions during the Games. The results showed that

> 24 per cent of respondents postponed non-essential orders, 19 per cent used alternative delivery methods, 18 per cent had deliveries at different times, 13 per cent used alternative suppliers and 15 per cent ordered larger quantities in a smaller number of deliveries. (London Chamber of Commerce, 2012)

Company inaction was due either to their local areas being unaffected or because client requirements prevented deliveries outside normal working arrangements.

Research carried out by TfL into goods vehicle traffic volumes indicates reductions of about 10% in volumes of longer vehicles (those greater than 5.2 m in length) during the Olympic period against levels that would otherwise be expected (TfL, 2012b).

In terms of changes in the time of goods vehicle operations in London as a whole, the data suggest a relative shift towards a greater proportion of LGV journeys being made overnight. However, there appears to have been no relative reduction in van traffic in the morning peak period. For HGVs, the data indicate substantial relative proportionate increases in journeys made overnight, together with reductions in the proportion of lorry traffic across the working day. In central London, these changes in the time of goods vehicle operations during the Olympics were even more marked than in London as a whole for both LGVs and HGVs with greater relative use during the night, and less relative use during the day than in 2011 (TfL, 2012b).

The London Chamber of Commerce survey reported that 54% of respondents experienced no delivery disruptions during the Games. Many respondents had no difficulty in continuing their usual delivery schedules, with some freight operators and suppliers finding no interest for night deliveries among their customers. Only 14% of respondents reported supply disruptions during the Games (London Chamber of Commerce, 2012). This suggests that changes in road traffic conditions in London during the Olympics are likely to have played a role in the prevention of freight transport disruptions as well as the actions taken by companies.

7. Legacy of the London 2012 Games for freight transport

Despite the adoption of the initiatives discussed above by businesses and freight operators it is rather unclear how necessary they were in order to avoid supply chain disruptions given the reductions in total road traffic in central and inner London during the Games. However, the Games did provide an opportunity for companies to implement a wide range of measures that they may not have otherwise ever attempted. TfL and other public bodies are hopeful that having adopted these initiatives during the Games, companies will continue to use them. This would constitute an important legacy for freight transport in London and would thereby potentially have a long-term downward impact on freight intensity and the negative impacts of freight. In addition companies located outside London may also choose to adopt such practices based on the experiences of businesses operating in London and the publicity surrounding the Games.

In terms of the lessons learned from the Games experience by respondents to the CLFQP survey, parcel carriers reported: the importance of correct and timely information in coping with such an event and ensuing that operations could be successfully maintained in a worst case scenario but that achieving this had a negative impact on operating costs; the important role of communication within companies, between supply chain partners and with public sector bodies; that forecasts of increased road traffic levels during the Games were over-estimated; and that carriers would now be more prepared for similar other future major events. Other operators and receivers reported that lessons learned included: the planning of details with all partners in the supply chain both public and private were very important; road information is essential for pre-planning and day-to-day operations in such a situation; obtaining and then transmitting information and knowledge throughout the organization was valuable to success; and that communication with local residents in situations where out-of-hours deliveries were to take place was helpful (CLFQP, 2012).

Research has indicated that only a small proportion of businesses and freight operators continued to persist with the operational measures they took (i.e. the '4Rs') during the London 2012 Games. Approximately 10% of businesses and 7% of freight operators that reduced deliveries during the Games continued to do so afterwards (which is equivalent to approximately 1.5% of all businesses and freight operators surveyed). Approximately 5% of all businesses and 3% of all freight operators surveyed have continued to make deliveries at revised times following the London 2012 Games (TfL, 2013a).

Business respondents noted barriers to reducing the number of deliveries once the 2012 Games had finished that included lack of support from customers, and the difficulties of reducing deliveries in the case of perishable goods. In the case of retiming deliveries, reported barriers to continuing these practices after the end of the Games included operating cost increases, lack of support from customers and delivery time restrictions (TfL, 2013a).

In terms of the impact of reducing the number of deliveries during the 2012 Games, approximately half of businesses and freight operators that adopted this measure experienced no change in operating costs, approximately one-quarter reported cost increases, approximately 5% experienced cost savings, and the remainder did not know the effect on their costs (TfL, 2013a). When asked about expected cost impacts if continuing with this practice after the end of the Games approximately 60% of businesses and freight operators expected no cost savings or increases, while most of the remainder expected increases in operating costs (TfL, 2013a).

Approximately half of all businesses and freight operators that revised the times of deliveries during the London 2012 Games experienced no change in operating costs, while approximately one-third reported cost increases, only 3% experienced cost savings, and the remainder did not know the effect on their costs. However, most of these businesses and freight operators surveyed expected costs to increase if they continued to revise their delivery times after the 2012 Games (TfL, 2013a).

Some of these measures taken by companies to avoid freight transport disruption during the Games have been reported by other sources as leading to extra effort and additional costs (Chapman, 2012; London Assembly Transport Committee, 2012; London Chamber of Commerce, 2012).

In the case of freight transport measures that incur additional costs and efforts for companies it will be necessary for such measures to also provide commercial benefits if a business case is to be made for adopting and continuing with them in the long term. Without such a business case the implementation of such operating measures are only likely to be adopted by companies for a short period of time during exceptional situations to ensure business continuity. As noted by TfL (2013a), 'It is therefore difficult to see night time deliveries being used extensively by the industry without any other motivational factor in place'.

However, although only a small proportion of businesses and freight operators have continued to reduce the number of deliveries or revise the timing of their operations outside of peak hours following the end of the London 2012 Games, this demonstrates that for some organizations the Games has instigated new ways of working. Also, the far higher proportion of organizations that adopted these practices during the Games indicates the scope for far greater levels of change given a suitable business case in which benefits outweigh costs.

TfL has recognized that the 2012 Games has led to much progress in identifying shared priorities between the public and private sectors in relation to road freight transport, and the potential that exists for long-term change in freight operating practices in London. TfL ran workshops with industry representation after the close of the 2012 Games to reflect on lessons learned and scope for achieving legacy outcomes for freight transport in London. This has led to the publication of a report in which TfL has noted the positive engagement and collaboration that was developed with the freight industry during the Games, especially through the 'London Freight Forum' which became the central focus for improving communication between TfL and the industry (TfL, 2013b).

In this report TfL has outlined a range of steps it will take to help ensure such a legacy. As well as building on the 2012 Games freight initiatives, this legacy needs to also take account of the forecast growth in London (with 1.25 million more people and 750,000 new jobs by 2031) and the efforts to improve road safety and encourage greater levels of cycling. These steps include: improving TfL road planning to ensure that freight activities are paid due consideration in the design and management of TfL-funded road schemes; developing means by which revised off-peak times for delivery and collection work can be encouraged; and further enhancing communication with and to the freight industry, for both planning and increasing awareness of potential solutions (TfL, 2013b).

TfL and the freight industry are viewing the potential for increased levels of out-of-hours delivery work as a desirable operational change resulting from the Games. Studies and trials had already been exploring this topic in recent years. The Games has given this initiative much publicity and has also given companies the opportunity to see that it is practical. It is hoped that this will result in more companies adopting it in future than was the case prior to the Games (FTA, 2012; TfL, 2012b). To progress this TfL is setting up the 'London Out-of-Hours Consortium', consisting of key boroughs, retailers, and trade associations to carry out a review of re-timing activity; initiating a long-term demonstration trial for re-timing deliveries; and developing guidance for boroughs and operators on retiming deliveries including how to go about amending existing operating (TfL, 2013b). The Mayor has indicated the potential to further encourage the uptake of delivery and servicing planning including greater use of load consolidation in freight transport operations serving both new and existing developments in London' (Mayor of London, 2012).

Other aspects of the Games legacy for freight transport include: the electronic provision of traffic information by TfL to the freight industry (which the industry is keen to see continue), and the further development of tools such as the Freight Journey Planner, which was made freely available by TfL to help companies and drivers with vehicle routeing and to find a legal loading space. TfL had already invested in the Freight Journey Planner but the Games gave the project an impetus to make it available sooner than originally planned (TfL, 2013b).

A close working relationship developed prior to and during the Games between public sector bodies (especially TfL and the London boroughs) and the freight transport industry including companies and trade associations. TfL and the freight industry have expressed a desire to continue this level of engagement and collaboration. This will include maintaining and strengthening the London Freight Forum that was established, and to work together to build on innovative and flexible freight practices employed during the Games (FTA, 2012; TfL, 2012b, 2013b). Other city authorities and public bodies in the rest of the UK and elsewhere may also decide to follow the example provided by fostering closer working relationships with industry to address freight transport issues, and to develop approaches and solutions promoted and used during the Games. Some companies also reported that they hoped to continue the closer working relationships that they had developed during the Games with other commercial partners in their supply chains.

In general, the publicity provided by the media to freight transport in the run up to and during the Games has also helped to increase public awareness of the industry. That freight transport operations managed to continue to function reliably during the Games resulting in goods and services continuing to be available as and when required by businesses and individuals has meant that this media coverage and attention has been positive.

8. Conclusions

Prior to the London Olympic and Paralympic Games there had been concerns that the traffic levels combined with the road restrictions that needed to be implemented to ensure the transportation of the Games family, athletes, and goods destined for the venues took place in a rapid and reliable manner could have major negative impacts on delivery and servicing activity in London. It was thought that these impacts would primarily involve reductions in freight vehicle journey speeds and journey time reliability, and could cause significant difficulties for businesses in terms of receiving goods and services. The modelling work carried out indicated a potential increase of up to 12% in vehicle hours required in some sectors (with a need for operators to either use more vehicles or operate longer shifts).

TfL produced guidance about how organizations could alter their freight and logistics systems to avoid problems during the Games. It also worked closely with freight operators and businesses receiving deliveries to put in place suitable plans in advance of the Games. This included shifting the time at which freight transport activities take place to the night when the ORN/PRN restrictions were not in force, and increasing the grouping of freight transport to reduce the necessary deliveries. TfL also made traffic information available to businesses throughout the Games period, and provided other tools such as the Freight Journey Planner.

Modelling of the proposed mitigations suggested that the expected impacts of the road restrictions on journey time and journey time reliability could be overcome if the advice provided by TfL about grouping deliveries and shifting the timing of operations was followed. The analysis indicated that these measures would help organizations to continue to receive the goods and services they required, and limit the increase in total goods vehicle operating hours necessary.

As a result of the actions taken by TfL, freight operators and other businesses, together with the reduced demand for road space as a result of TfL's effort to encourage car drivers to either avoid making journeys or use public transport, businesses continued to receive goods and services as they required during the Games period. TfL is keen to ensure that close and productive collaboration with the freight industry continues beyond the London 2012 Games. TfL is also taking steps to support industry so that the most promising of the freight transport actions taken by companies to cope during the Games, such as changing the time of delivery and collection activities to the off-peak, and consolidating goods flows will continue and grow in future, thereby reducing the negative impacts of freight transport through greater efficiency while maintaining high levels of service to customers. The importance of developing business models for these actions in which the economic benefits to companies outweigh the costs will be of central importance to their widespread adoption in the freight transport industry. If this can be achieved then the 2012 Games will have acted as a crucial catalyst to the fulfilment of more sustainable freight transport in London.

Funding

This work was supported by Transport for London.

References

Alleyne, R., & Ford Rojas, J.-P. (2012, July 31). We're bleeding, darling' – London's theatres, shops and hotels claim they are suffering because of the Olympics. *The Daily Telegraph*. Retrieved from http://www.telegraph.co.uk/sport/olympics/news/9440230/Were-bleeding-darling-Londons-theatres-shops-and-hotels-claim-they-are-suffering-because-of-the-Olympics.html

BBC. (2012, September 20). Retail sales hurt by Olympics in August. *BBC*. Retrieved from http://www.bbc.co.uk/news/business-19659806

Bovy, M. (2001). *Transport issues for the Sydney 2000 Olympics*. Paper presented at the UITP 54th world congress 20–25 May, London. Retrieved from http://www.mobility-bovy.ch/resources/My-Publications/49_UITP.London.01.pdf

Bovy, M. (2004). *Athens 2004 Olympic games transport*. REVUE VSS. 7-8. 45–48. Retrieved from http://www.mobility-bovy.ch/resources/My-Publications/34_VSS-JO-04.pdf

Bovy, M. (2009). Beijing 2008 Olympic games success: Massive public transport developments and major road traffic reduction. *Public Transport International, 3*, 52–55. Retrieved from http://www.mobility-bovy.ch/resources/My-Publications/05_UITP_Beijing-EN.09.pdf

Bovy, M. (2010). No transport white elephants. *Siemens ITS magazine for Intelligent Traffic Systems, 2*, 16–18. Retrieved from http://www.mobility-bovy.ch/resources/My-Publications/11.ITS-2010.PDF

Central London Freight Quality Partnership. (2012). *Survey of members' views and experiences concerning freight transport during the Olympic and Paralympic games: Summary report*. London: Author. Retrieved from http://www.londonsfqps.co.uk/LinkClick.aspx?fileticket=ND5Wn56ODOY%3D&tabid=178&mid=538

Chapman, N. (2012). Crossing the finishing line... *Freight,* October, 25–27.

Currie, G., & Delbosc, A. (2011, January). *Travel demand management for the summer Olympic games – approaches and impacts*. Paper presented at Transportation Research Board Annual Meeting, Washington, DC.

Department for Transport. (2004). *Survey of privately owned vans: Results of survey, October 2002 – September 2003*. SB (04) 21. London: Author.

Department for Transport. (2008). *Road freight statistics 2006*. SB (06) 23. London: Author.

Department for Transport. (2010). *Data provided by the road freight statistics Team*. London: Author.

Department for Transport. (2012). *Transport statistics Great Britain 2012: Spotlight on transport statistics during the London 2012 Olympic Games and Paralympics*. London: Author. Retrieved from https://www.gov.uk/government/statistical-data-sets/tsgb10

Frantzeskakis, J., & Frantzeskakis, M. (2006). Athens 2004 Olympic games: Transportation planning, simulation and traffic management. *ITE Journal, 76*(10), 26–32.

Freight Transport Association. (2011). *Managing deliveries and servicing during the Olympic games*. Tunbridge Wells: Author.

Freight Transport Association. (2012). *Logistics legacy: Celebrating logistics achievement and innovation during summer 2012*. Tunbridge Wells: Author.

Hensher, D., & Brewer, A. (2002). Going for gold at the Sydney Olympics: How did transport perform? *Transport Reviews, 22*(4), 381–399.

Hughes, D. (2012). *House of Lords library note: Debate on 8 November: Olympic and Paralympic games legacy*. LLN 2012/037. London: House of Lords.

London Assembly. (2010, November 3). *Concerns raised over impact of 2012 delivery*. Press release. London: Author. Retrieved from http://www.london.gov.uk/media/press_releases_london_assembly/concerns-raised-over-impact-2012-transport-plans

London Assembly Transport Committee. (2012). Committee meeting, transcript of Item 6: 2012 transport, 13 March. London: London Assembly. Retrieved from http://www.london.gov.uk/moderngov/ieListDocuments.aspx?CId=173&MId=4374&Ver=4

London Chamber of Commerce. (2012). *2012 the final hurdle: Securing a business legacy*. London: Author. Retrieved from http://www.londonchamber.co.uk/docimages/10783.pdfhttp://www.londonchamber.co.uk/docimages/10783.pdf

London Travel Watch. (2012). *2012 games legacy for London transport users*. Board meeting 25 September 2012. London: Author.

Lui, X., Guo, J., & Sun, Z. (2008). Traffic operation with comments during Beijing Olympic games. *Journal of Transportation Systems Engineering and Information Technology, 8*(6), 16–24.

Mayor of London. (2012). *Leaving a transport legacy: Olympic and Paralympic transport legacy action plan*. London: Greater London Authority. Retrieved from http://www.london.gov.uk/sites/default/files/leaving-a-transport-legacy.pdf

Minis, I., & Tsamboulas, D. (2008). Contingency planning and war gaming for the transport operations of the Athens 2004 Olympic games. *Transport Reviews, 28*(2), 259–280.

Office for National Statistics. (2012a). *Economic review – October 2012*. London: Author. Retrieved from http://www.ons.gov.uk/ons/dcp171766_285083.pdf

Office for National Statistics. (2012b). *Overseas travel and tourism – August 2012*. London: Author. Retrieved from http://www.ons.gov.uk/ons/rel/ott/overseas-travel-and-tourism—monthly-release/august-2012/stb-monthly-overseas-travel-and-tourism–august-2012.html

Olympic Delivery Authority. (2010a). *On time: London 2012 – Olympic route network and paralympic route network*. London: Author.

Olympic Delivery Authority. (2010b). *Keep on running*. London: Author. Retrieved from http://www.london2012.com/mm%5CDocument%5CPublications%5CTransport%5C01%5C24%5C08%5C97%5Ctraveladviceforbusiness-handbook.pdf

Smithers, R. (2012, October 9). UK tourist attractions suffer plunge in visitor numbers. *The Guardian*. Retrieved from http://www.guardian.co.uk/business/2012/oct/09/uk-tourist-attractions-plunge-visitor

Transport for London. (2011a, February 9). *Transport for London assumes responsibility from Olympic delivery authority for delivery of key 2012 Games transport programmes*. Press release. London: Author. Retrieved from http://www.tfl.gov.uk/corporate/media/newscentre/archive/18237.aspx

Transport for London. (2011b). *Analysis of road traffic data provided by Road Network Performance Team*. London: Author.

Transport for London. (2012a). *Operators' guide for the 2012 games*. London: Author.

Transport for London. (2012b). *Travel in London report 5*. London: Author. Retrieved from http://www.tfl.gov.uk/assets/downloads/corporate/travel-in-london-report-5.pdf

Transport for London. (2013a). *Olympic legacy monitoring: Adaptations to deliveries by businesses and freight operators during the games* (Travel in London Supplementary Report). London: Author. Retrieved from http://www.tfl.gov.uk/assets/downloads/corporate/olympic-legacy-freight-report.pdf

Transport for London. (2013b). *Delivering a road freight legacy: Working together for safer, greener and more efficient deliveries in London*. London: Author. Retrieved from http://www.tfl.gov.uk/assets/downloads/delivering-a-road-freight-legacy.pdf

Visa Europe. (2011). *A golden opportunity: London 2012 Olympic and Paralympic games expenditure and economic impact*. Visa Europe. Retrieved from http://www.visaeurope.com/en/newsroom/news/articles/2011/visa_2012_economic_impact.aspx

Zhou, Y., Wua, Y., Yang, L., Fu, L., He, K., Wang, S., Hao, J., Chen, J., & Li, C. (2010). The impact of transportation control measures on emission reductions during the 2008 Olympic games in Beijing, China. *Atmospheric Environment, 44*, 285–293.

Developing a local research strategy for city logistics on an academic campus

Thomas Hagen Zunder, Paulus Teguh Aditjandra and Bruce Carnaby

NewRail–Newcastle Centre for Railway Research, School of Mechanical and Systems Engineering, Newcastle University, Stephenson Building, Newcastle upon-Tyne, UK

This paper investigates the relative suitability of data and methodologies to assess the determinants of urban freight activity, based on a case study that has been carried out in a city centre university campus, in a medium-sized British city. Data, from procurement/purchasing and traffic surveys, have been used to set a baseline model of freight activity in the development of Delivery and Servicing Plans. A focused literature review of urban freight studies has been completed, in order to address identified urban freight challenges in meeting sustainability objectives. The study demonstrates imperfect data and raises questions that identify new research opportunities with new data collection, including focus group interviews, staff questionnaires, and stated preference surveys. These and other methodologies are identified to address the data gap, in order to develop a localized research strategy adapted to a local campus sustainability initiative.

1. Introduction

City logistics is a current concern, in many cities across the world, in improving sustainability, especially in the areas of noise, air quality, congestion, and carbon emissions. In Europe, the most urbanized continent in the world, over 60% of the European Union (EU) population currently lives in urban areas that make up 85% of the EU's GDP (European Commission, 2007). Recent literature reports various urban freight strategies, such as low emission zones (LEZs); urban consolidation centres (UCCs); and freight quality partnerships, all intended to reduce social and environmental impacts (see, for example, Allen & Browne, 2010; Browne, Allen, Nemoto, Patier, & Visser, 2012). These strategies have replaced previous foci of urban freight research in the 1970s, which were concerned mostly with the safety of heavy goods vehicles (HGVs), following a period when the UK saw little interest in the field, whilst Germany embarked on over 85 initiatives, most of which did not lead to viable success (Flaemig, 2003). Since the mid-1990s, this has been followed by an emerging interest in the logistics of collection and delivery services in town and city centres (Allen & Browne, 2010). Another observation on the dynamics of urban freight research from the past 20 years demonstrated a shift focus, from optimization of the supply chain, into organization and management of city logistics, to address urban freight issues (Gonzalez-Feliu, Semet, & Routhier, 2014). The implication of the organization and management of city logistics is particularly planning and transportation management; city freight transportation planning is not normally adopted by city authorities (Ballantyne & Lindholm, 2014) and, as a result, freight in the cities is becoming difficult to organize and to manage (Dablanc, 2007; Lindholm & Behrends, 2012; Muñuzuri, Cortés, Guadix, & Onieva, 2012).

Freight transport has become a significant problem for many cities. The objective of this paper is to demonstrate an avenue for the development of strategic freight planning, unfortunately often bypassed by most cities when developing strategic plans. Here we show an example of how freight transport greatly affects the functioning of an academic campus. We report on our investigations into the relative suitability of data and methodologies to assess the potential efficacy of interventions in urban freight activity on a typical city centre campus. Newcastle University is located in a medium-sized British city, in the North East of England. We present problems identified locally; a review of the literature; the local context and available data; the gaps in that data; potential research approaches; the developed research strategy; and conclusions.

2. Problem definition

We adopted an inductive approach to local problem definition, based on a critical realist approach to human systems, in that we accept the reality of vehicles, logistics systems, purchasing policies, and sustainability targets, but also that these 'real' objects are not always spontaneously apparent; that behaviour has meaning to the participants that can be different to rules, regulations, organograms, and procedures. We accept that, whilst an organization such as a university appears an objective reality, with hierarchies and rules, it is in fact a construct, mixing both apparent and hidden processes. To that end, we work in the mathematics and economics of quantitative data, whilst also employing interpretivist techniques to understand why behaviour occurs and to develop a systems approach that models (however imperfectly) the interaction of stakeholders (Bhaskar, 1989; Bryman, 2012; Reynolds & Holwell, 2010).

This approach is consistent with the view that city logistics is particular to a location; that the combination of 'why' (the goals), 'who' (the actors), 'with what' (the techniques), 'where' (the environment), and 'when' allows a systems approach that can localize the available intervention strategies to the unique nature of each urban case (Zunder & Dellinger, 2005). This is consistent with the fact that logistics networks in the Single European Market operate in multiple cities and nation-states, sometimes on the same day, for example, in France–Benelux–Germany (CITY FREIGHT, 2002).

2.1. *Local problems*

Newcastle University launched a Coherent Campus initiative in July 2008 following a 'Think Tank' workshop hosted by the Vice-Chancellor. Its aim is to improve the spaces between buildings to create a sense of place that is welcoming, with well-designed, well-linked social spaces. The campus aims to be permeable; pedestrian and cyclist friendly; safe; clean and tidy; visually recognizable; clearly defined; and environmentally sustainable. This has led to road closure on campus; parking space reduction; new buildings; new-build living accommodation; and pedestrianization. There was no brief to address freight, nor did the advising consultants address freight issues. The first transport focus was on sustainable travel planning, part of the 'Smarter Choices' programme introduced by the UK Department for Transport as soft policy measures, largely well known for promoting a reduction in carbon-based travel to school and workplace, via a personalized travel plan (Cairns et al., 2004). This work was carried out working closely with the local city council.

Within the university, the presence of freight vehicles generates a steady flow of complaints from senior management, generating pressure on the Estates Service and the purchasing function. Traffic data analysis shows that the proportion of freight on campus is high, at around 20% of all traffic entering university campus sites – above the norm for standard urban freight flows. Furthermore, unstructured observation of the campus shows a high level of illegal parking on the periphery (Zunder, Aditjandra, & Carnaby, 2012). Meetings and a stakeholder workshop in 2012 led to an agreement that the following issues needed to be addressed: how does a campus, with reducing vehicle access and increasing staff and student numbers, manage freight; increase sustainability; and prevent subsidiary impacts on the city?

3. Review of literature

This section comprehensively reviews urban freight studies from as early as the 1970s and focuses on recent researches of urban freight strategies that address the sustainability agenda. The subsections that follow then describe a review of city logistics literature, to address the local compact city campus freight issue, as well as to address large public organizations that aim to be green champions that promote sustainability.

Urban freight studies have emerged in transport academic literature since the 1970s, following concerns about urban goods movement, rather than the movement of trucks in cities (Ogden, 1977). The term 'urban goods movement' has been defined as the movement of goods (as distinct from people) to, from, within, and through urban areas and can comprise goods or services that are produced and consumed in an urban system (Ogden, 1992). Since the main concern of urban freight was goods movement, the literature about urban freight focused on the optimization of urban freight transport network operation (Button & Pearman, 1981), leading to the establishment of the city logistics concept (Taniguchi, 2001). Whilst this led to a better understanding of how to model urban freight traffic flow in the city environment, recent urban freight studies have focused on issues such as environmental impacts, sustainable economic growth, and quality of urban life. The need for urban freight policy, as part of city strategies, has begun to be realized and cross-nation, urban freight logistics best practices have been promoted (Zunder & Ibanez, 2004). Then the urban freight policies have been criticized as inefficient, despite the growing and changing needs of urban logistics services (Dablanc, 2007). Aspects such as the lack of urban freight data; uninformed public authorities in managing freight; and home deliveries became new areas for urban freight studies.

Alongside the classic issues of urban freight studies, discussed above, sustainability – encompassing economic, social, and environmental aspects, within the context of urban freight – has been the centre of discussion amongst urban freight researchers in the past decades (see, for example, Anderson, Allen, & Browne, 2005; Behrends, Lindholm, & Woxenius, 2008; Quak & De Koster, 2005, 2007). The initial focus leaned towards addressing the negative environmental aspects of transport, as identified by the United Nations following the Rio Earth Summit in 1992 and the Kyoto Protocol agreement of 1994, which target nations to reduce carbon emissions. The issue of urban transport of freight was also well acknowledged, alongside passenger transportation, on the European agenda for creating greener towns and cities (European Commission, 2007). In the UK, the research council funded the 'Green Logistics' project (2006–2010) that aimed to answer the call. Sustainability strategies for city logistics was a particular focus of the project, with a number of urban freight initiatives being discussed, including LEZs; UCCs; and freight quality partnerships (Allen & Browne, 2010). At the European level, 'BESTUFS – Best Urban Freight Solutions', an European Commission-funded project (2000–2008), had been promoted as a tool for urban freight professionals/practitioners to learn, to exchange, or to adopt best practices in urban freight strategies, centred on three main strategies: goods vehicles access and loading in urban areas; last mile solutions; and UCCs (Allen, Thorne, & Browne, 2007). Green Logistics and BESTUFS demonstrate industry's acknowledgement of urban freight strategies. A summary of recent urban freight strategies that have featured in academic literature can be seen in Table 1.

In Table 1, a number of strategies were given higher sustainability credit (i.e. ++ remarks) because those studies found a positive impact.[1] The +/− remarks indicate that such strategies were evidently beneficial in particular circumstances, but might not be applicable in different circumstances due to city planning, local (community) issues, location, etc. Additionally, the +/− remark can also be scored by a strategy considered to have a potential but untested benefit, for example, the freight tram case, and Delivery and Servicing Plans (DSPs).

Whilst the list of urban freight strategies is long and can be seen from various perspectives, including local administrations/urban communities (Muñuzuri, Larraneta, Onieva, & Cortés, 2005), product-type distribution channels (Danielis, Rotaris, & Marcucci, 2010), and urban planning (Allen, Browne, & Cherrett, 2012a; Hesse & Rodrigue, 2004), the strategies can be classified into six categories of urban freight policy, as defined by Stathopoulos, Valeri, and Marcucci (2012):

- market-based measures that aim to alter the market prices of goods (road pricing system);
- regulatory measures that refer to regulations enforced by control systems (vehicle access; out-of-hours delivery);
- land-use planning measures, such as zoning of commercial/residential activities (LEZs, UCC);
- infrastructural measures that aim to encourage modal shift (use of not-road modes; use/design of environmentally friendly goods vehicles: bicycles);
- new technological measures that aim to encourage exchange of data between logistics company agents and other parties (lorry routing schemes when road congested; loading/unloading bays management); and
- management measures that aim to promote cooperation between urban freight stakeholders (public–private partnership (PPP); DSP).

Five of the six measures above are interventionist approaches impacting mainly on the relationship between carriers, forwarders, and receivers – known as the traditional actors in the goods movement systems, as described in Ogden (1992). The sixth measure addresses the importance of the role of policy-makers in urban freight activities and is the main focus of recent urban freight research (Lindholm & Browne, 2013; Stathopoulos et al., 2012).

3.1. *DSPs as an intervention strategy*

DSPs are one of the recent strategies being promoted in the UK to address current urban freight issues (Cherrett et al., 2012). The DSP strategy is centred on the receiver within the supply chain, as opposed to traditional urban freight intervention strategies that have focused on the transport operator. Whilst the European-funded (Intelligent Energy Europe) TRAILBLAZER project (Wagdahl, 2010) promotes DSP as a soft urban freight transportation

Table 1. Recent urban freight strategies in academic literature.

Urban freight strategies	Location	Research findings	+/− to sustainability
LEZs	London, UK	Operators would generally comply LEZ (Browne, Allen, & Anderson, 2005)	+
Urban consolidation centre (UCC)	Across European cities	If applied properly can generate benefits but financial sustainability is an issue (Allen, Browne, Woodburn, & Leonardi, 2012)	+/−
Joint working public private partnership (PPP)	Paris, Utrecht, Linkoping, Gothenburg, London	Strong management and knowledge exchange with support of political involvement and focus on long-term possibilities (Lindholm & Browne, 2013)	+
Vehicle access weight/size/time restrictions	The Netherlands	Time windows harmonized between cities lead to fewer negative environmental effects (Quak & De Koster, 2007)	++
Out-of-hours delivery and reduced noise from operations	USA	The total savings to the carriers are not large enough to compensate the costs to receivers (Holguín-Veras, 2008)	−
Use of home delivery locker banks and collection points	Lyon, France	Home delivery induces about 13% of the road occupancy rates in urban areas (Gonzalez-Feliu, Ambrosini, & Routhier, 2012)	+/−
Use of non-road modes, e.g. tram	Barcelona, Spain	Waste tram scenario is better than retail delivery scenario (Regué & Bristow, 2013)	+/−
Lorry-routing schemes	Worldwide	Improvements in technology and logistics practices lead to efficient and less expensive transport (Hensher & Figliozzi, 2007)	++
Use/design of environmentally friendly goods vehicles, e.g. bicycles	London, UK	The use of UCC, bicycle, and electric vehicle reduced travel distance by 20% and CO_2 emissions fell by 54% (Browne, Allen, & Leonardi, 2011)	++
Road pricing systems	New York, USA	Cordon toll cannot be transferred to the receivers as it is a fixed cost; receivers are key to carriers' behaviour change (Holguín-Veras, 2011)	−
Delivery and servicing plans (DSPs)	UK cities	Load consolidation via DSPs and out-of-town freight consolidation centre with last mile in shared vehicles can be beneficial (Cherrett et al., 2012)	+/−

policy, still little is known of its effective deployment and use. Many unanswered questions remain about DSP as an urban freight strategy: how does it work; what advantage and/or disadvantage does the strategy bring; what is the impact on the organization's stakeholders; and, finally, what are the key drivers behind freight activity around (geographically) compact sites of a large organization?

When we talk about DSP here, it is not merely the optimization of a single operation within the last leg of a supply chain, but management and organization of multiple operations of last mile deliveries that can be optimized by efficient freight planning in an organization. We feel that this approach would suit compact campus university sites, which have a number of buildings with many deliveries across different locations. In addition, the many unknown aspects of DSP deployment in the urban freight literature provide another driver for us to look closely at this approach, to shed light on a new research avenue.

DSP is originally an urban freight strategy promoted by Transport for London in 2007, as part of the London Freight Plan sustainable freight distribution (Transport for London, 2007). This looks to assist retailers and other companies to consider the steps they can take to reduce the freight activity associated with their deliveries and collections that may benefit the reliability and cost of these operations. Whereas Cherrett et al. (2012) have defined DSP targeting high street retail businesses, we have focused on the case of DSP from a public sector viewpoint.

DSP has been promoted in the London Freight Plan, targeting high street retail businesses and other companies but, the early evidence of DSP effectiveness, as reported by Transport for London, was from the public sector experience. The pilot case of DSP concerned the relocation of a portion of Transport for London's own offices (Transport for London, 2009). The report describes how overall deliveries were reduced by 20%, within which catering, archives, and stationary deliveries were reduced by 40%. Additionally, best practices in facilities management were highlighted, with central storage and management of consumables (including paper, ink, tea, coffee, milk, sugar, etc.); consolidation of deliveries; and increased out-of-hours delivery activity. Responsible purchasing, via the evaluation of contracts with suppliers using vehicles registered to the Fleet Operator Recognition Scheme (FORS), was also highlighted. FORS is a subsidized certification scheme (i.e. a form of PPP policy measure) aimed at ensuring that fleet operators are aware of a range of exclusive, economically sound benefits to improve safety and reduce environmental impact. It is worth noting that this exercise was part of a major rationalization and consolidation of offices and considering whether the results are more to do with the DSP or with the efficiencies of co-location. The old maxim that 'the amount of stock held is the square of the number of stock locations' may be what we see here. To what extent can DSP improve urban freight activity without relocation? To what extent is DSP an incomplete framework that actually requires other methods to build it into a coherent research strategy?

3.2. *Organizational purchasing literature*

The focus of DSP is centred on the logistic receiver and, for that reason, the purchasing background of an organization, be it public or private, becomes relevant to the investigation. Logistics is an induced activity and derives from purchases. To understand the role of purchasing we need to identify the interests, drivers, and meanings of the profession, which can be quite different to those of transport practitioners and planners. Unlike the above urban freight studies, which have been the subject of transport and logistics disciplines, purchasing is drawn across business and management disciplines. Notwithstanding the difference, the agenda of the recent purchasing literature has demonstrated similar themes to recent urban freight studies. Socially and Environmentally Responsible Purchasing (Hoejmose & Adrien-Kirby, 2012), also known as 'sustainable purchasing', is the pursuit of sustainable development objectives through the purchasing and supply process, incorporating social, environmental and economic aspects (Walker & Brammer, 2009).

A recent comprehensive survey of sustainable purchasing in the UK public sector (Walker & Brammer, 2009) assessed a number of sustainable purchasing practices encompassing a number of dimensions, including environment, diversity, human rights, philanthropy, and safety. The analysis has shown that, relative to other sectors (e.g. health and education), local authorities place a particularly strong emphasis on buying from local and small suppliers and that education appears to place emphasis on recycling; buying from minority and female-owned suppliers; waste reduction; avoiding sweatshop labour suppliers; and reducing packaging. The challenges in the health sector were due to conflicting priorities, with patient care considerations taking precedence over sustainability in purchasing choices; moreover, medical consumables and clinical products may be less substitutable than products purchased by other public sector bodies. Cost has been found to be the leading barrier to sustainable purchasing, rather than the facilitation of supportive top management.

Purchasing does have a sustainability agenda, which could encompass DSP to improve freight efficiency in a sound manner, but we also need to note the role of cost, as a key driver in the profession, and look to how that can be incorporated into any intervention strategy. Since transparency, accountability, and achieving value for money for citizens and taxpayers is the basic principle of public procurement (Walker & Brammer, 2009), there is a degree of experimentation involved in this research, to test how far and to what extent transparency of delivery costs, incurred by the university as a public organization and as a purchaser, can be explained and understood.

4. Local context and available data

Newcastle University lies at the heart of a city with a population of circa 300,000 within a conurbation of circa 900,000, which lies on both sides of the river Tyne. The university main campus is integral to, but separated from, the main city, but there are also other campuses and sites integral to the city (Figure 1). The scope of the study is the main campus only since it can be clearly isolated, whereas many other sites have dual ownership or use, often with local National Health Service (NHS) hospitals. The university has over 144 schools/departments/institutes and over 80 buildings. There are around 5000 staff and 20,000 students, making it the second largest employer in the city. Even on the main campus, there are organizations that are autonomous or semi-autonomous to the university proper. These include the Students Union and the Northern Stage theatre. Catering outlets, whilst integrated, run separate purchasing and logistics systems.

Analysis of traffic count data, collected from 30 April 2012 to 4 May 2012, and analysis of purchasing data, from September 2011 to September 2012, has identified key facts about both the freight activity and buying patterns. The initial results were presented and reported by Zunder et al. (2012). The analysis was extended by identifying a research strategy to cover data gaps. The salient points are that the university is a key freight generator; 27% of all traffic attracted to the main campus is freight, using a mix of 82% light goods vehicles (LGV), with a flow of around 600 unique vehicles per day (traffic counted at four critical points). The reported usual European urban freight activity is between 10% and 18% (European Commission, 2006). Approximately one freight vehicle enters or departs

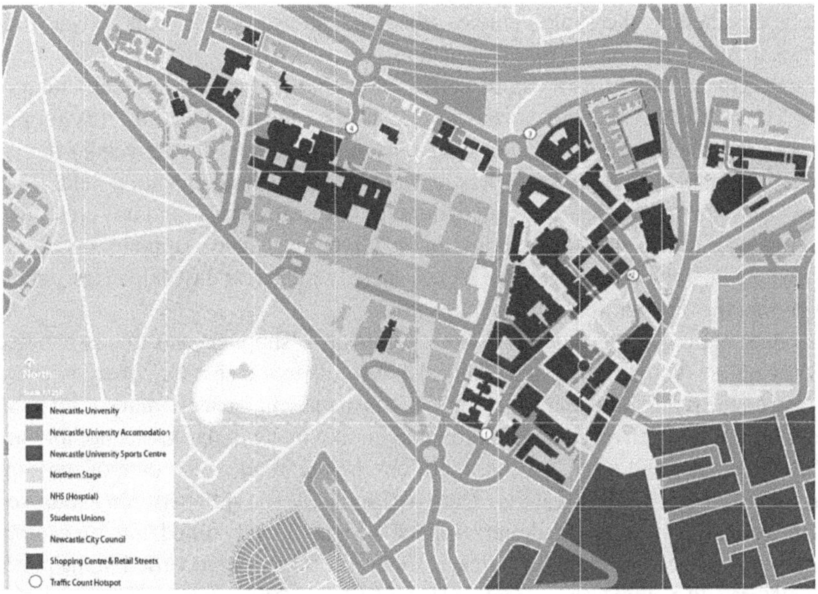

Figure 1. Main campus of Newcastle University with traffic count points numbered.

the main site every four minutes.[2] The vehicle make-up is also quite different from, for example, the local shopping centre, which has a majority HGV share within its delivery vehicles. The weekly flow of freight is quite stable through the working week (Monday to Friday); we see little of the daily differences that is evident at the adjacent hospital, deliveries are fairly flat save for a small and non-significant rise on Wednesday – traditionally a 'sports afternoon' in British universities – although no causal link has been shown.

Analysis of the purchasing data shows a similarly flat ordering pattern, and one might expect this to be reflected in the deliveries. However, analysis of the nature of purchase orders (PO) and the varying processes that underlie the activity shows that this is not the case. The university has 144 schools/departments/institutes that can raise a PO, via 466 expert buyers and 1058 shoppers (or requisitioners). Purchasing is highly decentralized, with the purchasing team focusing their efforts using a Pareto rule: that 80% of spend will be with 20% of suppliers and that these, plus the legal regulations on the spending of public money, take precedence. Of interest to urban freight researchers is the proportion of goods deliveries versus service visits, which the data (from September 2011 to September 2012) suggest is 70% goods and 20% services, with a tail of professional services and other works.

5. Data gaps

5.1. *Purchasing data*

Whilst the data allow insight into the freight entering and leaving the site and the top-level purchasing activity, it is problematic for our purpose, due to the fact that the system is designed to meet the financial needs of the institution, not the analysis of freight activity. Further understanding of the purchasing data shows that the volume of PO does not relate to delivery activity. Some PO represent a single item of medical equipment that is delivered with tens of others in the same vehicle; others are 'blanket' orders that cover a month's deliveries to multiple sites, on many occasions.

The catering function uses a wholly separate system, as does the Student Union and the theatre. The purchasing data are partial with respect to delivery location; it is not possible, in the majority of cases, to map a PO with a delivery location. The university has a single postcode with many (if not most) buyers failing to use the storage location field. Requested delivery dates are unreliable – the system defaults to the next day – and it is clear that many buyers place all orders with this default value. Given that many suppliers operate a 'next day' service, the university is sending a clear message for next day deliveries, and yet it is not clear that this is intentional.

The buyer is processing a demand from a user or a 'shopper' and this is handled by a secondary online requisition system. This also defaults to the next day; there is no systems link between the requisition and the resulting PO, so matching user demand with final PO is not possible. Actual delivery date is unreliable, in that many departments do not have staff to process receipts, and a receipt can, therefore, be recorded as the date of the supplier's despatch note, or just the date that the record was updated. The split between goods, services, and professional services is also doubtful, since we immediately noted that, for example, the university travel agent, who delivers tickets to the site all day, is recorded in the purchasing data as all three. In conclusion, we realized the difficulty of using purchasing data to estimate activity type and link it to vehicle trips. Positively however, this led to further steps being taken to engage university suppliers to gain a better understanding of delivery patterns and what strategies might be employed to reduce the negative impact of the current state of deliveries and servicing.

5.2. *Traffic count data*

The literature suggests that a dwell time of 7–35 minutes is a delivery (Browne, Allen, Steele, Cherrett, & McLeod, 2010; Cherrett et al., 2012) and this was adapted, using our knowledge of the site, to 5–35 minutes, with shorter than 5 minutes being through traffic, and longer than 35 minutes being a service visit. The traffic count data (all survey points combined) reveal a dwell time split of 27% longer than 35 minutes; 55% between 5 minutes and 35 minutes; and 18% less than 5 minutes. We also see a noticeable peak of freight between 08:30 and 10:30 each day. The 06:00–12:00 period is considered by the literature to generate the most urban deliveries for high street businesses (Cherrett et al., 2012), so the concentration between 08:30 and 10:30 at the university prompts a question: is this due to the university's perceived demand for just-in-time, next day deliveries? The traffic count also shows 18% as through traffic, yet the points monitored were not through roads; additionally, it would be very difficult to make a delivery at these points, due to the position of reception areas, relative to the road. When this was discussed in a wider forum, it was suggested that in fact this was so-called kiss and ride activity, where the driver of an LGV drops off or picks up their spouse/partner at work. Indeed, the degree to which the suppression of passenger traffic has created non-typical behaviour *requires further exploration*.

The traffic survey showed a very low record of courier, parcel, and post carriers, including a total absence of FedEx, UPS, or DHL. This could have been put down to poor recording of company deliveries but, after walking the site for a few days, it became apparent that illegal parking on the periphery of the campus – possibly a consequence of campus pedestrianization – means that such services are no longer entering the campus at all, preferring to 'stop and run' to make a delivery, before driving on to possibly the next illegal stop.

6. Research strategy

At the beginning of this paper, we stated our adopted epistemological position as 'critical realist', where we accept the reality of the natural order but accept also that the observable pattern of events alone does not make the reality identifiable. We also stated an adopted ontological position that was 'constructionist', asserting that social phenomena (such as the buying, selling, and transportation of goods) are constructed through social interaction and subject to constant revision (Bryman, 2012). We believe that the first inductive results of our research support the approach as sound for this case. This is because the observable patterns of events, such as traffic counts, or PO, or delivery records, are artefacts of behaviour which has meaning and that meaning has to be derived through a systems approach that includes the actors/stakeholders.

Three types of stakeholder within the university are considered to play important roles in shaping the current freight behaviour. Each of the stakeholder groups will be dealt with by a different approach, with the objective of fully understanding how decisions are made that create a freight delivery at university sites.

The first stakeholder group considered are the end users and the buying agents that pass their demand through to the supplier. Amongst the approximately 5000 staff employed by the university, 1058 are eligible to raise a PO (shoppers) on the university procurement system and, within that group, 466 are categorized as 'expert' buyers. Whilst the purchasing data reveal the end PO, they do not reveal a variety of issues, such as the validity of requested delivery date, the underlying demand, and the degree to which the delays in the administrative process change the original requirement.

The second group of stakeholders considered is based on all staff and research-based students. The rationale for selecting this category, separately from the shoppers, is the identification of employee personal orders delivered to the work place. This activity, which may be sustainable, generates freight operations around the sites, which may or may not be incremental to the needs of the organization itself.

The third type of stakeholder considered is the university's supplier base. The procurement data show that circa 2700 vendors supplied the organization in the period analysed, categorized into four vendor types: 'goods', 'professional service', 'service', and 'works'. Each month there are around 500 vendor orders recorded for goods, with a similar figure for the sum of the remaining vendor types.

Allen, Browne, and Cherrett (2012b) listed various survey techniques to elicit quantitative data for the analysis of both freight deliveries and the originating demand; however, before designing the data collection, we must better understand how to analyse the data, as discussed next.

7. Methodologies considered

7.1. *Systems approaches*

Systems approaches managing complex issues date back to the 1950s. They recognize that both human and engineering problems can be 'messy', but they vary in their degree of objectivism versus constructionism and group- or expert-led approaches. We have evaluated five approaches, each with a proven track record of over 25 years. The five approaches (adapted from Reynolds & Holwell, 2010) are the following:

- System Dynamics (SD) developed originally in the late 1950s by Jay Forrester;
- Viable Systems Model (VSM) developed originally in the late 1960s by Stafford Beer;

- Strategic Options Development and Analysis (SODA: with cognitive mapping) developed originally in the 1970s by Colin Eden;
- Soft Systems Methodology (SSM) developed originally in the 1970s by Peter Checkland; and
- Critical Systems Heuristics (CSH) developed originally in the late 1970s by Werner Ulrich.

Each of the aforementioned approaches was assessed for the Newcastle University study, as shown in Table 2.

More than one of these methods being appropriate to our required approach in addressing the issues, we shall adopt the more interpretivist one, which has an available software suite, as well as being clearly led by the actors' view of process, problems, and meaning. Our choice for the first identified stakeholder group – the university 'buyers' – is therefore SODA, a systems approach well suited to designing interventions able to work with 'messy' problems. We shall utilize workshops with the 466 'expert buyers' to understand how they understand the process of buying and how they meet the needs of their internal customers. It is likely that we will explore the degree to which the institutional 'message' to suppliers, regarding service delivery methods, is consciously constructed, or whether in fact it is an unintended consequence of people and procedures. It will also be of great interest to explore the extent to which the university is in fact one organization at all, or whether it is more akin to a small town or high street. As part of this technique, the different potential interventions will be developed, and/or changed, as a better understanding is reached of the desired outcome of the final demand. This will be accompanied by better mapping of PO and locations and also a reshaping of the data to better equate the small frequent PO of a medical researcher with the single catering order that triggers hundreds of deliveries over an extended time span.

7.2. *Multivariate statistical analysis*

A multivariate analysis is an examination of observed behaviour. This analysis attempts to explain, rather than merely describe, what is going on. A questionnaire-based survey is targeted at all staff and students (the second identified stakeholder group) to capture data about purchasing behaviour, attitudes, and preferences, which encompass the social, environmental, and economic aspects of urban freight transportation. This simple low-level survey aims to identify the level of private purchases delivered to the university. This may well also include a section for staff about their perceptions of customer service, to corroborate the SODA results.

7.3. *Revealed/stated preferences*

There are several reasons why revealed preference (RP) data will not be easy to collect/use, although RP data could be used to analyse how suppliers (stakeholder group 3) currently respond to demand from the university. This would be problematic, given the effect of lack of detail upon the quality of the data collected to match purchasing to deliveries. It seems unfeasible to restructure the ICT systems to focus on delivery data, when the institution's primary focus is teaching and research, not logistics management. It may be possible to further enrich the revealed data by requesting data sets, for the dates of the traffic count, from our suppliers' systems, since they are indeed focused on logistics. We shall do this, but are left with a core problem of RP: that to evaluate the effect of change, it must be piloted to see how the behaviour changes. This can be problematic in that it may involve

Table 2. Comparative systems approaches, adapted from Reynolds and Holwell (2010).

System approach	Summary	Strength	Rating for Newcastle University study
SD	An approach for thinking about and simulating situations and organizations of all kinds and sizes by visualizing how the elements fit together, interact, and change over time. Uses feedback structure and behaviour, causal loop diagrams, and dynamics	Strategic planning and evaluation	++ for planning and evaluation −− for understanding from actor perspective −− use of equations not sympathetic to non-technical actors −− stated as 'difficult' for novices −− 'hard' objective systems thinking
VSM	A conceptual model built from the axioms, principles, and laws of viable organization. It can be used as a comparison against an actual organization to identify weaknesses, mismatches, or missing elements in diagnosing a problem and then as a framework for organization design to resolve a diagnosed problem. Understands that autonomy exists within an apparently hierarchical and objectively 'real' organization	Modelling difference between reported and perceived organizational structures	++ weakness identification −− process is not actor led and therefore relies on the practitioner's interpretation not the users/actors −− 'hard' objective systems thinking ++ adopts constructionist approach to organizations
SODA	Enables a group or individual to construct a graphical representation of a problematic situation and thus explore options and their ramifications with respect to a complex system of goals or objectives. In addition, the method aims to help groups arrive at a negotiated agreement about how to act to resolve the situation	Group-focused negotiated construct to explore options	++ actor led, group focused ++ adopts constructionist approach to organizations + inductive − less focused on solution planning + off the shelf software and accompanying process available
SSM	An approach for tackling problematical, messy situations. It is an action-oriented process of inquiry into problematic situations in which users learn their way from finding out about the situation, to taking action to improve it	An organized process in which the situation is explored using a set of models of purposeful action	++ predicated on differing world views, which may never be resolved ++ looks for solutions that are feasible −− appears to assume problems are objective
CSH	A framework for reflective professional practice organized around the central tool of boundary critique. Boundary critique is presented as a participatory process of unfolding and questioning boundary judgements rather than as an expert-driven process of boundary setting	Working constructively with tensions between opposing perspectives as they arise	++ adopts constructionist approach to organizations + addresses interventions and methodology −− literature shows an expert-driven method

infrastructure, operational, or commercial changes which are costly to set up. It may also be difficult to obtain sufficient variation in the RP data to examine all the variables of interest, in order to develop utility functions.

Stated Preference Survey refers to a family of techniques that use individual respondents' statements about their preferences to estimate utility functions. This technique is particularly helpful when there are variables that are not immediately apparent to the researcher, since the process can allow for such 'unknown' factors to be inferred through analysis. There are some criticisms with any stated preference survey. People may not act as they say they will; there are problems inherent in a major customer, such as a university, asking its suppliers how they will react commercially to changes in purchasing practice. However, if we use the relative utility and not the absolute utility of the resulting survey, and triangulate it with qualitative data, then we may either detect bias or be able to set aside a tendency to overstate responses (Kroes & Sheldon, 1988).

There are several approaches to this method. Discrete choice experiments is one that can elicit preferences through understanding the behaviour of humans or human preferences (supported by a long-standing, well-tested, theory of choice behaviour – random utility theory) as opposed to the behaviour of number systems, as demonstrated in conjoint analysis (CA) studies (Louviere, Flynn, & Carson, 2010). Although CA has some positive strength in marketing research (i.e. a technique for measuring buyers' trade-offs amongst multi-attributed products and services with a substantial ability to predict market share, etc.; Green & Srinivasan, 1990), we will not pursue CA on this study because CA-related research has been predicting outcomes, rather than understanding decision processes and is thus not suitable for use in applied economics, in particular on policy assessment, as reported by Louviere et al. (2010). In freight transport, a key method has been the Leeds Adapted Stated Preference, introduced by Fowkes and Shinghal (2002), which uses a software suite that repeatedly adapts itself to a single respondent, effectively repeatedly sampling an individual to generate ranked results. This is well suited to very small sample sizes (such as an oligopoly), but can also be questioned for bias from the process. Another method, often used in passenger transport, is discrete choice stated preference surveys, which offer combinations of choices to respondents and ask for simple binary selection of preferences. Through factorial design and randomizing the questionnaire presented to each party, quite complex combinations of choices can be sampled.

We have a large potential supplier base to sample; we hope that the commercial relationship will engender a high response rate and we are going to be surveying discrete choices in response to interventions, rather than mode choice, which may well be better suited to ranking. We shall adopt a discrete choice stated preference survey, using the purchasing spend to stratify the sample and to achieve higher sample size validity.

8. Conclusions

The research strategy developed adopts a mixed methods approach, utilizing quantitative soft operations research – systems approaches, staff questionnaire, and stated preference surveys – combined with methods from social research that are qualitative in nature. Mixed methods research can be adopted for various reasons (Bryman, 2006) and we have a research strategy that adopts integration between the various methods in an iterative fashion and looks to achieve a holistic view that incorporates mutual corroboration through triangulation, offsets the strengths and weaknesses of each method (and associated data), and achieves a more comprehensive account of the purchasing, policy, and logistics activity in the studied

Table 3. Research strategy to support campus sustainability initiative addressing freight.

	Stakeholders	Methodology considered	Data collection
1	Staff as end users (buying agents)	Systems approach using SODA methodology	Focus group and interview
2	All staff and research-based students	Multivariate statistical analysis	Questionnaire survey
3	University's supplier base	Stated preferences (discrete choice experiments)	Interview and questionnaire survey

area. Table 3 demonstrates the summary of the research strategy identified. This leads to further data collection of three studies employing the university's stakeholders. Each study aims to address a different hypothesis. The first study aims to contest the relationship between the buying system and freight activities. The second study aims to understand the relationship between private purchasing and freight activities. The third study aims to understand the response of university suppliers to potential freight interventions, to optimize freight activities.

We have seen that the inductive approach has yielded a plethora of imperfect data and raised multiple questions, many thought provoking and also possibly unanswerable by the revealed data from the traffic counts and purchasing records. The dissemination of the results, within the management of the university and with local partners, such as the city council and the NHS, has led to the recognition that there are issues to be resolved, but that opportunities exist to improve the university's sustainability. This may be by reducing the overall carbon footprint, reducing intrusion by illegal parking and/or looking to save money through more efficient or more appropriate supply choices and consequent delivery systems – a DSP.

Notes

1. As reported in the associated literature.
2. In addition to this, there is an observed and persistent level of illegal parking along the periphery of the site, largely by couriers, but also by catering supplies' vehicles.

References

Allen, J., & Browne, M. (2010). Sustainability strategies in city logistics. In A. McKinnon, S. Cullinane, M. Browne, & A. Whiteing (Eds.), *Green logistics – improving the environmental sustainability of logistics* (pp. 282–305). London: CILT, Kogan Page.

Allen, J., Browne, M., & Cherrett, T. (2012a). Investigating relationships between road freight transport, facility location, logistics management and urban form. *Journal of Transport Geography, 24*, 45–57.

Allen, J., Browne, M., & Cherrett, T. (2012b). Survey techniques in urban freight transport studies. *Transport Reviews, 32* (3), 287–311.

Allen, J., Browne, M., Woodburn, A., & Leonardi, J. (2012). The role of urban consolidation centres in sustainable freight transport. *Transport Reviews, 32* (4), 473–490.

Allen, J., Thorne, G., & Browne, M. (2007). *BESTUFS good practice guide on urban freight transport*. BESTUFS consortium. Karlsruhe: PTV Planung Transport Verkehr AG.

Anderson, S., Allen, J., & Browne, M. (2005). Urban logistics how can it meet policy makers sustainability objectives? *Journal of Transport Geography, 13* (1), 71–81.

Ballantyne, E. E. F., & Lindholm, M. (2014). Identifying the need for freight to be included in local authority transport planning. In J. Gonzalez-Feliu, F. Semet, & J.-L. Routhier (Eds.),

Sustainable urban logistics: Concepts, methods and information systems (pp. 37–48). Berlin: Springer.

Behrends, S., Lindholm, M., & Woxenius, J. (2008). The impact of urban freight transport: A definition of sustainability from an actor's perspective. *Transportation Planning & Technology, 31* (6), 693–713.

Bhaskar, R. (1989). *Reclaiming reality: A critical introduction to contemporary philosophy*. London: Verso.

Browne, M., Allen, J., & Anderson, S. (2005). Low emission zones: The likely effects on the freight transport sector. *International Journal of Logistics Research and Applications: A Leading Journal of Supply Chain Management, 8* (4), 269–281.

Browne, M., Allen, J., & Leonardi, J. (2011). Evaluating the use of an urban consolidation centre and electric vehicles in central London. *IATSS Research, 35* (1), 1–6.

Browne, M., Allen, J., Nemoto, T., Patier, D., & Visser, J. (2012). Reducing social and environmental impacts of urban freight transport: A review of some major cities. *Procedia – Social and Behavioral Sciences, 39*, 19–33.

Browne, M., Allen, J., Steele, S., Cherrett, T., & McLeod, F. (2010). Analysing the results of UK urban freight studies. *Procedia: Social and Behavioral Sciences, 2*(3), 5956–5966.

Bryman, A. (2006). Integrating quantitative and qualitative research: How is it done? *Qualitative Research, 6* (1), 97–113.

Bryman, A. (2012). *Social research methods* (4th ed.). Oxford: Oxford University Press.

Button, K. J., & Pearman, A. D. (1981). *The economics of urban freight transport*. London: The Macmillan Press Ltd.

Cairns, S., Sloman, L., Newson, C., Anable, J., Kirkbride, A., & Goodwin, P. (2004). *Smarter choices – changing the way we travel. Final report of the research project: 'The influence of soft factor interventions on travel demand'*. London: Department for Transport. Retrieved from www.dft.gov.uk

Cherrett, T., Allen, J., McLeod, F., Maynard, S., Hickford, A., & Browne, M. (2012). Understanding urban freight activity – key issues for freight planning. *Journal of Transport Geography, 24*, 22–32.

CITY FREIGHT. (2002). *CITY FREIGHT Work package 1: Final report: Comparative survey on urban freight, logistics and land use planning systems in Europe*. Brussels: STRATEC S.A.

Dablanc, L. (2007). Goods transport in large European cities: Difficult to organize, difficult to modernize. *Transportation Research Part A: Policy and Practice, 41* (3), 280–285.

Danielis, R., Rotaris, L., & Marcucci, E. (2010). Urban freight policies and distribution channels. *European Transport/Trasporti Europei, 46*, 114–146.

European Commission. (2006). *Urban freight transport and logistics – an overview of the European research and policy*. Brussels: Author.

European Commission. (2007). *GREEN PAPER towards a new culture for urban mobility*. Brussels: Author.

Flaemig, H. (2003) Wirtschaftsverkehr in Staedten – 'vergessener' Planungsgegenstand? *Internationales Verkehrswesen, 55*(10), 489–490.

Fowkes, A. S., & Shinghal, N. (2002). *The Leeds adaptive stated preference methodology. Transport.* Institute of Transport Studies, University of Leeds, Leeds.

Gonzalez-Feliu, J., Ambrosini, C., & Routhier, J. (2012). New trends on urban goods movement: Modelling and simulation of e-commerce distribution. *European Transport/Trasporti Europei, 50*, 1–23.

Gonzalez-Feliu, J., Semet, F., & Routhier, J. (2014). Preface. In J. Gonzalez-Feliu, F. Semet, & J. Routhier (Eds.), *Sustainable urban logistics: Concepts, methods and information systems* (pp. v–ix). Heidelberg: Springer.

Green, P. E., & Srinivasan, V. (1990). Conjoint analysis in marketing new development with implications for research practice. *Journal of Marketing, 54*(4), 3–19.

Hensher, D., & Figliozzi, M. (2007). Behavioural insights into the modelling of freight transportation and distribution systems. *Transportation Research Part B: Methodological, 41*(9), 921–923.

Hesse, M., & Rodrigue, J. (2004). The transport geography of logistics and freight distribution. *Journal of Transport Geography, 12*(3), 171–184.

Hoejmose, S. U., & Adrien-Kirby, A. J. (2012). Socially and environmentally responsible procurement: A literature review and future research agenda of a managerial issue in the 21st century. *Journal of Purchasing and Supply Management, 18*(4), 232–242.

Holguín-Veras, J. (2008). Necessary conditions for off-hour deliveries and the effectiveness of urban freight road pricing and alternative financial policies in competitive markets. *Transportation Research Part A: Policy and Practice, 42*(2), 392–413.

Holguín-Veras, J. (2011). Urban delivery industry response to cordon pricing, time–distance pricing, and carrier–receiver policies in competitive markets. *Transportation Research Part A: Policy and Practice, 45*(8), 802–824.

Kroes, E. P., & Sheldon, R. J. (1988). Stated preference method: An introduction. *Journal of Transport Economics and Policy, 22*(1), 11–25.

Lindholm, M., & Behrends, S. (2012). Challenges in urban freight transport planning – a review in the Baltic Sea Region. *Journal of Transport Geography, 22*, 129–136.

Lindholm, M., & Browne, M. (2013). Local authority cooperation with urban freight stakeholders: A comparison of partnership approaches. *European Journal of Transport and Infrastructure Research, 13*(1), 20–38.

Louviere, J. J., Flynn, T. N., & Carson, R. T. (2010). Discrete choice experiments are not conjoint analysis. *Journal of Choice Modelling, 3*(3), 57–72.

Muñuzuri, J., Cortés, P., Guadix, J., & Onieva, L. (2012). City logistics in Spain: Why it might never work. *Cities, 29*(2), 133–141.

Muñuzuri, J., Larraneta, J., Onieva, L., & Cortés, P. (2005). Solutions applicable by local administrations for urban logistics improvement. *Cities, 22*(1), 15–28.

Ogden, K. W. (1977). An analysis of urban commodity flow. *Transportation Planning and Technology, 4*, 1–9.

Ogden, K. W. (1992). *Urban goods movement*. Aldershot: Ashgate.

Quak, H. J., & De Koster, M. B. M. (2005). The impacts of time access restrictions and vehicle weight restrictions on food retailers and the environment. *European Journal of Transport and Infrastructure Research, 6*(2), 131–150.

Quak, H. J., & De Koster, M. B. M. (2007). Exploring retailers' sensitivity to local sustainability policies. *Journal of Operations Management, 25*(6), 1103–1122.

Regué, R., & Bristow, A. L. (2013). Appraising freight tram schemes: A case study of Barcelona. *European Journal of Transport and Infrastructure Research, 13*(1), 56–78.

Reynolds, M., & Holwell, S. (2010). Chapter 1: Introducing systems approaches. In M. Reynolds & S. Holwell (Eds.), *Systems approaches to managing change: A practical guide* (pp. 1–24). London: Springer London.

Stathopoulos, A., Valeri, E., & Marcucci, E. (2012). Stakeholder reactions to urban freight policy innovation. *Journal of Transport Geography, 22*, 34–45.

Taniguchi, E. (2001). City logistics. *Infrastructure Planning Review, 18*(1), 34–45.

Transport for London. (2007). *Transport for London Freight Plan sustainable freight distribution: A plan for London Foreword by Mayor*. London: Transport.

Transport for London. (2009). *A pilot delivery servicing plan for TfL's Palestra Offices in Southwark: A case study*. London: Author.

Wagdahl, K. (2010). *TRAILBLAZER (Transport And Innovation Logistics by Local Authorities with a Zest for Efficiency and Realization) deliverable D2.1 report on the state of the art*. Eskilstuna, Sweden: Climate Protection Agency, Sweden for Intelligent Energy Europe (IEE).

Walker, H., & Brammer, S. (2009). Sustainable procurement in the United Kingdom public sector. *Supply Chain Management: An International Journal, 14*(2), 128–137.

Zunder, T., Aditjandra, P., & Carnaby, B. (2012). *Delivery service plan to make urban freight greener: A soft measure?* Proceedings of the 17th annual logistics research network conference, Cranfield University, Cranfield.

Zunder, T. H., & Dellinger, J.-C. (2005). Chapter 14: City freight: Evaluation methodology for urban freight transport. In G. Ambrosino, M. Boero, J. Nelson, & M. Romannazzo (Eds.), *Systems and advanced solutions for eLogistics in the sustainable city* (pp. 299–309). Rome: ENEA Italian National Agency for New Technologies, Energy and the Environment.

Zunder, T. H., & Ibanez, J. N. (2004). Urban freight logistics in the European Union. *European Transport/Trasporti Europei, 28*, 1–8.

Collaboration in urban logistics: motivations and barriers

Lindawati[a], Johan van Schagen[a], Mark Goh[a,b,c] and Robert de Souza[a]

[a]*The Logistics Institute – Asia Pacific, Singapore, Singapore;* [b]*NUS Business School, Singapore, Singapore;* [c]*Business Logistics and IT, RMIT University, Melbourne, Australia*

Urban logistics activities, while essential to the development of cities, also contribute to congestion and pollution if poorly managed. Synchronizing the last mile of delivery is critical, but challenging to implement. Collaboration between the stakeholders is thus needed and timely to improve the efficiency of last mile delivery in a growing city while advancing environmental sustainability. This paper is an exploratory study undertaken in Singapore, to identify the motivations and barriers to collaboration in urban logistics, which may influence a stakeholder's decision to participate. Our initial results suggest that the expected benefits (motivation) and the competitive intelligence risks (barrier) influence the participation decision.

1. Introduction

Urban logistics is essential for the economic development of cities and supply to city residents. However, such logistics activities contribute to the congestion, pollution, and resource depletion that can impede delivery efficiency, mobility, and the environment and human health (Anderson, Allen, & Browne, 2005). Solving these issues is difficult as urban logistics involves complex processes which need to engage many stakeholders who may have potentially conflicting interests and incommensurate objectives (Ballantyne, Lindholm, & Whiteing, 2013).

Urban logistics initiatives seek to increase supply chain efficiency in terms of cost, time, and resources by changing the methods and means of transport while maintaining sustainability. These initiatives encompass a variety of measures, including education programmes for improving driving behaviour, improvement of public information provision, vehicle pooling, standardization of loading units, fuel technology advancement, terminal facilities for consolidating loads known as urban consolidation centres, and policy measures regulating traffic flow (Russo & Comi, 2011).

Many urban logistics initiatives unfortunately fail at the proposal stage (Köhler & Groke, 2003). Quak (2011), in a study of 106 such initiatives, find that more than half of them fail during implementation, agreeing with Allen, Browne, Woodburn, and Leonardi (2012) who have reported that only 50 of the 114 initiatives studied are operational. Allen et al. (2012) also note that the lack of participation from the stakeholders prevents their practical implementation.

Stakeholder behaviour is influenced by the difference in their objectives and by the interactions between them (Taniguchi, Yamada, & Okamoto, 2007). In some urban logistics initiatives, stakeholder participation is enforced through regulations. For instance, Gonzalez-Feliu (2008) reports that the local governments in two Dutch cities have implemented restrictive time-based cordon policies for transportation carriers within the city. Other initiatives depend on the willingness of the stakeholders to participate, for example, by consolidating the goods or by having a third party to organize trucks to optimize load utilization. We focus on such initiatives, where information and resources are shared under an agreement between the stakeholders. The reasons for joining such urban logistics collaborations remain unexplored in the literature.

In this paper, we investigate the factors that influence the stakeholders' decision to participate in urban logistics collaboration initiatives for Singapore. We base our study on Singapore for the following reasons. Singapore is unique in that it is a small island-based city state that is still aspiring to enlarge its population by at least 20%. This poses a constraint and challenge for urban logistics activities (particularly in last mile delivery) and the need to rein in congestion and pollution through better use of transportation assets, information sharing, and shared cargo consolidation facilities.

To undertake this initial study, we originally design a research model that includes one motivational factor, expected benefits, and three barrier factors, namely, internal capability, trust, and competitive intelligence risks. We then validate the research model through an exploratory field study in Singapore using data triangulation of focus groups, semi-structured interviews, and questionnaire survey. Our preliminary results show that only expected benefits as a motivator and competitive intelligence risks as a barrier have significant effects on the participation decision.

This paper is structured as follows: Section 2 reviews the literature on stakeholder participation in urban logistics initiatives. Section 3 presents the research model and the hypotheses on the motivation and barriers for stakeholder participation in urban logistics initiatives. Section 4 describes the research method. Section 5 presents the survey results, while Section 6 discusses some implications for theory and practice. Section 7 concludes with limitations and directions for future research.

2. Theoretical background

The literature on collaboration in urban logistics covers a variety of initiatives, building on different concepts, with different requirements and modes of stakeholder participation. We discuss approaches in the existing literature that conceptualize categorization frameworks to group initiative types for analysis. Ville, Gonzalez-Feliu, and Dablanc (2013) propose categorization into infrastructure, technologies, funding, regulation, logistics organization, and communication. Quak and Tavasszy (2011) distinguish between policy initiatives, physical infrastructure initiatives, transport reorganizing initiatives (e.g. auctions and intermodal freight), and company-driven initiatives. This last category emphasizes that participation modes are important characteristics, but at the same time recognizes, for example, that auctions cannot always be company-driven (Wang, Potter, Naim, & Beevor, 2011). Russo and Comi (2011) propose a typology in which the initiatives are divided into four categories: material infrastructure, governance, equipment, and non-material infrastructure (including intelligent transportation systems (ITS)). The role of ITS in urban logistics is also emphasized in Taniguchi and Shimamoto (2004) who consider advanced information sharing to be a core component. This is echoed by Crainic, Gendreau and Potvin (2009, p. 543) who consider 'obtaining, processing, and distributing information for better use of the transportation system, infrastructure and services' the core of ITS.

Indeed, urban logistics collaboration depends very much on voluntary stakeholder participation. Players in the logistics sector have a major stake in these collaborations (Dablanc, 2007), and the literature has evidence of their efforts, for example, supplier-initiated inventory consolidation and routing for a grocery purchasing firm supplying to large retailers in the Netherlands (le Blanc, Cruijssen, Fleuren, & de Koster, 2006), proposed collaboration for the delivery and consolidation of eight food distributors in Uppsala, Sweden (Gebresenbet, Nordmark, Bosona, & Ljungberg, 2011), and supplier-driven industrial park settlement in the German automotive sector (Pfohl & Gareis, 2005). Stakeholder participation in urban logistics collaboration initiatives is evaluated on the basis of the different criteria due to the specific stakeholder objectives (Taniguchi & Tamagawa, 2005).

The research in which urban logistics stakeholders are involved broadly covers three topics: (1) development of government strategies for urban freight, (2) evaluation of the impact of specific government policies for urban freight, or (3) the assessment of requirements for a specific urban logistics initiative.

Hensher and Brewer (2001) have documented the development of a government freight strategy using action learning for New South Wales, Australia, by involving 60 stakeholders from various interest groups, while Lindholm and Behrends (2012) assess the quality of the urban freight system in four cities around the Baltic Sea by interviewing different stakeholders (city administration, customers, freight forwarders, transport operators, and research institutes). Concurrently, Awasthi and Chauhan (2012) use a board of five decision-makers drawn from different stakeholder groups to determine the desired impact of a urban freight strategy.

In evaluating the impact of government policy, Thompson and Hassall (2005) asked stakeholders from the public sector to rank different urban logistics initiatives in terms of the stakeholder's objectives. Anderson et al. (2005) have assessed the potential impact of public policy on instituting low emission zones, time window and weight restrictions, and congestion charging based on interviews with seven distribution companies in the UK. The level of impact on company operations was found to depend on fleet size, diversity of vehicles, and preferred times for delivery. Stathopoulos, Valeri, and Marcucci (2012) use focus groups to rank the preferred policy initiatives with traders and producers, freight operators, and policy-makers, as well as a questionnaire of preferred hours for delivery with freight operators in Rome, Italy. They report that the resistance to implementation of an urban distribution centre stems from a fear of the loss of control and legal responsibility over the supply chain, and doubt that the benefits could be distributed fairly. A stated-preference survey on the different policy options to encourage collaboration between retailers and carriers to plan deliveries outside of the peak traffic hours in New York City is discussed in Holguín-Veras, Silas, Polimeni, and Cruz (2008). They find that the most cited reason for carriers to not partake in such off-peak deliveries is that their customers are not flexible enough in planning and call for a comprehensive policy approach targeting both carriers and receivers. Puckett and Hensher (2008) used a stated choice experiment to understand the behaviour of both shippers and transport operators in terms of the price and trip choice under different congestion charging schemes in Sydney, Australia.

On the assessment of stakeholder requirements in urban logistics initiatives, Marcucci and Danielis (2008) use a stated-preference survey to determine the demand potential for an urban consolidation centre for the retail business in Fano, Italy. They find that retail products with specific logistics needs (e.g. perishable items) are less likely to support such an initiative. Regan and Golob (2005) who have surveyed 700 logistics managers of trucking companies to determine the desired services in an urban consolidation centre for California, the USA, find that companies which have already adopted third-party logistics (3PL) services and IT infrastructure had a stronger demand for urban logistics initiatives. McKinnon and Ge (2006) who surveyed 27 grocery companies in the UK on the backhaul opportunities find that grocery product requirements and a general lack of transparency in the road freight market are limiters. Recently, an assessment of the expected benefits from intelligent systems for truck parking in Sweden was conducted by Sochor and Mbiydzenyuy (2013) on 30 drivers and 20 company representatives from transportation providers. They find a low willingness to pay for the service, hinting at the fact that cost can be either a motivator or barrier, depending on the elasticity effect.

3. Research model and hypotheses

Indeed, participation in urban logistics initiatives requires collaboration from stakeholders, such as shippers, carriers, customers, regulators, vehicle makers, and business councils (Ballantyne et al., 2013). This participation is a major enabler in urban logistics (Sengpiehl, 2010). Howard, Vidgen, and Powell (2006) mention that the motivations and barriers influence the participation decision. In the extant literature, several motivations and barriers are identified (Anderson et al., 2005; Quak, 2011). However, these papers focus on evaluating the outcomes of the initiatives and do not discuss the relationship between the motivations and barriers and the participation decision.

We derive our research model (Figure 1) from a review of the urban logistics literature and the IT, information, and knowledge risk literature. We initially identify four constructs that may influence the participation decision. Expected benefits are considered to be a motivation for participation, believed to have a positive impact that can encourage and change behaviour (Howard et al., 2006). As for barriers, we identify three: internal capability, trust, and competitive intelligence risks (Tsai, Liao, & Han, 2008).

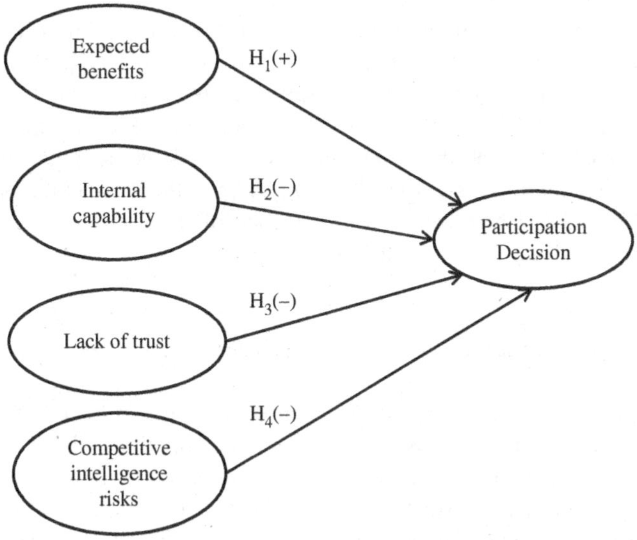

Figure 1. Research model.

Expected benefits are defined as the perceived positive effect from participating in urban logistics collaboration. This construct includes measures such as the cost of delivery, quality of service, and delivery time, as well as the social and environment benefits like total social cost (Nemoto, 2003), environmental sustainability (Anderson et al., 2005), social reputation (Quak, 2011), and IT-related benefits (Howard et al., 2006). Expected benefits in cost efficiency motivate collaboration and interaction for participation as studied in automotive e-hub collaboration by Howard et al. (2006). Besides efficiency, sustainability benefits can also increase a stakeholder's willingness to collaborate (Anderson et al., 2005). Stakeholders are motivated by the expected gains derivable from efficiency and sustainability. Expected benefits can increase the willingness of stakeholders to take part in urban logistics collaboration initiatives. Thus, we posit:

Hypothesis 1: Expected benefits increases participation in urban logistics collaboration.

Internal capability focuses on a stakeholder's ability to meet the requirements of urban logistics. This factor includes the resource, organizational, and implementation capability. Capability risks indicate a possible loss or damage by not being able to meet the demands of urban logistics collaboration, such as the failure to develop internal IT infrastructure or employee know-how in the implementation of the initiative (Tsai et al., 2008). The lack of internal capability drives the cost that a stakeholder needs to bear when participating in urban logistics collaborations. These internal capability risks can be derived from a technical, top management, and strategic perspective (Ratnasingam, 2006). For instance, a shortage of vehicles may delay the fulfilment of demand and ruin a company's reputation, and incompatible technical solutions hinder integration with an urban logistics IT platform. Risks may also arise when there is no top-level management support. Further, participation in urban logistics collaboration may not be aligned with a stakeholder's strategy. The internal capability risk may decrease the willingness of a stakeholder to participate in urban logistics collaboration. Thus, we hypothesize the following:

Hypothesis 2: Internal capability risk affects participation in urban logistics collaboration.

Trust is a complex issue surrounding collaborative relationships. In this paper, we define trust as the perceived quality of the technical system, but not the quality of the collaboration. Many factors influence trust such as security, usability, reliability, availability, external audit, and interoperability (Lai, Tong, & Lai, 2011). Further, we limit the definition of trust to only the urban logistics IT platform, which includes the stakeholder organization that hosts the IT platform. Trust plays a significant role in shaping the participation and adaptation of a system (Markus & Christiaanse, 2003). A lack of trust may have a negative effect on a stakeholder's willingness to participate in urban logistics. Thus, we hypothesize the following:

Hypothesis 3: Lack of trust affects participation in urban logistics collaboration.

Competitive intelligence risks concern the problem of sharing information and the disclosure of sensitive information, possibly resulting in a loss of competitive advantage. Urban logistics collaborations rely on the submission of information (either to a coordinating 3PL or through a collaborative platform) that is then processed in order to support the urban delivery processes. This disclosure may allow competitors to have the same access to the information. Different from IT security risk, such as information security breakdown, competitive intelligence risks are more focused on the intellectual property right and information leakage to other stakeholders. This includes the risk of poaching experts and customers (Faisal, Banwet, & Shankar, 2007; Trkman & Desouza, 2012). The fear of exposing information to other stakeholders may hinder a firm from collaborating in urban logistics initiatives. Thus, we hypothesize the following:

Hypothesis 4: Competitive intelligence risks affect participation in urban logistics collaboration.

4. Research design

Given that this study, based in Singapore, is largely exploratory, we followed the suggestions in the literature which called for a field study involving a focus group, semi-structured interviews, and a survey (McKinnon & Ge, 2006; Puckett & Hensher, 2008; Stathopoulos et al., 2012).

The focus group discussion was held on March 2013, with senior industrialists and researchers in the logistics industry. It confirmed the viability of urban logistics collaboration in Singapore. The focus group also revealed some challenges to implementing urban logistics collaboration initiatives in Singapore such as effective solutions to managing traffic congestion in commercial zones and how to coordinate multiple parties for overall system efficiency and cost productivity (de Souza, Goh, Lau, Ng, & Tan, 2013).

We then interviewed six industry partners from the food, electronics, logistics, and retail sectors. We used semi-structured interviews to identify the motivations and barriers to urban logistics collaboration participation. The responses were varied. One respondent considered the company's supply chain management practices to be a competitive advantage which is to be protected; another felt that the information about service level is highly confidential and must never be revealed to competitors. Other concerns raised were the unequal treatment of participants and the low level of information system adoption in the company at the time of the interview. Meeting minutes were produced to assure the validity and reliability of the interview. To validate the findings in the semi-structured interviews, we developed a questionnaire comprising 30 items (Table 1). In conducting our survey, we queried the respondents on their willingness to collaborate in urban logistics activities, predicated on the five urban logistics initiatives discussed in de Souza, Lindawati, Zhang, and Goh (2014). Specifically, the five initiatives are as follows: (1) goods consolidation in a warehouse with automated goods moving systems in an industrial estate, in which information is exchanged with a third-party service provider, (2) data harmonization and analytics across firms for better business intelligence, demand forecasting, and finding improvement opportunities, in which information is voluntarily shared with a shared platform, (3) collaborative multi-objective planning resource scheduling, with service level and contract performance management as enablers for a fairer distribution of the benefits, as well as simulating the solutions, which require shared and thus known guidelines for performance contracts, (4) collaborative vehicle routing optimization taking into consideration the environmental impact with only operational data being shared, and (5) an online platform for stakeholders to bid and negotiate on spare truck capacity, delivery, timing, and load consolidations.

We listed 10 items for expected benefits and asked the respondents for their views on the expected benefits if collaborating in urban logistics and the importance of the benefits to their operational performance. To minimize uncertain/neutral responses (Matell & Jacoby, 1972), we used a 4-point Likert scale (1 = very low; 4 = very high). The barriers were

Table 1. Items for motivation and barriers.

Factor	Item	Source
Expected benefits	1. Reduce total last-mile logistics cost	Howard et al. (2006)
	2. Improve reliability	Howard et al. (2006)
	3. Improve visibility	Interview
	4. Reduce congestion and traffic delays	Anderson et al. (2005)
	5. Reduce pollution	Anderson et al. (2005)
	6. Improve business analysis	Interview
	7. Improve benchmarking	Interview
	8. Improve supply chain risk mitigation	Interview
	9. Improve reputation/CSR	Quak (2011)
	10. Improve scalability	Interview
Internal capability	11. No top management commitment	Ratnasingam (2006)
	12. No competent staff	Howard et al. (2006)
	13. No time to learn to use shared system	Hartley, Lane, and Duplaga (2006)
	14. Employee resistance to initiative	Tsai et al. (2008)
	15. Insufficient IT capacity	Wu and Zhu (2012)
Trust	16. Inaccurate or inconsistent data	Tsai et al. (2008)
	17. Lack of visibility in the system	Interview
	18. No fair distribution of benefits	Interview
	19. No secure encryption	Lai et al. (2011)
	20. Inadequate service level	Interview
	21. Lack of company participation	Quak (2011)
	22. No information security/confidentiality	Tsai et al. (2008)
	23. Sabotage/cyber-attack	Smith, Watson, Baker, and Pokorski (2007)
	24. False information	Wu and Zhu (2012)
	25. Long-term partnerships not possible	Hartley et al. (2006)
Competitive intelligence risks	26. Information leakage	Interview
	27. No sufficient authentication	Lai et al. (2011)
	28. Poaching customers	Interview
	29. Strategy/best practice exposure	Interview
	30. Poaching experts	Trkman and Desouza (2012)

Note: CSR, corporate social responsibility.

Table 2. Respondent company profile.

Company role	Number of respondents
Carrier	1
3PL	12
Shipper	10
Retailer	4
Forwarder	1
Government	2
Others	4
Incomplete	3

measured via 20 items, with 5 for internal capability, 10 for trust, and 5 for competitive intelligence risks, respectively, again using the same 4-point Likert scale. We again used a 4-point Likert scale (1 = not likely; 4 = very likely) to measure the participation decision. In addition, the respondent's background information was captured: company, industry, company's dominant role in urban logistics, job role, number of years in the company, and firm size.

We ascertained the validity of the constructs with a content validity test (Litwin, 1995) on a panel of five experts from industrialists and researchers with extensive background in logistics. We then revised the wording of the questionnaire based on their opinions.

A hundred questionnaires were distributed to senior industrialists in roles such as Senior Supply Chain Analyst and Vice President, representing multi-national and local firms that have an office/representation in Singapore and with various primary roles in urban logistics. In all, 37 responses were received, but only 34 were valid (Table 2). SPSS version 22 was used for the statistical analysis involving data reduction (exploratory factor analysis – EFA) and relationship estimation among the constructs (regression analysis).

5. Results

Invoking principal components analysis (PCA) on the survey data set yielded 2 factors which helped to reduce the data into a parsimonious set of 10 component items. The other 20 items were removed due to the high cross-loadings between the factors. Tables 3 and 4 contain the results of the PCA and EFA, respectively. We label the factors based on the item with the highest loading score. Factor 1 is labelled as competitive intelligence risks, while Factor 2 is labelled as expected benefits. This effectively reduces the independent variables to expected benefits and competitive intelligence risks as shown in our revised research model in Figure 2.

To assess the internal consistency of the component items, we compute Cronbach's alpha, which assumes that our model has differences in the means rather than the variance within a category (Nunnally, 2010). Cronbach's alpha values, shown in Table 4, exceed 0.7, indicating good internal consistency for an exploratory study.

The linear regression result of the revised research model is shown in Table 5. Both expected benefits and competitive intelligence risks have significant influence on participation decision. Therefore, Hypotheses 1 and 4 are supported.

Table 3. Results of PCA.

	Initial eigenvalues			Extraction sums of squared loadings		
Component	Total	% of variance	Cumulative %	Total	% of variance	Cumulative %
6	4.570	45.696	45.696	4.570	45.696	45.696
7	1.812	18.118	63.814	1.812	18.118	63.814
21	0.980	9.802	73.616			
22	0.844	8.441	82.057			
25	0.557	5.572	87.629			
26	0.465	4.654	92.283			
27	0.343	3.429	95.712			
28	0.236	2.356	98.067			
29	0.193	1.933	100.000			
30	0	0	100.000			

Table 4. EFA results.

Variable	Item description	Factor 1 (competitive intelligence risks)	Factor 2 (expected benefits)	Cronbach's alpha
6	Improve business analysis	.089	.926	.831
7	Improve benchmarking	−.038	.902	
21	Lack of company participation	.866	−.084	.887
22	No information security/confidentiality	.786	.114	
25	Long-term partnerships not possible	.703	.207	
26	Information leakage	.866	−.084	
27	Insufficient authentication	.818	−.041	
28	Poaching customers	.570	−.142	
29	Strategy/best practice exposure	.662	−.177	
30	Poaching experts	.719	.131	

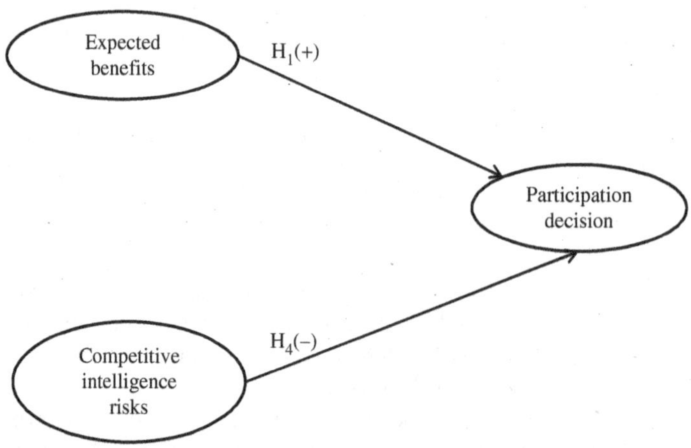

Figure 2. Revised model.

Table 5. Regression results.

	Participation decision	
Model	Coefficient	Adj. R^2
Constant	2.824*	0.202
Expected benefits	0.397*	
Competitive intelligence risks	−0.126*	

[a]$p < .05$.

6. Discussion

The prior research on urban logistics has only qualitatively mentioned stakeholder participation as being critical to successful urban logistics collaboration initiatives, albeit they do not lend much attention to the motivation and barriers behind the participation decisions of the stakeholders (Allen et al., 2012; Quak, 2011; Sengpiehl, 2010). Our work offers some new perspectives to address this gap about the motivation and barriers to stakeholder participation in such initiatives.

We also advance the current understanding of stakeholder participation decision in urban logistics collaboration initiatives by identifying the key factors of influence, namely expected benefits and competitive intelligence risks. Our findings support the research on stakeholder participation in policy initiatives, notably in the encouragement of information sharing between stakeholders (Stathopoulos et al., 2012) and the assessment of stakeholder requirements (Regan & Golob, 2005) with their focus on the expected benefits. Further, by including competitive intelligence risks, we supplement the existing literature on the urban logistics collaboration initiatives (Taniguchi & Tamagawa, 2005). Clearly, companies operating in a small marketplace such as Singapore are concerned about information leakage and rightly so.

For policy-makers and business decision-makers, when prioritizing and evaluating the options for motivating stakeholders to decide on whether to collaborate in urban logistics initiatives, one key consideration should be on making the cost–benefits analysis transparent to all stakeholders. At the same time, top management of business must be well aware of the underlying competitive intelligence risks and be prepared to put in place the requisite mitigation strategies for their firms to be forearmed optimally. Clearly, the competitive intelligence risks may also pose a stronger concern for stakeholders, especially those smaller businesses who rightfully worry that they might lose their competitive advantage to business rivals by sharing even the most mundane operational data or information. This indirectly places a constraint on public policy intervention in the realm of urban logistics, again concurring with Ville et al. (2013) and the feedback from the interviewees of our study.

7. Conclusion

This paper has examined the factors that motivate and hinder stakeholders from deciding to participate in urban logistics collaboration initiatives. We find that two factors matter – the perceived benefits of collaboration and the risk of losing competitive intelligence. Other factors such as trust in the shared IT platform and the internal capability of the firms are not as statistically significant. As with all papers, there are limitations which can make our conclusions guarded. One limitation in our paper is the small sample size. Also, as the empirical context of our study, Singapore's industrial features and cultural factors may limit the general applicability of our conclusion. Singapore, being a small but cosmopolitan island state with more than 3000 multi-national corporations, has been a pioneer in the adoption of various road transport technologies and urban transport policies such as electronic road pricing. Not many countries in Asia are similar to Singapore or are as forward-looking in the use of innovative urban transport technologies. Further research could extend this study across different industries and cultural settings, and countries to enhance its generalizability.

Funding

This work was supported by Science and Engineering Research Council (SERC) of the Agency for Science, Technology and Research (A*STAR) [Grant numbers 1224200003 and 1224200004].

References

Allen, J., Browne, M., Woodburn, A., & Leonardi, J. (2012). The role of urban consolidation centres in sustainable freight transport. *Transport Reviews*, *32*(4), 473–490.

Anderson, S., Allen, J., & Browne, M. (2005). Urban logistics – how can it meet policy makers' sustainability objectives? *Journal of Transport Geography*, *13*(1), 71–81.

Awasthi, A., & Chauhan, S. S. (2012). A hybrid approach integrating affinity diagram, AHP and fuzzy TOPSIS for sustainable city logistics planning. *Applied Mathematical Modelling*, *36*(2), 573–584.

Ballantyne, E. E. F., Lindholm, M., & Whiteing, A. (2013). A comparative study of urban freight transport planning: Addressing stakeholder needs. *Journal of Transport Geography*, *32*, 93–101.

Crainic, T. G., Gendreau, M., & Potvin, J. Y. (2009). Intelligent freight-transportation systems: Assessment and the contribution of operations research. *Transportation Research Part C: Emerging Technologies*, 17(6), 541–557.

Dablanc, L. (2007). Goods transport in large European cities: Difficult to organize, difficult to modernize. *Transportation Research Part A: Policy and Practice*, *41*(3), 280–285.

Faisal, M. N., Banwet, D. K., & Shankar, R. (2007). Information risks management in supply chains: An assessment and mitigation framework. *Journal of Enterprise Information Management*, *20*(6), 677–699.

Gebresenbet, G., Nordmark, I., Bosona, T., & Ljungberg, D. (2011). Potential for optimised food deliveries in and around Uppsala city, Sweden. *Journal of Transport Geography*, *19*(6), 1456–1464.

Gonzalez-Feliu, J. (2008). *Models and methods for the city logistics: The two-echelon capacitated vehicle routing problem* (Doctoral dissertation). Politecnico di Torino, Turin, Italy.

Hartley, J. L., Lane, M. D., & Duplaga, E. A. (2006). Exploring the barriers to the adoption of e-auctions for sourcing. *International Journal of Operations & Production Management*, *26*(2), 202–221.

Hensher, D. A., & Brewer, A. M. (2001). Developing a freight strategy: The use of a collaborative learning process to secure stakeholder input. *Transport Policy*, *8*(1), 1–10.

Holguín-Veras, J., Silas, M., Polimeni, J., & Cruz, B. (2008). An investigation on the effectiveness of joint receiver–carrier policies to increase truck traffic in the off-peak hours. *Networks and Spatial Economics*, *8*(4), 327–354.

Howard, M., Vidgen, R., & Powell, P. (2006). Automotive e-hubs: Exploring motivations and barriers to collaboration and interaction. *The Journal of Strategic Information Systems*, *15*(1), 51–75.

Köhler, U., & Groke, O. (2003, June). *New ideas for the city-logistics project in Kassel*. Paper presented at the 3rd international conference on city logistics, Madeira, Portugal.

Lai, I. K. W., Tong, V. W. L., & Lai, D. C. F. (2011). Trust factors influencing the adoption of internet-based interorganizational systems. *Electronic Commerce Research and Applications*, *10*(1), 85–93.

le Blanc, H. M., Cruijssen, F., Fleuren, H. A., & de Koster, M. B. M. (2006). Factory gate pricing: An analysis of the Dutch retail distribution. *European Journal of Operational Research*, *174*(3), 1950–1967.

Lindholm, M., & Behrends, S. (2012). Challenges in urban freight transport planning – a review in the Baltic Sea Region. *Journal of Transport Geography*, *22*, 129–136.

Litwin, M. S. (1995). *How to measure survey reliability and validity* (Vol. 7). Thousand Oaks, CA: Sage.

Marcucci, E., & Danielis, R. (2008). The potential demand for a urban freight consolidation centre. *Transportation, 35*(2), 269–284.

Markus, M. L., & Christiaanse, E. (2003). Adoption and impact of collaboration electronic marketplaces. *Information Systems and e-Business Management, 1*(2), 139–155.

Matell, M. S., & Jacoby, J. (1972). Is there an optimal number of alternatives for Likert-scale items? Effects of testing time and scale properties. *Journal of Applied Psychology, 56*(6), 506–509.

McKinnon, A. C., & Ge, Y. (2006). The potential for reducing empty running by trucks: A retrospective analysis. *International Journal of Physical Distribution & Logistics Management, 36*(5), 391–410.

Nemoto, T. (2003, June). *Experiment on co-operative parcel pick-up system using the Internet in the central business district in Tokyo.* Paper presented at the 3rd international conference on city logistics, Madeira, Portugal.

Nunnally, J. C. (2010). *Psychometric theory.* Noida: Tata McGraw-Hill Education.

Pfohl, H. C., & Gareis, K. (2005). Supplier parks in the German automotive industry: A critical comparison with similar concepts. *International Journal of Physical Distribution & Logistics Management, 35*(5), 302–317.

Puckett, S. M., & Hensher, D. A. (2008). The role of attribute processing strategies in estimating the preferences of road freight stakeholders. *Transportation Research Part E: Logistics and Transportation Review, 44*(3), 379–395.

Quak, H. (2011). Urban freight transport: The challenge of sustainability. In C. Macharis & S. Melo (Eds.), *City distribution and urban freight transport: Multiple perspectives* (pp. 37–56). Cheltenham: Edward Elgar Publishing.

Quak, H., & Tavasszy, L. (2011). Customized solutions for sustainable city logistics: The viability of urban freight consolidation centres. In J. A. E. E. Nunen, P. Huijbregts, & P. Rietveld (Eds.), *Transitions towards sustainable mobility* (pp. 213–233). Heidelberg: Springer.

Ratnasingam, P. (2006). Perceived risks in supply chain management e-collaboration. *Journal of Internet Commerce, 5*(4), 105–124.

Regan, A. C., & Golob, T. F. (2005). Trucking industry demand for urban shared use freight terminals. *Transportation, 32*(1), 23–36.

Russo, F., & Comi, A. (2011). A model system for the ex-ante assessment of city logistics measures. *Research in Transportation Economics, 31*(1), 81–87.

Sengpiehl, C. (2010). *Towards the development of a holistic planning framework for a Logistics City-Cluster: A multinational modified Delphi study* (Doctoral dissertation). Victoria University, Melbourne, Australia.

Smith, G. E., Watson, K. J., Baker, W. H., & Pokorski, J. A., II. (2007). A critical balance: Collaboration and security in the IT-enabled supply chain. *International Journal of Production Research, 45*(11), 2595–2613.

Sochor, J., & Mbiydzenyuy, G. (2013). Assessing the benefits of intelligent truck parking. *International Journal of Intelligent Transportation Systems Research, 11*(2), 43–53.

de Souza, R., Goh, M., Lau, H. C., Ng, W. S., & Tan, P. S. (2013, July). *Collaborative urban logistics – synchronizing the last mile a Singapore research perspective.* Paper presented at the 8th international conference on City Logistics, Bali, Indonesia.

de Souza, R., Lindawati, Zhang, X., & Goh, M. (2014, January). *Supply chain and logistics challenges and opportunities in Asia: Innovative urban logistics concept.* Paper presented at the international conference on industrial engineering and operations management, Bali, Indonesia.

Stathopoulos, A., Valeri, E., & Marcucci, E. (2012). Stakeholder reactions to urban freight policy innovation. *Journal of Transport Geography, 22*, 34–45.

Taniguchi, E., & Shimamoto, H. (2004). Intelligent transportation system based dynamic vehicle routing and scheduling with variable travel times. *Transportation Research Part C: Emerging Technologies, 12*(3–4), 235–250.

Taniguchi, E., & Tamagawa, D. (2005). Evaluating city logistics measures considering the behavior of several stakeholders. *Journal of the Eastern Asia Society for Transportation Studies, 6*, 3062–3076.

Taniguchi, E., Yamada, T., & Okamoto, M. (2007). Multi-agent modelling for evaluating dynamic vehicle routing and scheduling systems. *Journal of the Eastern Asia Society for Transportation Studies, 7*, 933–948.

Thompson, R. G., & Hassall, K. (2005, July). *A methodology for evaluating urban freight projects.* Paper presented at the 4th international conference on City Logistics, Langkawi, Malaysia.

Trkman, P., & Desouza, K. C. (2012). Knowledge risks in organizational networks: An exploratory framework. *The Journal of Strategic Information Systems, 21*(1), 1–17.

Tsai, M. C., Liao, C. H., & Han, C. S. (2008). Risk perception on logistics outsourcing of retail chains: Model development and empirical verification in Taiwan. *Supply Chain Management: An International Journal, 13*(6), 415–424.

Ville, S., Gonzalez-Feliu, J., & Dablanc, L. (2013). The limits of public policy intervention in urban logistics: Lessons from Vicenza (Italy). *European Planning Studies, 21*(10), 1528–1541.

Wang, Y., Potter, A., Naim, M., & Beevor, D. (2011). A case study exploring drivers and implications of collaborative electronic logistics marketplaces. *Industrial Marketing Management, 40*(4), 612–623.

Wu, Y., & Zhu, W. (2012). An integrated theoretical model for determinants of knowledge sharing behaviours. *Kybernetes, 41*(10), 1462–1482.

An estimation of freight flow using secondary data: a case study in Belo Horizonte (Brazil)

Leise Kelli de Oliveira[a] and Lílian dos Santos Fontes Pereira[b]

[a]Department of Transport and Geotechnical Engineering, Federal University of Minas Gerais, Belo Horizonte, Brazil; [b]Civil Engineering, Federal University of Tocantins, Palmas, Brazil

This paper presents a methodology to estimate freight flows using secondary data. Problems associated with urban freight are of increasing concern to both public and private institutions. Low efficiency due to traffic congestion, lack of policies and restricted information for decision-making are common in the Brazilian context. Thus, this paper aims at describing a simple, but effective methodological approach for data processing in order to support decision-making in the context of urban freight in Brazil. The proposal consists of gathering common available data in the country as well as Minas Gerais State and applying the method in a study area defined according to a set of different parameters. The results achieved for the Belo Horizonte central region indicate the effectiveness of the methodology as well as the need for a systematic data collection in order to improve future results.

1. Introduction

The transportation of freight is of paramount importance for the efficient and sustainable operation of different systems in urban areas. Nonetheless, its importance is often downplayed by transport policy makers, which can heavily impact urban freight movements. In Brazil, the requirements and the complexity of the sector are not well understood and the management of the systems and operations can be fully transferred to the shipper. Hence, as the private sector often proves unable to manage its operations properly, we tend to experience lack of information and/or data unreliability, which makes it difficult to estimate the impacts of policy changes in the context of transport planning (Bolland, Weir, & Vincent, 2005).

At one end of the spectrum, different tools have been proposed by researchers and practitioners. Among these, origin–destination (O–D) matrices have shown excellent results, but their application is expensive, laborious, time consuming and taxing in relation to the gathering and processing of data. At the other end, modelling demand for freight transport is complex due to the need to consider different dimensions (i.e. types of cargo, volumes and weights). It is also necessary to include in the analysis the different actors/decision makers (e.g. shippers, carriers and drivers) that collectively interact in the dynamic freight transport environment, often making its application impractical (Souza, Silva, & D'Agosto, 2010).

In this context and considering the usual scenario of low data availability in Brazil for freight transport planning as well as the urgent need to improve current practices in the country, this paper proposes a methodology to estimate freight flow in urban areas using secondary data. We evaluate the proposed methodology through a case study in Belo Horizonte (Brazil) because of its considerable relevance to the national economic scenario: the Belo Horizonte metropolitan area comprises over 2.5 million people, has an estimated gross domestic product – GDP – of R$45 billion and plays a key role in mining, service and tourism activities in the Minas Gerais State.

The paper also discusses findings concerning the importance of acquiring reliable data/information for policy making in the context of city logistics and the main challenges to the implementation of holistic and efficient freight planning in Brazil. The paper is divided into five sections. After this introduction, the importance of freight flows in urban logistics analysis is presented. In the third section, the proposed methodology is described and the case study results are discussed in the fourth section. The last two sections concern the implications of the results for policy and research contributions and conclusions.

2. Urban freight transport demand modelling

City logistics aims to reduce nuisances associated with freight transportation while supporting the sustainable development of urban areas (Benjelloun & Crainic, 2009). Thus, it is the process of optimizing the logistics and transport activities undertaken by private companies with the support of advanced information systems in urban areas, considering the traffic environment (congestion), safety and energy savings within the framework of a market economy (Taniguchi, Thompson, Yamada, & Duin, 2001). In relation to this, Comi, Site, Filippi, and Nuzzolo (2012) stress the need to find solutions whereby it is possible to simulate the effects of policies/measures before their implementation, applying an ex ante assessment framework to the investigation of demand models to estimate freight O–D flows. To Cascetta (2001), the models applied to simulate urban freight transport demand on a national scale are derived from a two-level integration process. This process comprise: (i) macroeconomic models that simulate the quantity and spatial distribution of the goods traded among different zones, providing the O–D flows and (ii) models that simulate the modal split and route choice in road networks representing the transport service.

Historically, Ogden (1992) was among the first researchers to study the topic. In his initial study, he proposed models to manage and control urban freight movements. He also presented the first results from a series of case studies in different cities around the world. Regan and Garrido (2002) presented a summary of research on freight demand modelling and carrier behaviour. The authors categorized models according to the nature of the data and the geographic extent considering five levels: aggregated, disaggregated, international, intercity and urban areas. Finally, Ambrosini and Routhier (2001) conducted a comprehensive international comparative study on the methods developed for freight movement modelling and the results obtained.

In this conceptual backdrop, two main approaches derived from the four-step model (trip generation, trip distribution, modal split and traffic assignment) have become popular for freight travel demand modelling: (i) the use of models based on travel volume and (ii) the use of models based on freight volume. Hence, freight modelling can be divided into multi-stage models (Ogden, 1992), input–output models (Harris & Liu, 1998) and spatial price equilibrium models (Oppenheim, 1994).

An evolution of the multi-stage model was proposed by Russo and Comi (2005). This model takes into consideration consumer demand and allows flows to be split between passenger shopping flows and freight flows for urban movements. Models based on freight volume focus on freight quantity, allowing the mechanisms that guide the freight movements to be identified. The diagnosis stage provides all necessary information for developing the model according to real-life needs. Initially, trip-generation data should be used to estimate the rates of freight generation or regression models for individual areas, disaggregated for each different type of goods. The outcomes provide modelling information for the running of the freight distribution model, which then can be used to assign distribution and production flows between the zones (i.e. O–D flows) for the different kinds of goods. The next step concerns the modal split in which the use of the logit model makes it possible to estimate the volume between the different zones according to the freight type and transport mode. Following the modal split, it is necessary to convert freight volume into trips according to typical freight densities and vehicle fleet characteristics (e.g. load, capacity) in the country or region. Finally, the traffic assignment step is performed in which trips are allocated within the transportation network.

Trip-based travel models focus on traffic flow and consider the partition mode. The diagnostics step provides information, disaggregated by mode of transport, necessary for the model. The next step is trip generation, which requires the definition of the trip-generation rates or the use of regression models for each specific area by mode of transport. The result of this step provides information for the trip distribution model, assigning freight trip production and attraction so that O–D flows for each mode of transport can be estimated. The last step is trip distribution (usually performed using gravity models), which allocates the O–D flows within the transportation network. In this context, Russo and Comi (2005) conducted a study to identify the various decision-making processes involved in urban freight movement. In their study, the authors proposed as the first step the identification of the role of passenger models to establish a connection between freight and passenger movements and second to develop an integrated model for a specific case. The study shows that urban scale models can be divided into two levels: (i) models that estimate the demand for types of freight using socioeconomic data and (ii) models that determine the service, time and vehicle use as well as the routes chosen. Both models use probabilistic base approaches to determine the utility consumption patterns for each zone studied (Russo & Comi, 2005).

The trip-generation step corresponds to transportation planning activity related to the forecasting of the number of trips of people or vehicles. Researchers have studied trip generation over the years and there are several models, each with their advantages and limitations. Holguín-Veras et al. (2011) examined factors that challenge current practices and concluded that the models' accuracy in relation to freight generation and freight trip generation depends on the consistency between the structure of the model and the actual patterns of freight generation and freight trip generation, the internal degree of heterogeneity with regard to the aggregate economic use/land used to estimate the model and the adequacy of spatial aggregation procedures used to obtain estimates of load generation and travel load generation. The results that Holguín-Veras et al. (2011) obtained indicate that it is usually correct to assume that proportionality between freight trip generation and the size of the business and the use of constant rates could be problematic. For example, only 18% of industry sectors in New York City have a constant rate for trip-generation charge by employee.

A delivery model, FRETURB, was used to refine the diagnosis of freight on agglomeration in terms of road occupancy, allowing also to assess the extent of the possible effects of various urban policies (Routhier & Aubert, 1999). In this model, the modelling unit is neither the trip nor the quantity of goods, as in many literature works seen before, but the number of pickup and delivery operations. The model requires two types of variables: the variables characteristics, used to calculate the various parameters of the model output in the processing modules; and the sensitivity variables, used to boost the results according to scenarios, allowing the model to be sensitive to different measures tested. The model parameters were firstly estimated based on various surveys applied to the cities Dijon, Bordeaux and Marseille. Bonnafous, Gonzalez-Feliu, and Routhier (2013) showed that the essential variables of the model, the number of movements and the durations of parking can be calculated independently of the city of application of the model and the third variable average distances generated by the movements can be calculated using information easily obtainable on the morphology of the city. The results show the FRETURB model could be applied to several dozen cities in Europe without it being necessary to perform a specific survey.

Other less common models in Brazil are the Activities-Based Models and Integrated Land Use and Transport Models. Activity-Based Models recognize the existence of complex interactions between participation in activities and the standard of travel. Generating demand activities become the focus of the modelling, and no more trips (Arruda, 2005). The Integrated Land Use and Transportation Models, besides studying the connection with activities, seek to identify the impacts of land use changes in the transport system and vice versa, in a cyclical relationship. That allows predicting patterns of urban land use and transportation systems development.

In an analysis of integrated land use and transport models, Rosenbaum and Koening (1997) suggest that, in general, the freight transport have been considered as exogenous data in urban analysis, not allowing to capture the impacts of management measures in the urban environment. The integrated models allow deepening the analysis, from the identification of these relationships.

One existing Integrated Land Use and Transport Model is TRANUS, which starts with the assumption of a link between location of activities in space, land use and the transportation system. TRANUS is composed by three different modules: transport, land use and integration, which combine the other two. This model has been used for many studies of transport networks and impacts of investments measurement. The main applications are the models of Swindon, England (Modelistica, 2009), Aveiro, Portugal (Bandeira, 2009), Sapporo, Japan (Vichiensan, Sato, Miyamoto, & Kitazume, 2003) and Oregon, USA (Parsons Brinckerhoff Quade & Douglas Inc. & Urban Analytics, 1999). Among these main applications, only the application of Oregon also modelled the freight transport, based on the economic data flow between the industrial sectors that comprised the model.

The application of an Integrated Land Use and Transport Model to study the freight transport demands proves to be quite interesting, since it is possible to establish relations of consumption quite explicit in that there is a producer sector and a consumer sector well-defined and spatially located to each type of load (Modelistica, 2009).

The methodology proposed in this paper assumes that, knowing three variables (location, activity and explanatory variable of the trip-generation model) obtained from secondary bases, one can design a model to estimate flows of a particular distribution channel. It was made an effort to use variables present in a database existent in most Brazilian municipalities, and that has a great reliability. That is an important point of the proposal, once lack of data is a problem for many municipalities.

3. The proposed methodology

The methodology proposed in this paper assumes that we can develop a model to estimate the flows of a particular distribution channel, in having three variables obtained from secondary databases, currently existent in Brazilian cities, used by municipalities for tax control. The proposal is based on the principle of Activity Based and Integrated Land Use and Transport Models. Thus, as part of the process, it is necessary to identify the activities that most represent the relations of production and consumption. Once consumer relationships have been identified, it is necessary to geographically locate the points where these activities are carried out, as well as the points of attraction and trip generation.

The treatment of the database allows the classification of the facilities under analysis, distinguishing the points of production (trip generation) and the consumption points (trip attraction) according to the description of their activity. This distinction should be based on an understanding of the supply chain characteristics and the type of freight studied, considering establishments that serve as trip attractors or trip producers.

Once ranked and spatially located, such establishments and the trips produced and attracted in each defined area, namely zones, are calculated. This calculation considers the area of the establishment as an explanatory variable of trip generation. The study suggests using equations described in the available literature, according to the type of freight, as shown in the application description. In the case of not existing a previous trip-generation model appropriated for the segment, it is necessary to make a complementary field research, to investigate generation trip parameters. This kind of survey has not the same complexity and difficulties for implementation as an O–D research. Following the above-mentioned steps, the trip-generation results are used as inputs for distinct travel distribution models. In this particular study, in order to aggregate the concepts of models based on activities, stage distribution was performed using the TRANUS software; this relates the location of activities in space, land use and the transportation system. To conduct this step, it was necessary to model the road network, using the attributes of capacity, speed, direction of travel, costs involved and others that geometrically characterize the road network.

Finally, it was necessary to calibrate the matrix volume according to the actual classified traffic count. This procedure consists of allocating the matrix in software that allows the calibration of traffic volumes per link, for example, TransCAD.

The proposed methodology is divided into seven steps: (i) definition of planning and study area, (ii) zoning, (iii) definition of type of freight, (iv) data collection and processing, (v) trip generation, (vi) trip distribution, (vii) parameters and calibration.

3.1. *Definition of planning and study areas*

The initial step aims to define both planning and study areas. The study area should include an area in which secondary data can be collected for the model. It must have a range such that it includes cities that have direct relations with the planning area.

The planning area used to evaluate impacts and propose intervention measures. In this methodology, the selection of the planning area considers the availability of updated freight flows, according to field research, which will allow the comparison of results derived from the proposed methodology and the assessment of their validity.

For this first step, it is of great importance to consider several factors that may interfere with the choice of the study area. First, the study area must be greater than the planning area. Second, consideration should be given to a buffering area that has an influence over the planning area to support field observations in the planning area.

3.2. *Zoning*

After defining the study and planning areas, they should be divided into zones with similar characteristics to enable data collection activities. Nguyen-Luong (2008) applied an integrated land use and transportation model in the case of Paris and after four years of study gathered some lessons that can serve as guidance for future research. Nguyen-Luong (2008) highlights the importance of the approach to zoning adopted in ensuring the consistency of existing data with the desired level of disaggregation.

Complementarily, Parsons Brinckerhoff Quade & Douglas Inc. & Urban Analytics (1999) recommend that the limits for the zones should be compatible with official divisions, preferably with the basic units in census data, as they can be aggregated without any information loss. Furthermore, the zoning must be compatible with the scale of analysis desired: local, metropolitan or region. For application in transport planning, it is also recommended that access points are defined according to the given road system.

3.3. *Definition of type of freight*

The freight sector presents the modeller with considerable complexity as it transports a range of products and the characteristics of logistics activities depend on the type of goods carried. As the intention is to estimate an O–D matrix, it is necessary to select a type of freight or commodities to be studied. In this context, the methodology proposes selection criteria according to the extent to which the segment is representative in proportion to the total freight circulated in the city.

3.4. *Data collection and processing*

The availability of consistent and reliable data is crucial to the performance of the proposed model. The intended database, which should allow a good application of the methodology, is the registration of businesses along with the identification of activities performed by the establishment. A common source is the authority which holds the information on taxes paid according to different transport activities. In Brazil, the Municipal Taxpayers' Registry of Securities Taxes is the register of legal entities engaged in any economic activities in the city, which are subject to payment of service tax of any nature. These data associated to the National Classification of Economic Activities, in Brazil, are the recommended source for this purpose.

Furthermore, the database needs to classify the establishments according to the freight sector for the subsequent evaluation of the sector defined in the study. Following the sector classification, trip generation and attraction are estimated by establishment. This activity allows the identification of the main zones for trip generation and attraction by freight sector and the estimation, based on practical knowledge, of the area of use of each establishment and the number of trips produced and attracted.

It should be noted that in the case that no database is available for the entire study area but only for the planning area, field research might be required to identify the dynamic urban freight distribution in the study area.

3.5. *Trip generation*

Trip-generation data can be collected by conducting survey interviews to identify average number of trips produced and attracted in each zone. The survey can be conducted with businesses by telephone and the questions relate the number of trips produced and attracted, the size of the business in terms of floor area and various other aspects.

Although this kind of interviews is simpler and much less expensive than an O–D traditional research, it requires formal support and the involvement of transport operators to obtain a valid sample. Whenever this approach fails, a second alternative should be considered in order to gather the necessary data. The alternative is to adopt models of freight trip generation previously studied that are recognized in the scientific community and the boundary conditions of which are similar to the conditions of the current research. It is important to define, in this case, if it will be adopted a model of generation of goods flow or generation of trips of vehicles, because this will influences in the distribution modelling.

3.6. *Distribution modelling*

After estimating trip generation, the next step is to create the network. In this case, a number of readily available software packages can be adopted. It should be highlighted that the software can also be used for trip generation according to parameters that establish the relationship between the demand sectors. However, a more precise method involves the estimation of trips produced and attracted by the methods previously described.

In the modelling process, the first step is to define the sectors that compose the model. To estimate O–D flows, it is necessary to define the parameters for each type of freight, the producer sector and the consumer sector. After defining the sectors, it is necessary to determine the relationship sector from which economic flows will be generated and to spatially link the demands of the production sectors to each zone. Following this, the data transport network should be included in the model; this is necessary to define the categories of trips, travel time, waiting time, trip-generation rate and the parameters of the utility function of the logit model. It is also crucial in providing information on routes and road capacity and operational speed. The distribution model is

$$D_i^n = \sum_m D_i^{mn} + D_i^{*n}, \tag{1}$$

$$U_{ij}^n = \lambda^n (p_j^n + h_j^n) + t_{ij}^n, \tag{2}$$

$$\Pr_{ij}^n = \frac{(A_j^n)^{a^n} \mathrm{e}^{-\beta^n \tilde{U}_{ij}^n}}{\sum_j (A_j^n)^{a^n} \mathrm{e}^{-\beta^n \tilde{U}_{ij}^n}}, \tag{3}$$

$$X_{ij}^n = D_i^n P_{ij}^n, \tag{4}$$

where D_i^n is the total demand n in zone i, in this case substituted by trip generated, D_i^{*n} an exogenous demand n in i, p_j^n the production cost of the sector n in production zone j, h_j^n the dummy production cost of the sector n in production zone j, t_{ij}^n the disutility transport of the sector n from production zone j to consumer zone i, λ^n the parameter that adjusts the relative importance of price and disutility of transport, considering the utility, X_{ij}^n the production in n that it is located in the zone j induced by activities in i, A_j^n the attractor to production n in zone j, a^n the parameter that adjusts the relative importance of the production attractor, that is related with utility function of the location in sector n; $\tilde{U}_{ij}^n$ the marginal utility of the production location n in zone j to supply the demand in zone i and β^n the parameter that adjust the distribution in logit function.

To generate the economic flows, it is necessary to convert unit values from transport module and land use module, considering volume and time factors:

$$F_{ij}^s = \sum_n \left(X_{ij}^n \frac{\mathrm{vol}^{ns}\, \mathrm{pc}^{ns}}{\mathrm{temp}^{ns}} + X_{ji}^n \frac{\mathrm{vol}^{ns}\, \mathrm{cp}^{ns}}{\mathrm{temp}^{ns}} \right), \tag{5}$$

where F_{ij}^s is the transport flows s from the origin i to destiny j, X_{ij}^n the production of the sector n located in j and demanded by i, i.e. the socioeconomic flows between i and j, vol^{ns} the factor to change volume to socioeconomic flows n, in transport categories, temp^{ns} the temporal factor between socioeconomic flows n and transport flows s, cp^{ns} the proportional flows from consumers to production and pc^{ns} the proportional flows from production to consumer.

When the demand does not represent the number of trips, but the goods flow, it needs to be transformed in trips using the following equation:

$$T_{ij}^{s} = F_{ij}^{s}[v_{\text{min}}^{s} + (v_{\text{max}}^{s} - v_{\text{max-min}}^{s})\,e^{(-\eta^{s}c_{ij}^{s})}], \tag{6}$$

where F_{ij}^{s} are the flows between i and j in transport category s, v_{min}^{s} is the minimum number of the trip that the category s performs, independent of disutility, v_{max}^{s} is the maximum number of the trip that the category s performs when the disutility tends to zero and η^{s} is the elasticity of the category s for trip disutility.

In order to optimize the performance of the modelling task, it is recommended that the road network be simplified by considering only the collector, arterial and regional connection roads. Transport networks consist of links (line segments representing the road axis) and nodes (connectors between two or more links). The zones are connected to the road network, represented by the centroids of each zone. The selection of the centroid depends on the analysis on the internal network of the zone and how it connects to the road network. An existing point in the road network can be chosen as the centroid or a dummy point can be created which connects the network by one or more fictitious links, as long as the movement in the existing network is not compromised.

For each link, the road capacity, length and type of link must be specified. The link types are defined according to the road hierarchy and other characteristics that could interfere in the speed of the trucks. For each type of link, the operator, mode of transportation allowed to travel on the link and its corresponding speed are defined.

In addition to the attributes of the road network, it is also necessary to configure the modes of transport and related costs. To do so, transport categories, related to each sector of freight analysis, are to be defined by the modeller. Once all the transport data are logged into the system, activity data, sectors and information on the zones should be loaded into the system to perform the calibration step.

3.7. *Calibration*

The calibration of the model is performed by verifying the convergence of the activities model and the transport model. The convergence of the activities model is undertaken by varying the elasticity of sectors and incorporates the approximation values calculated by the software and those supplied from the database. Elasticity represents the response capacity of the sector in relation to the price changes: the higher the value of the elasticity, the greater the sensitivity and reaction to the price, whereas the lower the elasticity, the lower the reaction to the price.

Another element that can be adjusted is inter-sectoral demand. From this point, travel can be calculated. In this case, as the trips were calculated previously and the amount for each sector refers to the number of trips produced and attracted in each zone, this ratio can be set to one, i.e. each unit in the production sector generates a unit in the consumption sector. If the input data do not comprise the number of trips, the model allows the adjustment of volume and time factors as the transport model works with daily trips or peak hours and the activity model works with the quantity of product per month. These factors allow the units to match the two models.

There is also the possibility of adjusting demand according to its elasticity. In this context, lower elasticity implies more trips being generated. Elasticity can be also modified to consider the occurrence of internal trips in the zone, which are not estimated in the proposed model.

Finally, these parameters are adjusted to approximate the total number of trips in relation to the actual number observed. The distribution of trips between zones is usually estimated using the model of maximum entropy. The resulting matrix is a calibrated data set of classified volume counts performed on the main road network nodes. This procedure is commonly undertaken in an updating O–D matrix and can be done using multiple software platforms.

4. Results

The proposed methodology was applied in the city of Belo Horizonte (Brazil). This is the capital of Minas Gerais State and the metropolitan area comprises an area of 331 km^2 in which approximately 2.4 million people live. The study area was chosen considering various factors, the main one being the availability of data that would allow assessment of the results of the proposed model and the verification of the model's validity in the context given in the previous section.

First, the zoning was obtained by aggregating neighbourhoods defined according to administrative boundaries for the nine municipalities included in the metropolitan area of Belo Horizonte. In total, 30 zones, 12 of which were in metropolitan areas, were chosen for the case study, as shown in Figure 1.

Due to its level of representation in the total number of freight vehicles circulating in Belo Horizonte metropolitan region, the food and beverage sector was chosen for the study:

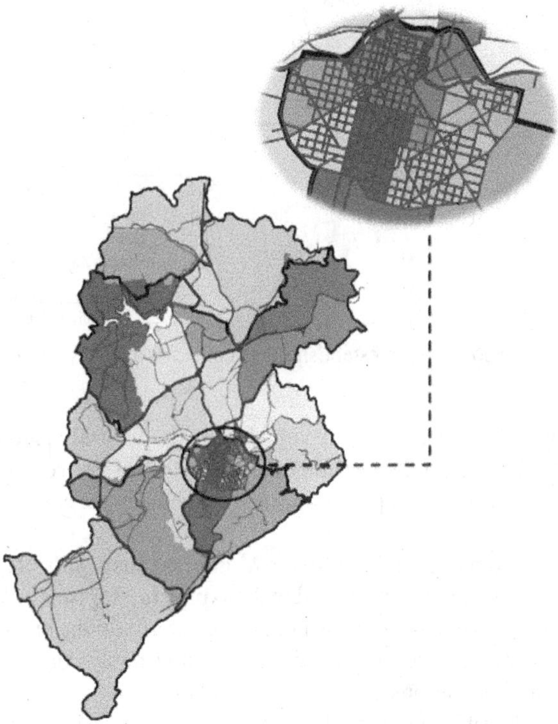

Figure 1. Zoning and the main road system of Belo Horizonte (central area highlighted).

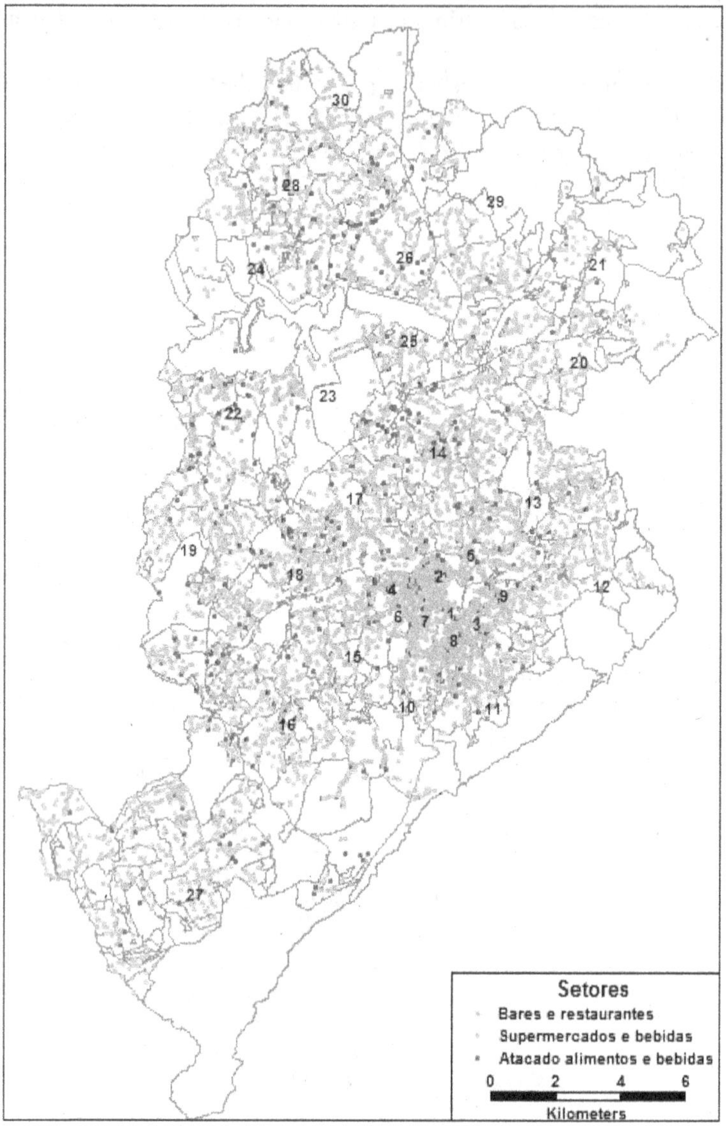

Figure 2. Distribution of commercial establishments considered in this research.

this sector represents 42% of all freight vehicles in the central region (Oliveira, 2014; Oliveira & Dias, 2014). Knowledge of the characteristics of the segment studied and its distribution channel is important for processing and structuring the next steps in the proposed methodology.

The original database obtained belongs to the Municipal Taxpayers' Registry provided by the Belo Horizonte City Council. The Municipal Taxpayers' Registry of Securities Taxes is the register of legal entities engaged in any economic activity in the city of Belo Horizonte, which are subject to the payment of service tax of any nature or transaction fees (e.g. inspection, location and operations, sanitary supervision).

Figure 2 shows the distribution of the three main groups of businesses related to the food and beverage sector. It should be noted that there is a concentration of pubs and restaurants

Table 1. Equations used for trip generation.

Dependent variable	Independent variable	Equation
Wholesale sector[a]	$X_1 = 1000\,\text{m}^2$ of the area built	$Y = 4.0X_1$
Supermarket[b]	X = area built	$Y = 1.1522 + 0.0012X$
Pubs and restaurants[b]	X = area built	$Y = 1.3334 + 0.0019X$

[a]Tadi and Balbach (1994).
[b]Melo (2002).

in the central area, whereas supermarkets and drinks trade are distributed evenly across all regions.

In the next step, the equations developed by Melo (2002) and Tadi and Balbach (1994) were used. Specifically, Tadi and Balbach (1994) studied the vehicle trips generated by the wholesale sector and the equations developed by Melo (2002) were adopted in this work as they were designed for the Brazilian context. The formulations are presented in Table 1.

For the wholesale sector, the equation is not specific to commodity type or adjusted to the food and beverage sector. In this case, we applied an adjustment factor to the values given by Tadi and Balbach's (1994) equation. The adjustment factor was obtained drawing on the survey data from Oliveira and Dias (2014) and Oliveira (2014), which revealed that 31% of deliveries in downtown Belo Horizonte are from Belo Horizonte. Therefore, we assumed that the total travel produced in Belo Horizonte should correspond to 31% of the trips attracted.

Based on the trip-generation model, the trip production and attraction results were analysed. For comparison purposes, areas sizes were standardized in each of the targeted zones. It can be observed that the areas that attract trips are proportionately located in the centre of the city, which is justifiable due to the great number of businesses in this area. Regarding trip production, considering the internal zones of Belo Horizonte, we highlight the area around the Hipercentro Region (2) and Antonio Carlos Avenue (14 and 17) and peripheral areas. Among these, we highlight the region north of the Pampulha Lake (24 and 26) and the western region (15 and 16) of Belo Horizonte.

However, most of the freight transported in Belo Horizonte, approximately 37%, originates from the city of Contagem (31) (Oliveira, 2014; Oliveira & Dias, 2014). Due to the lack of availability of data for Contagem, the data were considered exogenous to the model and the estimated number of trips produced in Contagem and other municipalities of the metropolitan area were acquired from Oliveira and Dias (2014) and Oliveira (2014). Figure 3 illustrates the result obtained from the trip-generation step for the city of Belo Horizonte.

Following trip generation, the trip-distribution step was conducted making use of the TRANUS software. This software calculates trip distribution using the maximum entropy method which is a very good fit for the present research. For modelling, the results from Oliveira and Dias (2014) and Oliveira (2014) were used to estimate trip production for other municipalities in the metropolitan region. Figure 3 shows the results according to the desire lines. It can be seen that the bulk of trade occurs with Contagem, in this case represented by a single zone (i.e. one centroid).

In order to allow a comparison between the data calculated and reference O–D matrix estimates (Oliveira, 2014; Oliveira & Dias, 2014), the data were grouped according to proposed zoning and zones 1–9 were grouped as constituting the central area. Moreover, percentages of trips between the zones were calculated considering the total travel from Belo

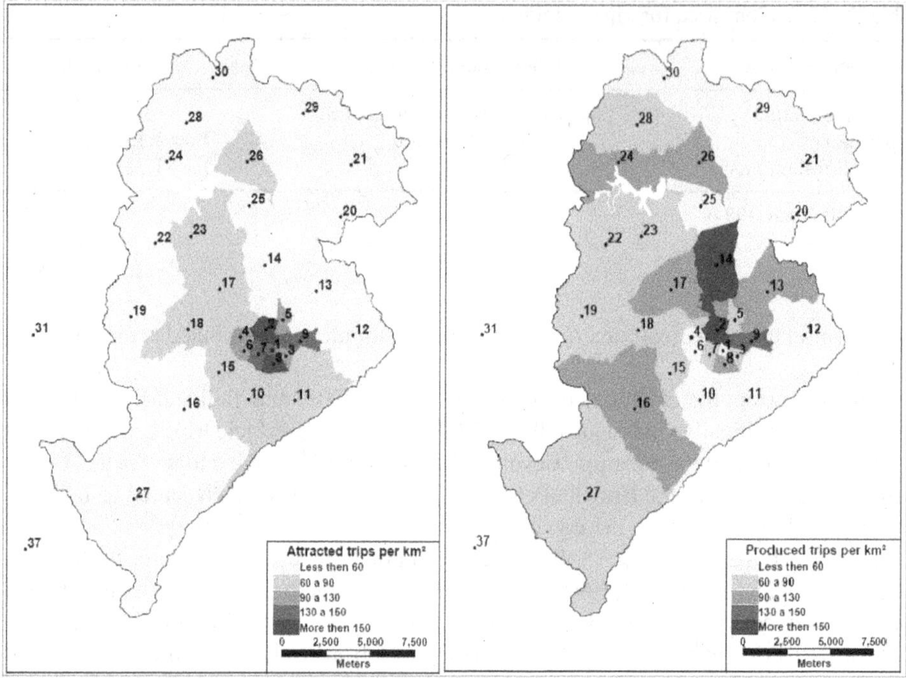

Figure 3. Trips attracted and produced per unit area in Belo Horizonte.

Table 2. Main origins in Belo Horizonte of trips with a destination in the central region.

Zone	Results from Oliveira and Dias (2013) adjusted	O–D calculated
Central area	2.9%	7.6%
17	3.4%	5.6%
18	0.8%	2.6%
22	3.0%	3.6%
23	2.6%	3.7%
25	0.5%	0.5%
27	10.2%	9.7%
28	6.7%	5.0%
29	2.0%	3.1%
Correlation	0.81	
Other zones	68%	59%

Horizonte. To obtain data only on the food and beverages segment, the total was corrected. This correction took into account the proportion of the number of wholesale establishments related to food and beverages in relation to all wholesalers in each zone. Table 2 shows the comparison of the results.

The correlation analysis between the two columns, excluding ‘Other zones’, reveals a correlation of 0.81. The category ‘Other zones’ should not be included in the comparative analysis because it adds zones with distinct characteristics and does not allow a direct comparison of O–D pairs. To check if the correlation value found has statistical significance, it was applied the t-test, verifying its significance at 5% level. The correlation analysis is used

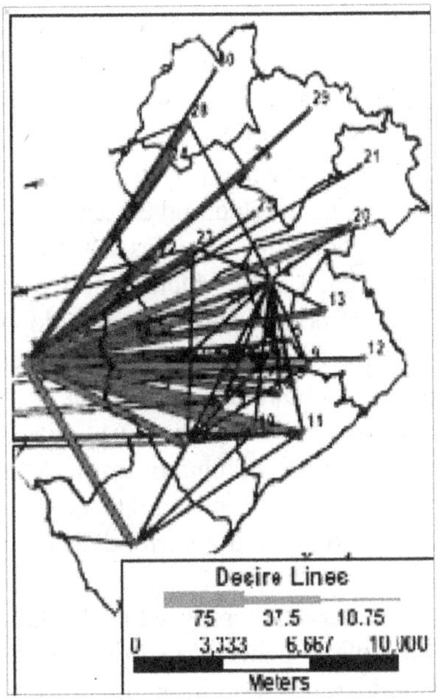

Figure 4. Desire lines and freight distribution of the food and beverage sector in Belo Horizonte.

to examine each pair of measurement variables and to determine whether the two variables tend to move together, or whether the high values of one variable tend to be associated with high values of the other (positive correlation), or the low values of one variable tend to be associated with high values of the other (negative correlation), or the values of the two variables tend to be unrelated (correlation near zero). The result indicates a high positive correlation. The scatter of the results reveals $R^2 = 0.6526$, higher than other applications TRANUS model, like Aveiro, $R^2 = 0.2113$ (Bandeira, 2009) and Sapporo, $R^2 = 0.6116$ (Vichiensan et al., 2003).

The desire lines, presented in Figure 4, show the important result of this work. The lines connect O–D areas and the thickness represents the number of trips between the pair of zones. It can be observed that major exchanges take place with Contagem, in this case represented by a single zone. According to Oliveira and Dias's (2014) study, approximately 37% of freight transported in Belo Horizonte originates in Contagem. This high proportion is explained by the concentration of industries in this city, as well as it being the location of Minas Supply Central (CEASA). Internally within the central area of Belo Horizonte city, Venda Nova (28 and 30) and Barreiro (27) are highlighted as destinations with significant numbers of deliveries.

The calculation of the number of vehicles that carry out daily deliveries takes into consideration the fact that the same vehicle performs more than one delivery per day. For this calculation, we considered that there are 25 daily deliveries by each truck in Belo Horizonte on average (Oliveira, 2014; Oliveira & Dias, 2014). In this study, we found that 630 vehicles made deliveries in the central area of Belo Horizonte per day.

The results achieved prove the practical application of the proposed methodology in the Brazilian context. Although one can argue the superficial contributions of the proposed method, it must be highlighted that in the general context of data availability and policy making in Brazil, like freight transport routes restrictions and facilities locations without specific traffic flows studies, this research can be of great support for both government associates and the private sector. For instance, a common practice adopted by the government is to make decisions on freight transport solely on anecdotal observations, which often generate more problems than solutions in urban transport. This approach is commonly see in the major urban centres (e.g. São Paulo, Rio de Janeiro and Belo Horizonte) and incurs further damage to the national economy and private institutions as most of the businesses and activities in the country are concentrated in these cities.

Furthermore, the proposed methodology provides urban freight players, mainly the government, with a systematic approach with which to collect/gather data, process results, represent information and support decision making, by allowing to estimate goods flows and to simulate different scenarios for urban policies. The method is of further support as it has spatial components and links both data and results to the existing road network in the study area. Its potentiality is confirmed when it is noted that the city of Belo Horizontè has no current information on the volume of traffic regarding urban freight. Hence, the development and improvement of this (and similar) methodologies will surely improve decision making in determining policy and contribute to improved and more sustainable operations.

Overall, for the specific case study, the proposed method proved to be applicable in the practical context as it was possible to generate O–D flows from the database provided by the Belo Horizonte city council. In general terms, the objectives were therefore achieved and the results were consistent when compared to data acquired from real traffic flows along the major roads in Belo Horizonte.

An important issue regards the reliability of the data utilized. In this study, although the available database is updated, it presents distortions in relation to certain types of business as assumptions had to be made using the address of the establishment due to the fact that no other information was available. This imposes limitations in relation to the study of specific sectors, such as civil construction or banking. In the sector studied, food and beverages, such distortions are not striking and do no prejudice the quality of the results; therefore, this was selected as the main sector for the case study.

5. Conclusion

The complexity of the urban freight distribution system is reflected in the conflict between the interests of the different stakeholders and the difficult task of managing goods deliveries and negative externalities resulting from these activities in urban areas. Understanding flow dynamics is of increasing importance for the implementation of public policies able to establish equilibrium in this complex system. However, traditional tools that may help in the planning process, such as the O–D matrix, are expensive and labour-intensive in relation to data collection and processing. Thus, research aimed at developing alternative methods is of vital importance as such methods may allow advances in the discussions of planning policies without requiring significant financial investment.

For the Brazilian context this situation is even worse, because there is rarely secondary data available for most of cities. So, to structure a model capable to estimate transport freight flow using the consolidated and uniform databases available, brings a new perspective to the Brazilian transport planners.

In general terms, the proposed methodology has shown to be applicable and it has achieved the goal of determining O–D flows using data from the Municipal Register of Contributors. Processing secondary data from the Municipal Taxpayers' Registry enabled the representation of dynamic urban freight distribution. Knowledge of the location, description of the activity and an explanatory variable in the model of trip generation for each establishment afforded better understanding and the design of the distribution channels of the freight segment under study, as well as the application of a model to estimate freight flows. Moreover, the suggestion to use public municipal databases allows the proposal to be replicated in other municipalities and also for other freight segments as such databases gather information about several segments. However, the application of the method requires careful consideration as the quality of the results is directly related to the quality of the database. For certain segments, there may be distortions in relation to the database and the dynamics of consumption, such as in the construction industry. For this sector, the data area is related to the construction headquarters, not to where the work is actually occurring.

In relation to the activity model, the study presents further possibilities to analyse freight flows. The model is coherent and relevant to logistics flows as its focus is on identifying the relationships that generate demand for transport. This allows better understanding of the dynamics of freight transport as part of the urban context, determined by urban relationships, rather than comprising an isolated system. This systemic view will enable decision makers to engage in integrated planning activities by incorporating its various dimensions.

The application of the TRANUS model to estimate freight flow was feasible with the available data, although it required some simplifications and adaptations, such as estimating trip generation using an alternative tool. The validation of the results obtained for the specific case of freight was compatible with other cases conducted for urban passenger transport in cities across the world, like the mentioned Swindon (England), Aveiro (Portugal), Sapporo (Japan) and Oregon (USA).

Thus, overall, the study conducted achieved its intended objectives. However, further considerations can be highlighted for future work:

- The end result could be improved by integrating other segments and classifying the traffic count, enabling a better fit for the O–D matrix.
- It is important to assess the results from the trip-generation step in relation to the reality of the city, and in some cases it might be necessary to investigate specific trip-generation equations.
- An important advantage of the proposed methodology lies in reducing the time and costs of building an important tool to assist in urban transport planning. Another benefit is its equivalence to instruments already established as routine in the use of data files of Brazilian cities, but employing a new function which brings an incentive to improve such databases.
- The research conducted focused on the distribution channel between wholesalers and retailers because of the limitations of the models adopted. However, the database allows the entire supply chain to be modelled and this is recommended for future work.
- Another important issue that was not addressed in the study and deserves investigation is the inclusion of land use in modelling. This research is highly relevant as we have observed a process of decentralization in activity in Brazil due to the flexibility of land use parameters which impacts on the dynamics of urban goods distribution.

Funding

This work was supported by the National Council for Scientific and Technological Development (CNPq), SETCEMG, Municipality of Belo Horizonte and BHTRANS.

References

Ambrosini, C., & Routhier, J. (2001, July 22–27). *Objectives, methods and results of surveys carried out in the field of urban freight transport: An international comparison.* Proceedings of the 9th world conference on transport research, Seoul.

Arruda, F. S. (2005). *Aplicação de um modelo baseado em atividades para análise da relação uso do solo e transportes no contexto brasileiro* (Doctoral thesis). Escola de Engenharia de São Carlos, Universidade de São Paulo, São Carlos. [in Portuguese]

Bandeira, J. F. M. (2009). Modelo de uso do solo de Aveiro: Impacto na mobilidade e qualidade do ar. Dissertação de Mestrado. Departamento de Ambiente e Ordenamento. Universidade de Aveiro. [in Portuguese]

Benjelloun, A., & Crainic, T. G. (2009). Trends, challenges, and perspectives in city logistics. *Buletin AGIR, 4*, 45–51. Retrieved from http://www.agir.ro/buletine/501.pdf

Bolland, J., Weir, D., & Vincent, M. (2005). *Development of a New Zealand national freight matrix* (Report no. 283). New Zealand: Booz Allen Hamilton. Retrieved from http://www.nzta.govt.nz/resources/research/reports/283/

Bonnafous, A., Gonzalez-Feliu, J., & Routhier, J. L. (2013). *An alternative paradigm to O-D matrices: The FRETURB model.* General proceedings of the 13th world conference on transport research, Rio de Janeiro, Brazil.

Cascetta, E. (2001). *Transportation systems engineering: Theory and methods.* Dordrecht, The Netherlands: Kluwer Academic Publishers.

Comi, A., Site, P. D., Filippi, F., & Nuzzolo, A. (2012). Urban freight transport demand modelling: A state of the art. *European Transport/Trasporti Europei, 51*(7), 1–17. Retrieved from http://hdl.handle.net/10077/6123

Harris, R. L., & Liu, A. (1998). Input–output modeling of the urban and regional economy: The importance of external trade. *Regional Studies, 32*(9), 851–862. doi:10.1080/00343409850118004

Holguín-Veras, J., Jaller, M., Destro, L., Ban, X., Lawson, C., & Levinson, H. S. (2011). Freight generation, freight trip generation, and the perils of using constant trip rates. *Transportation Research Record: Journal of the Transportation Research Board, 2224*, 68–81. doi:10.3141/2224-09

Melo, I. C. B. (2002). Avaliação da demanda por transporte de carga em áreas urbanas. Dissertação de Mestrado em Engenharia de Transportes, Instituto Militar de Engenharia, RJ. [in Portuguese]

Modelistica. (2009). A guide to the application of the TRANUS modeling system to the city of Swindon, UK. Modelística, 2009.

Nguyen-Luong, D. (2008). An integrated land use-transport model for the Paris Region (SIMAURIF): Ten lessons learned after four years of development. IAURIF/DTI/DNL. Retrieved from http://www.iau-idf.fr/ultisim/IMG/pdf/Paper_SIMAURIF_10_lessons_TRB_2009.pdf

Ogden, K. W. (1992) *Urban goods movement: A guide to policy and planning.* Aldershot, UK: Ashgate Publishing Company.

Oliveira, L. K. (2014). Diagnóstico das vagas de carga e descarga para a distribuição urbana de mercadorias: Um estudo de caso em Belo Horizonte. *Journal of Transport Literature, 8*(1), 178–209. doi:10.1590/S2238-10312014000100009 [in Portuguese]

Oliveira, L. K., & Dias, E. G. (2014). Methodology to diagnosis of urban goods distribution: A case study in Belo Horizonte City (Brazil). *Procedia – Social and Behavioral Sciences, 125*(20), 199–211. doi:10.1016/j.sbspro.2014.01.1467

Oppenheim, N. (1994). *Urban travel demand modeling.* New York: Wiley.

Parsons Brinckerhoff Quade & Douglas, Inc., & Urban Analytics, Inc. (1999). Development and calibration of the state wide land use-transport model – transportation and land use model integration program phase II, task 2.3. Prepared for the Oregon Department of Transportation, February 1999, New Mexico, USA.

Regan, A., & Garrido, R. A. (2002). Modelling freight demand and shipper behavior: State of the art, future directions. In D. Hensher (Ed.), *The leading edge of travel behaviour research* (pp. 185–216). New York: Pergamon Press.

Rosenbaum, A. S., & Koening, B. E. (1997). *Evaluation of modeling tools for assessing land use policies and strategies* (Technical Report). Systems Applications International, Inc.

Routhier, J. L., & Aubert, P. L. (1999). *FRETURB, un modèle de simulation des transports de marchandises en ville.* 8th WCTR Antwerp proceedings (pp. 531–544). Amsterdam: Elsevier.

Russo, F., & Comi, A. (2005, July). Demand models for city logistics: A state of the art and a proposed integrated system. In E. Taniguchi & R. G. Thompsom (Eds.), *Recent advances in city logistics – Proceedings of the 4th International Conference on City Logistics*, Langkawa, Malaysia (pp. 91–106). Amsterdam: Elsevier.

Souza, C. D., Silva, R. S. D., & D'Agosto, M. A. (2010). Modelos de geração de viagens para polos geradores de viagens de cargas. *Transportes, XVIII*(1), 46–57. doi:10.4237/transportes.v18i1.396 [in Portuguese]

Tadi, R. R., & Balbach, P. (1994). Truck trip generation characteristics of nonresidential land uses. *ITE Journal, 64*(7), 43–47. Retrieved from http://www.ite.org/membersonly/itejournal/pdf/JGA94A43.pdf

Taniguchi, E., Thompson, R. G., Yamada T., & Duin, R. V. (2001). *City logistics: Network modelling and intelligent transport systems*. Oxford: Pergamon.

Vichiensan, V., Sato, K., Miyamoto, K., & Kitazume, K. (2003). Introduction of land use model to improve travel demand forecasting in a metropolitan area: A case of Tranus application to Sapporo. *Journal of the Eastern Asia Society for Transportation Studies, 5*, 2863–2071. Retrieved from http://www.easts.info/2003journal/papers/2863.pdf

Index